M940757.8
9.99
D0270353
Introduction to
Business Economics
Return
will b
16
8
0
99
1
BIRMINGHAM CITY
UNIVERSITY
DISCARDED

First published in 1990 by:
Stanley Thornes (Publishers) Ltd
Ellenborough House
Wellington Street
CHELTENHAM GL50 1YD
England

Reprinted 1992
Reprinted 1993

British Library Cataloguing in Publication Data

Old, John
Introduction to business economics.
1. Economics
I. Title II. Shafto, Tony A. C. (Thomas Anthony Cheshire)
1929–
330

ISBN 0-7487-0412-4

Typeset by Tech-Set, Gateshead, Tyne & Wear.
Printed and bound in Great Britain at The Bath Press, Avon.

Contents

Preface

In recent years there has been a growing demand from tutors on business studies and business related courses for material which introduces students to the practical, business implications of economics. There is a realisation that the concepts and techniques of economic analysis offer much of value to managers who have to take business managerial decisions which are essentially economic in that they involve difficult choices for the use of scarce resources to achieve productive objectives. Nevertheless they feel, with some justification, that to concentrate on the kind of theoretical model building beloved by so many teachers and writers does little to stimulate the kind of economic awareness likely to prove really useful to those who wish to pursue a career in business.

We have sought to produce a book to meet this need. We have concentrated on the economic decisions that have to be made within the firm as they relate to objectives, marketing and production strategy, investment, pricing and finance. We have also examined some of the most important aspects of the relationship between government and business against the background of the profound changes that have been taking place in the ownership and control of the major public utilities and in public, and academic attitudes to business competition.

The book has been written to provide a well informed and, we hope, stimulating source of help for students to gain a deeper understanding of the business environment. Tutors will recognise that we have taken into account much of the recent research literature and academic debate surrounding many of our topics. We have not, however, cluttered the text with a snowstorm of references to learned texts which, in our experience, students feel obliged to repeat in their essays even though they and their tutors are well aware that the texts themselves are rarely disturbed. In the same way, the reading suggestions we provide at the end of chapters are intended to provide practical assistance to those who genuinely need and wish to pursue particular topics in greater detail. We have not listed works which are likely to be of little use to students and busy tutors nor have we set out to provide a bibliographical checklist for those with advanced specialist interest in particular areas of study.

We also hope that this book owes something to our own teaching and business experiences. We are well aware of the problems and pitfalls inherent in any attempt to convey fairly complex ideas in reasonably simple form. For much of our own careers we have tried to do just this and to put into practice the knowledge we have gained from our own studies. If we can help a wider audience to share our belief in the practical usefulness of basic economics we shall have achieved our main objective.

John Old & Tony Shafto
Coventry Business School, Coventry Polytechnic

1 An Economic Framework

Questions of Economics

A group of engineering students was once asked to suggest the correct materials for a particular job involving the machining of a fairly simple machine component. Surprisingly, they gave a variety of answers all of which were, in some sense, 'correct'. When the students were asked to defend their answers the following were typical of the answers they gave.

1 A particular material was, technically, superior to all others.
2 The problem with the 'best' method was that it was so expensive that no one would buy the finished product.
3 A particular material was easier to work with. Other materials would raise scrap costs. Others would cause such wear on the machines that they would need resetting or replacing very frequently.
4 Replacement costs for machines did not come into consideration if the number of components to be produced was small (and that might depend on the number to be sold which, in turn, depended on price, which, in its turn, depended on cost). The machine cost would also not be important if the machines were cheap enough, at least in relation to the number of components produced.

You might be able to think of other points you would want to consider if you were one of these students. The responses make it apparent that the question of what material was 'best' was not simply a matter of technology. It also involved answers to such questions as:

1 What were the costs of different materials?
2 What proportion of final costs was accounted for by material costs?
3 What other costs would be affected by the choice of material?
4 How was selling price related to cost?
5 How was the number sold related to price?

The original question was clearly not just one of technical efficiency but also of economic and commercial efficiency. The choice of material was affected by a whole series of questions whose answers would not be found in a purely engineering textbook.

They are, however, the very stuff of economics. Any course or text in any subject must start out by saying what the subject is or is not about. The central concern of economics is the fact that there is rarely only one course of action that people can take. There are nearly always several. All may appear attractive possibilities. In the case we have just looked at there were several differing engineering possibilities, all of which appeared plausible in some way. However, they all had different implications or consequences.

So, two basic economic questions are:

1 What is to be produced?
2 How is it to be produced?

A number of other technological questions flow automatically from these, i.e.

1 When and where is it to be produced?
2 Who is to do the production?

We also saw that it was very important to ask questions such as how many of the components were to be produced and who was going to buy them. So there are a number of other fundamental economic questions, including:

3 For whom is the production taking place?

In all these questions there is one basic, common idea, that is if we do one thing there are others that we cannot do. If we devote machine time to one product it is unavailable for another. If output goes to meet one customer's order it cannot be used to satisfy another. Economists refer to the **opportunity cost** of a decision. What is meant here is the real cost in terms of what has been given up or what cannot now be done. The cost of meeting an urgent order for one customer is not just the material costs, overtime and so on but also the fact that other customers may not get their orders on time with all the possible consequences of lost goodwill and future orders. The workers putting in overtime on the order are incurring an opportunity cost in that they cannot use the extra working time for watching television or weeding the garden. It is really only decisions which involve an opportunity cost that are problems at all. If there is no opportunity cost and nothing is being given up then there is no need to weigh alternatives before coming to a decision.

Economic Theory

This is not a pure textbook of economics in the conventional sense. It is a text that attempts to show how economics can help business people to tackle a whole range of problems. It is widely accepted that business people should 'know something about economics' but the criticism is often made that economics is too 'theoretical' meaning that economists seem to deal in abstract ideas that are all very well 'in theory' but have very few practical applications.

Is this fair criticism? Let us look at one area of economic theory and see what relationship it bears to practical experience.

The Theory of Demand

Factors affecting demand:	
1 Price	3 Incomes
2 Other prices	4 Tastes.

The theory of demand in economics says that the quantity of a commodity that is demanded will depend upon:

a the price of the commodity;
b the price of other goods and services, in particular:
  i substitutes – goods that could be substituted for this commodity, e.g. beef for pork,
  ii complements – goods that are typically consumed along with the commodity such as petrol with cars;
c the income of consumers;
d the tastes of consumers.

Furthermore **demand** is defined as the quantity that consumers are willing and able to purchase at a given range of prices.

It is common to focus simply upon the effect of price upon quantity, quantity demanded increasing as price falls, assuming that everything else that might influence buyers' intentions remains unchanged. These other influences include items **b** and **c** above together with some that are under the control of the firm itself – advertising, for example, and the general skill and resources which the firm is able to devote to marketing its products. A demand curve in its general form is shown in Fig. 1.1.

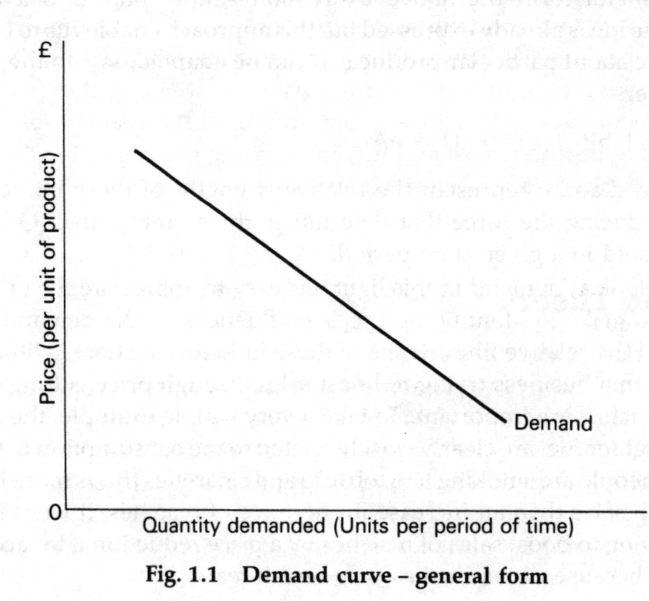

Fig. 1.1 Demand curve – general form

To many non-economists this may appear unnecessarily wordy and to be wrapping up a simple idea in a lot of 'ifs' and 'buts'. Even the idea of a 'demand curve' seems highly theoretical and impractical. Any attempt to derive a demand curve from real, observed demand relationships immediately comes up against very great difficulties. Moreover, the very basis for producing a demand curve – that all other things remain constant – is never fulfilled in practice.

The Practicality of the Theory of Demand

Economists, of course, are well aware that demand is subject to a set of constantly changing forces. This is implicit in our list of factors likely to influence demand. In fact, increasing familiarity with the computer to handle fairly complex mathematical models is helping many students to see demand in terms of what mathematicians call a **function**. We could, for instance, express the list of influences in the form:

$$D = f(P_o, P_a, Y_d, T, A)$$

where:

D = the demand for a product
P_o = the product's own price
P_a = the prices of other goods
Y_d = the average disposable (after-tax) income of buyers
T = taste
A = the marketing effort devoted to the product by suppliers

In this general form the above expression simply puts into a kind of shorthand the ideas already expressed but this approach enables us to be much more specific about particular products. It can be adapted, say, to the specific function where:

$$Q_x = aP_o + bP_a + cY_d + dT + eA$$

where a, b, c, d and e represent the relative strengths of these influences in together producing the force that determines the quantity of x (Q_x) that is likely to be sold in a given time period.

When we look at demand in this light it is easy to appreciate the effort that firms need to make to identify the precise influences on the demand for the products and the relative importance of these influences. There is little point, for instance, in a business trying to boost sales through price cutting if other things are much more important. To take a very simple example, the sales of matches or lighter fuel are clearly closely related to the consumption of tobacco products. If people are smoking less tobacco and cigarettes this is more likely to reduce match sales than an increase in the price of matches. It would not be much use trying to boost sales of matches by a price reduction if tobacco sales were falling because of tax increases or health fears.

Our approach to demand theory also teaches us to be very careful in the identification of substitutes and complements for a particular commodity. To many of us beef and pork may appear to be fairly obvious substitutes but in communities observing strict religious taboos on the consumption of either of these they are certainly not substitutes. We need to be aware of the true extent of substitutability. For instance, if we simply assume that a new car is a means of transport we might think that potential buyers of new cars are more influenced by the level of train or bus fares than is, in fact, the case. If, however, we see the new car as a form of spending that contributes to the general comfort and status of the family then we are more likely to recognise that stronger substitutes might be found in double glazing, fitted kitchens or packaged foreign holidays.

The commercial producer needs to be aware of potential as well as actual substitutes. For example, after the Second World War, US manufacturers of equipment for electricity generating stations became aware of the long-term possibilities of nuclear power as a substitute for coal and oil and began research into peaceful applications of atomic power to prepare for possible future substitutes.

We shall be looking at these and related points in greater depth in later chapters. For now, you might find it interesting to pick an everyday object such as a record player, microwave cooker, can opener or brand of pet food and subject it to this kind of analysis to try and work out for yourself the relative importance of price in relation to the other factors likely to affect its demand.

Prices and Costs

We have not yet finished with our economic theory of demand. Look again at the list of factors affecting demand. Notice not just what **is** there but also what **is not**. The price of the commodity is included but not the cost of production. This is not a trivial point. To the economist **price** and **cost** are not alternative terms for the same idea. The price of an article is what the buyer is invited to pay for that article. Its cost represents what its production has cost the supplying firm.

If the price changes we expect that it may affect the quantity demanded. However, there is no reason why people should be prepared to pay any more or less just because costs of production have changed. If a firm's costs rise and it tries to pass these on to buyers in the form of a price increase, the likely effect is a fall in quantity demanded, the usual result of a price increase. Only if there have been changes in other influences such as prices of substitutes or rises in consumer incomes can the producer hope that a cost induced price increase will not cause a reduction in total sales.

Note also the rather long-winded definition of **quantity demanded** as the amount that consumers are both willing and able to buy at a given range of prices. Demand is not the same as **want** or **need**. Just because people want more of something or feel that they need more of it does not mean that they will buy more. They can only do this if they have the necessary income or access to credit. Few people could have more of a want or need for food than the people of sub-Saharan Africa, yet there is widespread starvation in that area. Why? It is because there is little demand for food. This may appear an appallingly callous statement but it is factually correct. People starve in spite of the presence of large stocks of food in the world because they cannot afford to buy it. They are willing to do so but cannot because they have so little income. Demand implies ability to pay as well as willingness or need to consume.

In commercial terms, there is little point in producing something for which there is next to no demand. This means that firms need to think carefully, not only whether people 'want' something but also whether they are willing and able to pay for it. In 1987 there were reports that a device had been invented to allow people to remove their car radios when the vehicle was parked, thus avoiding theft of the equipment. Doubtless many people would 'want' such a device but its reported likely selling price was over £300, several times the cost of a typical car radio. How many people would be prepared to pay such a price?

Finally, look again at the demand curve of Fig. 1.1. We have noted that it could be criticised for being rather unrealistic and artificial especially in the assumption that nothing else has changed. In fact, if we are alert to the very artificiality of the demand curve we are likely to be protected from some common errors. For example, if we observe that the price of a product in 1980 was £1 when, say, the quantity sold totalled a million and, in 1987 the price was £1.50 when only 100 000 were sold, we might be tempted to draw a demand curve as in Fig. 1.2.

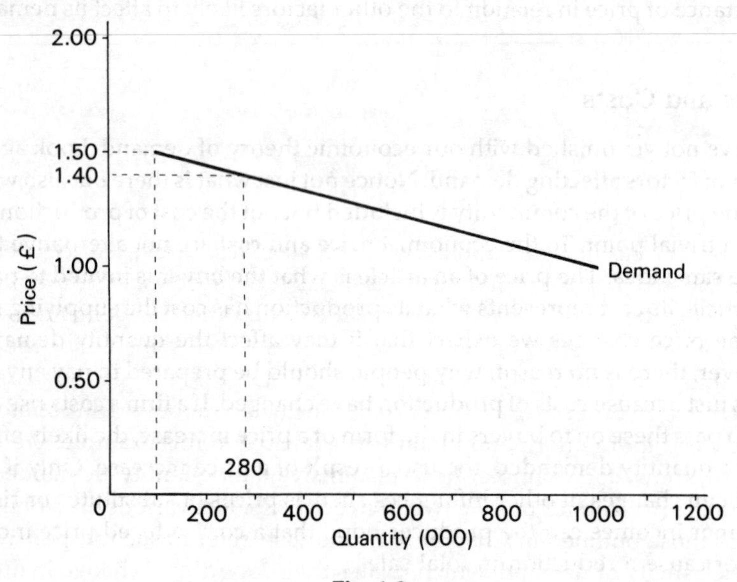

Fig. 1.2

In an effort to boost sales, we might suggest a small price cut. It appears that a 10p price reduction would boost sales from 100 000 to 280 000, an increase of 180 per cent. But remember that in drawing the demand curve we have assumed that all other things remained unchanged. Over a period of seven years this is hardly realistic. In fact, the true position may be closer to that illustrated in Fig. 1.3. DD_1 shows the position as it was in 1980. Over the years new, cheaper substitutes may have been developed. The price of complementary products may have increased sharply. Tastes could well have changed so that people no longer want this product in such quantities. The result of any or a combination of these influences could be that at any given price people want to buy less of this product. The result would be a new demand curve such as D′D″ in Fig. 1.3.

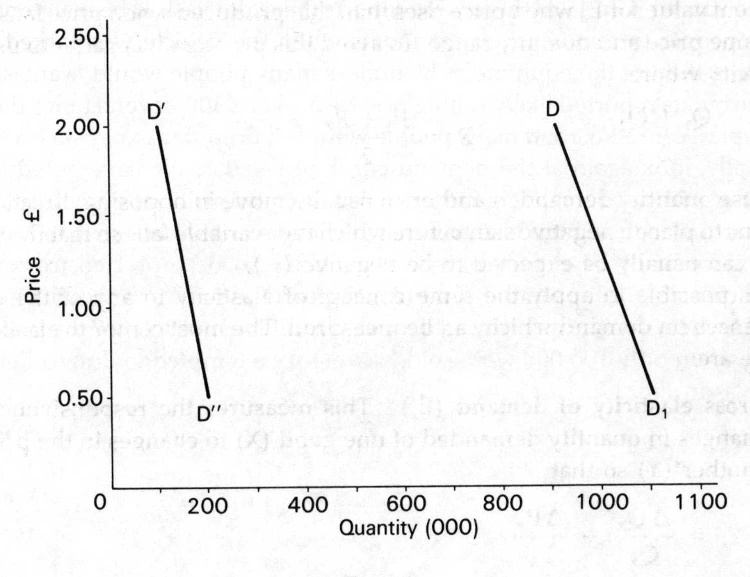

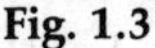
Fig. 1.3

Looking at this new demand curve we can see that, in fact, a price cut of 10p would cause only a very small increase in sales. Because we were aware of the scope of the theory of demand and of all the factors affecting demand, we were not deceived into drawing entirely erroneous conclusions about the likely effect of a price cut.

Of course, in order to draw the correct conclusions about pricing strategy we would need more information than was available in this example. We would need to know, for example, how **responsive** was quantity demanded to a change in price and for this we would need to conduct various marketing tests such as those outlined in Chapter 5. Economists refer to such responsiveness as the **elasticity of demand**, which relates the proportional change in quantity demanded to the proportional change in price:

$$\text{Price elasticity of demand} = \frac{\text{Proportional change in quantity demanded}}{\text{Proportional change in price}}$$

Price elasticity of demand, then, is the ratio of the **proportional change** in quantity demanded of a good to the **proportional change** in the price of that good. Using the Greek capital letter delta (Δ) as a symbol to represent a change in either quantity or price this ratio can be expressed in the form:

$$E_d = \frac{\Delta Q}{Q} \div \frac{\Delta P}{P}$$

where Q = the quantity before the change, P = the price before the change and E_d = price elasticity of demand.

It may occur to you that this formula, which is **point elasticity**, will produce a different value for E_d when price rises than that produced when price falls over the same price and quantity range. To avoid this problem it is better to use **arc elasticity** where:

$$Q = \frac{Q_1 + Q_2}{2} \quad \text{and} \quad P = \frac{P_1 + P_2}{2}$$

Because quantity demanded and price usually move in opposing directions it is usual to place a negative sign before whichever variable falls so that the value of E_d can usually be expected to be negative (−).

It is possible to apply the same concept of elasticity to any of the other influences on demand which can be measured. The most common elasticities in use are:

1 **Cross elasticity of demand (E_x)** This measures the responsiveness of changes in quantity demanded of one good (X) to changes in the price of another (Y) so that:

$$E_x = \frac{\Delta Q_X}{Q_X} \div \frac{\Delta P_Y}{P_Y}$$

2 **Income elasticity of demand (E_y)** This measures the responsiveness of changes in quantity demanded of a good (X) to changes in disposable income (Y_d) (income remaining after deduction of income tax and compulsory national insurance contributions). This measure is also a ratio of the two proportional changes so that:

$$E_y = \frac{\Delta Q_X}{Q_X} \div \frac{\Delta Y_d}{Y_d}$$

Both cross and income elasticity can be calculated as point or as arc measures as for price elasticity of demand.

Before leaving the present examination of demand you might like to ask yourself questions such as:

1 What would be the likely effect of an increase in income on the demand for such products as package holidays abroad, Mini cars, 'do-it-yourself' (DIY) tools, touring caravans?
2 What would you regard as substitutes for these goods and what would be the effect of increases in their prices?
3 What effect would increases in taxes have on the demand for these and similar goods?

The Law of Supply and Demand

This is one of those economic 'laws' and ideas – others include **diminishing returns** and **economies of scale** – which most people seem to have heard about and most would think they understand but which economists again seem to have made unnecessarily complicated and theoretical. What does it mean?

Most people would answer along the lines of 'If the demand for something increases, then somebody will supply it,' or 'There's no point in going on producing something if there is no demand for it.' In economics, however, this 'law' relates to a number of conclusions drawn from a number of interactions between the theories of demand and supply.

Background to the Theory of Supply

If anything, the theory of supply, as it appears from some economics texts, looks even more complicated and abstract than the theory of demand. Nevertheless we should look at some of its basic elements. Once again we can identify some fundamental factors affecting supply, which we can define as **the quantity of a commodity that producers are prepared to offer for sale at prices within a given range.** Notice that this is **not** the amount actually sold at a particular price. This depends on the interaction of both the forces of supply and of demand.

The influences on supply include:

1. The price of the commodity (a term used here in the general sense of any physical good or service or factor of production).
2. The prices that producers have to pay for production factors, e.g. wages paid for labour, and prices of goods, services and materials used in the production process. These all affect the cost of production. If the prices of production factors rise and it becomes more expensive to make certain products then producers will supply a smaller quantity of those products at the prevailing price which they receive, or they will seek to obtain a higher price if they are to continue producing the same quantity.
3. The prices of other goods and services that can be made using the same production factors and materials. If it becomes more profitable to make X than Y then producers of Y will switch production from Y to X if they have the means to do so. Even the finest quality farm land sited close to a large and overcrowded city is unlikely to continue in agricultural use if the government gives permission for it to be used for building purposes.
4. Taxes levied on producers at some stage in the production process. Producers will seek to recover the amount of tax from buyers through increased prices but their ability to do so – as in the case of increased input costs – will depend on the interaction of both demand and supply intentions.
5. The state of technology, advances in which usually mean that a given quantity of product can be produced using a smaller quantity of production factors, a tendency which reduces production costs and permits more to be

offered for sale at any given price – assuming as always that other things, including factor prices, remain the same.

The first four of the above supply influences are usually considered to affect supply **in the short run**, i.e. producers have to react fairly swiftly to such changes if they are to avoid substantial losses. Changes in technology are considered to affect supply **in the long run**. There is always a time lag between invention and its large-scale commercial exploitation. It is, of course, a feature of modern production that this time interval is much less than it was in the past but it does still exist.

As with demand we can represent supply by a curve, the supply curve, which relates quantity which producers are willing to supply, to price. This general point is illustrated in Fig. 1.4.

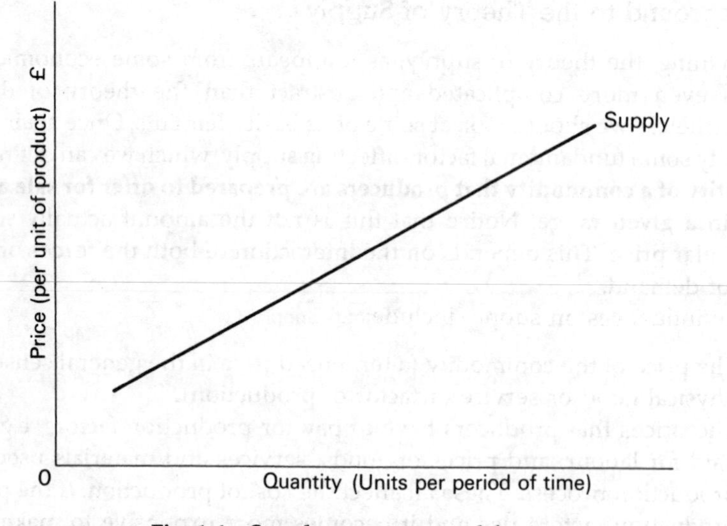

Fig. 1.4 Supply curve – general form

As in our analysis of demand, we recognise that matters other than price may be more important than price in affecting supply intentions. For example, an innovation such as the use of transistors in radios or microchips in computers may bring about very significant increases in the quantity of product that can be offered at a given price – or reduce the price at which a given quantity may be offered. A change in an influence other than the price of the commodity is shown by a shift in the supply curve from SS_1 to $S' S''$ in Fig. 1.5.

At this point you should work out for yourself the answers to questions such as:

1 What would be the effect on supply of:
a a rise in wages?
b a drought (for agricultural produce)?
c an increase in tax paid by producers?
(Notes on these questions are at the end of the chapter.)

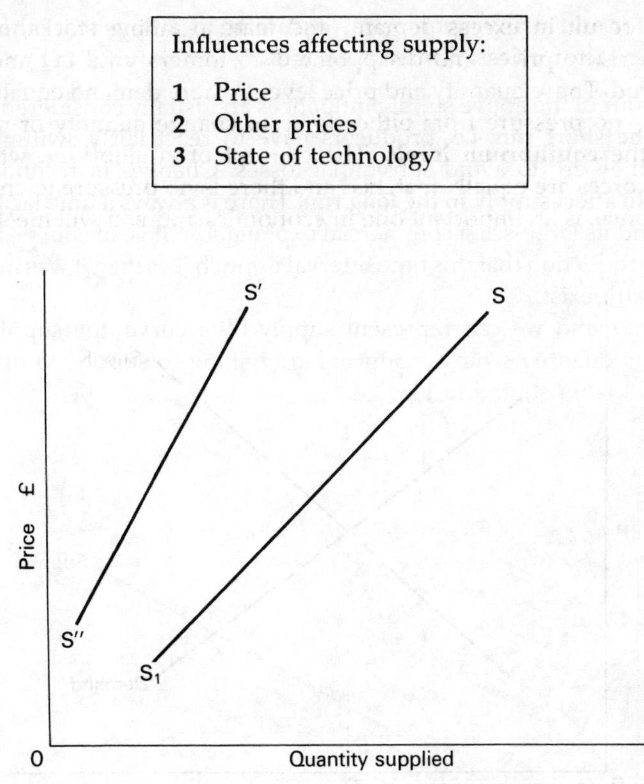

Fig. 1.5 Effect of a change in influence other than price on the supply curve

Supply, Demand and Price

In simple terms, and in the absence of any outside intervention, the price of a commodity is determined by the interaction of the separate forces of supply and demand where the intentions of buyers match those of suppliers. Graphically this condition is represented by the intersection of the demand and supply curves as illustrated in Fig. 1.6.

The significance of the price 0P in Fig. 1.6 is that at this price, and only at this price, the quantity demanded, i.e. the amount that buyers wish to buy, is the same as the quantity supplied, i.e. the amount that suppliers wish to supply, at 0Q. This may sound obvious but note that it is **not** the same as saying that the amount bought is equal to the amount sold. That must always be true if you think about it. However, it is quite possible for the amount demanded to differ from the amount supplied. For example, in Fig. 1.7, at price $0P_1$ there is excess supply. Firms are producing far more than customers are willing to buy at that price. In consequence, stocks will rise and some firms will respond by cutting production or ceasing to supply that commodity. Others are likely to reduce price so that there will be a tendency to move to the quantity (0Q) and price level (0P) where supply intentions equal demand intentions. Similarly a price of $0P_2$ will result in excess demand and lead to falling stocks, increased production, rising prices and disappointed customers until 0Q and 0P are again restored. These quantity and price levels, where demand equals supply, and there is no pressure from either force to change quantity or price, are known as the **equilibrium levels**. The concept of equilibrium, where two interacting forces are equally matched and there is no pressure to change the present balance, is an important one in economics and you will meet it many times.

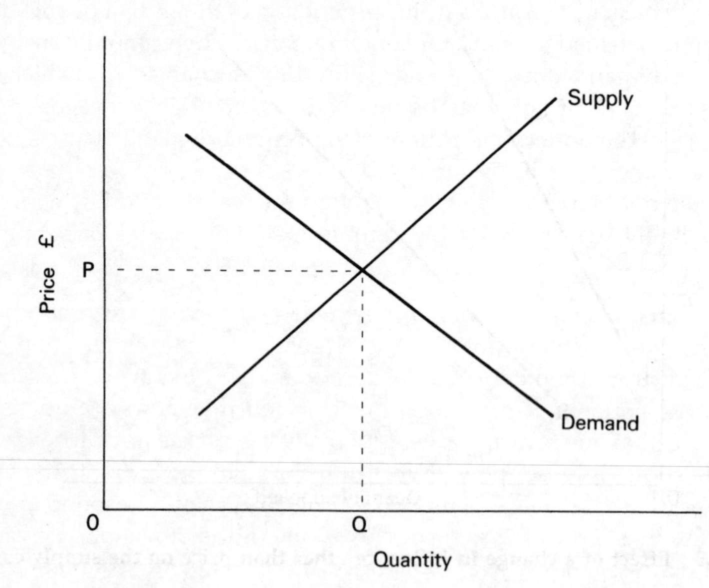

Fig. 1.6

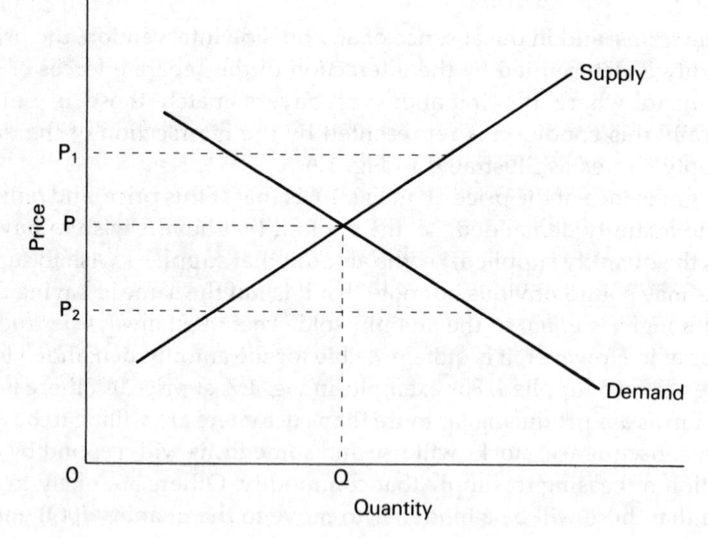

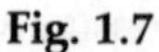

Fig. 1.7

The Operation of Supply and Demand in Practice

The process we have just outlined is the mechanism by which the interaction of supply and demand operates to 'clear the market' but a number of points should now be apparent. The law of supply and demand does not guarantee that everyone who wants something will get it, nor that there will always be a buyer for everything produced at the price wanted by the producer. It does not say that there will be no shortages and no gluts. It is quite possible for there to be, at least in the short term, a surplus production of things that people do not want or an unsatisfied demand for something else. The economic analysis of supply and demand does, however, show the mechanism by which such shortages and gluts are likely to be removed and the likely consequences of any changes in the underlying pattern of supply and demand. It also suggests how these changes are likely to arise.

We should note some key points that reflect the reality of the business world more accurately than some of the simple everyday notions of supply and demand.

1 All the customers and firms in this theory are reacting to price changes beyond their own control. Price is established by the interaction of the forces of supply and demand and they adapt their behaviour accordingly. But what happens if price is not established in this way? Suppose, for example, that one firm is so powerful that it can set the price. Then there is no question of the supplier having to respond to the 'going market price' because there is none. It is up to the firm concerned to respond to excess demand or supply as it wishes. This is one of the attractions for firms of securing the market power to fix price and of removing competitors who might otherwise upset the pricing strategy it chooses. It is also one of the reasons why governments tend to be hostile towards monopolies and price rings which enable firms to control price or quantity of production. When firms, either individually or in groups working together by agreement, gain this power the free interplay between supply and demand disappears and customers are the losers.
2 The way supply operates in the theory is based on the assumption that consumers have an absolutely free choice between suppliers while these cannot charge any price higher than those of competitors without losing all their business to their rivals. These assumptions sound highly artificial and this becomes even more apparent when you realise that the supply curves you have been examining have their roots in an economic concept called **perfect competition** which resembles hardly any real world conditions ever encountered. In this it is similar to the concept of the perfect vacuum developed by physical scientists and which cannot be found anywhere in the natural universe.

Perfect Competition

In economics the term **perfect competition** has no moral or ethical significance nor is it a guarantee that consumers will always be better off than in any other market situation. It simply describes a market in which the forces of supply and demand interact completely freely without the intervention of any non-economic influence or constraint. The requirements for such a perfect market to exist are:

1 The good traded in the market is homogeneous, i.e. any one unit is perceived as being the same as any other so that buyers are indifferent as to which they receive.
2 No individual supplier or buyer or group of suppliers or buyers acting together can influence the market price so that all have to accept the market price and current market conditions.
3 All suppliers and buyers are free to enter or leave the market in accordance with their own judgement and without any restraint.
4 Information is instantly available to all and no supplier or buyer has access to information not available to everyone else in the market and the good traded is available on the same terms in all parts of the market.
5 Each supplier and buyer is guided by economic considerations only and these are interpreted as the desire to maximise self-interest, i.e. buyers seek to maximise their utility from buying and suppliers seek to maximise their profits.

You can see that these are extreme conditions that are unattainable in the real world. To summarise, the conditions for perfect competition are:

1 Very large (infinite) number of suppliers;
2 Very large (infinite) number of consumers;
3 Identical products produced by all;
4 Perfect information about prices, products, etc., possessed by all;
5 Firms and customers at perfect liberty to enter or leave the market without cost.

Since very few real world markets approach the conditions required for perfect competition does this mean that the economic theory of supply and demand is dealing with an irrelevant, fantasy world? Not at all. It makes two important contributions to our understanding of the real economy:

1 It attempts to predict how markets will tend to adjust, how prices, output and consumption will change and adapt under **perfect** (in the economic sense) conditions. Anything less than perfect conditions will mean that the real world effects will be somewhat different.
2 It reminds us that things will only adjust in this frictionless, automatic way under highly unrealistic conditions. The simple view of how the law of supply and demand operates will not do for an understanding of how things happen in reality. In the real world, where products are not identical between firms, where it is expensive to break into new markets and where ignorance is widespread, not least concerning what is likely to happen tomorrow, firms and consumers are continually faced with the need to make decisions without the convenient assistance of automatic market signals like market prices to guide them.

Business Decision-making

This book is largely about business decisions. Sometimes economics can help to point the way to a decision; sometimes it simply provides a cautionary element by pointing out further aspects of a problem that may not have been obvious.

One thing is certain. In business, decisions are constantly having to be made. They cannot be avoided. Not making a decision can be as significant, sometimes more significant, than making one. Imagine being in a blazing room and not making a choice between going out through the door or jumping through the window! Nothing makes itself – materials, machines and people all have to be brought together and organised effectively. Nothing sells itself – potential customers have to be identified, likely market trends identified and competitors fought off. These are the concerns of the decision-maker, the person who, in economics texts, is often called **the entrepreneur**.

One Basic Tool

We have already come across one basic idea, developed and refined by economists, which can be continually used by business decision-makers. This is the concept of opportunity cost and it has been further developed into the notion of **marginal analysis**. The basic idea is that, when making any decision, you should pay attention to what are the **extra** benefits and **extra** costs that will result from that decision.

For example, a firm making reproduction furniture will be aware that its costs include not only material, labour and fuel charges but also the hire-purchase charges on its machines and the rent on its premises. Its selling price must cover all these if it is to break even, leave alone make a profit.

Suppose it has the possibility of meeting an extra order at a price that is slightly less than the firm has been charging for similar goods. To meet the order the employer would have to ask some workers to work overtime at higher wage rates. On the face of it the firm's costs would be higher and the receipts less than normal. Surely then the order should be rejected.

But should it? Remember that costs such as the hire-purchase charges and rent have already been met by normal production and sales. What the firm has to consider are the **marginal costs**, i.e. the **extra** labour, material and fuel costs, and it has to compare these with the **marginal revenue**, i.e. the extra sales receipts resulting from the order. If additional receipts are greater than additional costs – and if existing customers are not likely to be upset by finding out that one customer has been charged a lower price – accepting the order will increase the firm's profits.

We shall be using the idea of marginal analysis again later in the book. Marginal analysis is one of the key tools of economic analysis which are of practical use to business decision-makers. Although economic theories, such as those of demand, supply and competition, appear rather abstract, we have seen that their rigour alerts us to important facts about the business environment that might otherwise be overlooked.

Notes to the Suggested Exercises

Demand Curve

The likely result of an increase in income is a shift to the right of the demand curve – for most products more will be bought as incomes rise. Some products may be deserted for preferred, more expensive substitutes and so the demand curve would shift to the left. Much will depend on existing income levels. For example, as incomes rise more people spend time improving their homes. As incomes rise further they may decide to spend their time in travel and pay professional decorators to work on their homes.

A rise in the price of substitutes is likely to shift the demand curve to the right. At any given price, more people will buy the product rather than the more expensive substitutes.

If there is an increase in tax the demand curve does not change. Consumers are influenced by the price not by what happens to the money paid – whether it goes to the producers or to the government in the form of tax.

Supply Curve

A rise in wages will shift the supply curve to the left. An increase in costs means that firms will only offer the same amount for sale if they can obtain a higher price.

A drought would shift the supply curve to the left because farmers obtain less product for the costs they have to pay and the effort they make.

An increase in tax will shift the supply curve to the left. It has the same effect on producers as an increase in a factor or input cost.

You should now observe changes in the environment that take place during your studies and work out what effect, if any, they are likely to have on supply and demand curves.

Suggestions for Further Reading

This chapter has been concerned with the elements of basic microeconomic analysis. These are to be found in any good textbook. However, on the assumption that you are not pursuing a course that requires prolonged study of theoretical economics the following is recommended:

D. Blight and T. Shafto, *Microeconomics*, Hutchinson, 1989.

Appendix to Chapter 1

The Revenues of the Firm

Revenue is the gross amount received from sales of the firm's product during an accounting period. We refer to:

1 **Total revenue (TR)** which is the amount received from all sales during the period, e.g. if 200 articles are sold each at a price of £1 per article TR = £200.

2 **Average revenue (AR)** which is the total revenue divided by the number of units of the product sold, e.g. if TR = £200 and 100 units have been sold then AR = £2. If 200 units are sold for the same TR then AR = £1. If, at any given quantity of sales, all articles or units are sold at the same price then AR = Price (P)

3 **Marginal revenue (MR)** which is the change in the total revenue when there is a small (one unit) change in quantity sold in the accounting period, e.g. if, when 100 units are sold TR = £1000 but when 101 units are sold TR = 1009, then MR = £9.

The Firm as Price Taker

If the firm is able to (or can only) sell all it can produce at the same price (as illustrated in Fig. 1.8) then P = AR = MR. Notice that at quantity Q_n, TR = P × Q_n. Since AR is TR divided by Q_n then AR = P. When quantity rises by one unit to $Q_n + 1$ the addition to total revenue is the unchanged unit price. Since this addition is marginal revenue then MR = P. Under these conditions P = AR = MR.

The Firm as Price Maker

If the firm can increase quantity sold by reducing price or has to reduce price in order to increase quantity sold then the position changes, as illustrated in Fig. 1.9. Here the firm is able to sell quantity Q_n at a price of P but can only sell

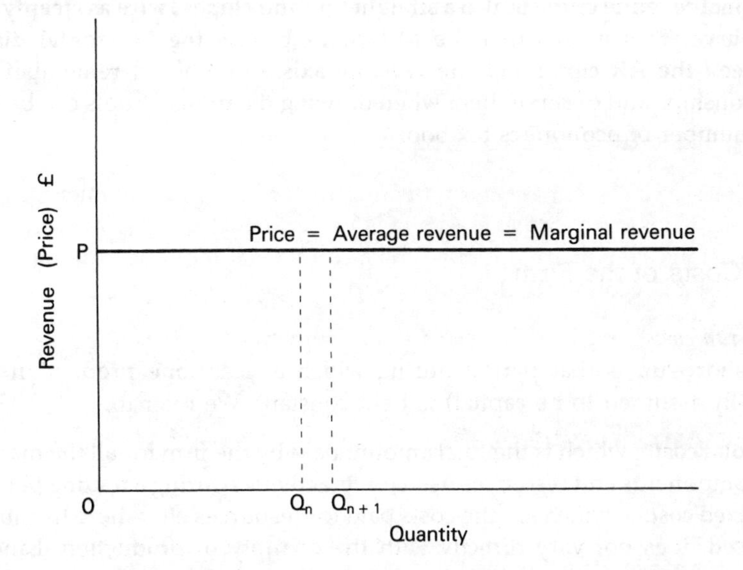

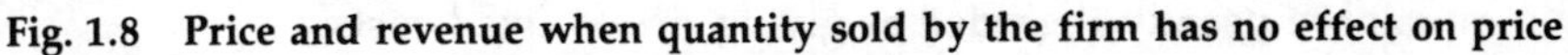
Fig. 1.8 Price and revenue when quantity sold by the firm has no effect on price

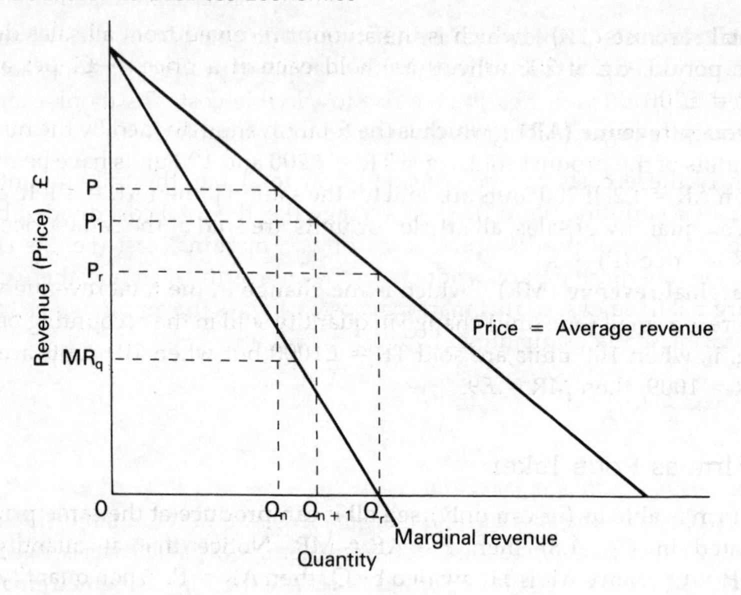

Fig. 1.9 Price and revenue when a rise in quantity sold results in a fall in price

$Q_n + 1$ if price is reduced to P_1. Since P_1 is lower than P then the marginal revenue (MR) can no longer equal price. The marginal revenue, being the change in total revenue, is now $P_1(Q_n + 1) - PQ$ and is, in fact, MR_q. Assuming that at any given quantity level the firm sells all units at the same price then this price is still the same as the average revenue.

When, as in Fig. 1.9, the price and average revenue curve is a straight line the marginal revenue curve is also a straight line and **slopes twice as steeply as the AR curve**. This means that the MR curve **bisects the horizontal distance between the AR curve and the revenue axis**. You should remember these relationships and observe them when drawing diagrams. Proofs can be found in a number of economics textbooks.

The Costs of the Firm

Short-run costs

The short run is that period during which at least one production factor (usually assumed to be capital) is held constant. We refer to:

1 **Total cost** which is the total amount paid by the firm for all the materials, components and resources used for its activities during a trading period.
2 **Fixed costs** which are the costs paid for resources etc. where the quantity used does not vary directly with the quantity of production. Land and capital are usually regarded as giving rise to fixed costs.

3 **Variable costs** which are the costs paid for resources etc. where the quantity used does vary directly with quantity of production. Raw materials used in production clearly give rise to variable costs. Textbook examples frequently regard labour as giving rise to a variable cost.

Each of these costs can be considered in **total** (i.e. the full amount paid during an accounting period), as an **average** (i.e. the total cost divided by the number of units of product produced) or as a **marginal cost** (i.e. the cost of producing one more unit of product). In the short run, of course, there can be no marginal fixed cost so that marginal cost is always the amount of change in total variable costs as quantity changes by one unit.

Graphical representation of short-run costs

Figure 1.10 shows the average and marginal costs and their relationships. The difference between average total costs and average variable costs is, of course, the averaged fixed cost. It is important to realise that **the rising marginal cost curve cuts both the average variable and the average total costs at their lowest points**.

As production is increased in the short run marginal costs will increase due to diminishing marginal returns, i.e. the tendency for increased increments of the variable production factors to add diminishing amounts to total production when at least one factor is kept constant. When marginal cost is above average cost the average must also rise. You can test this for yourself with any set of figures.

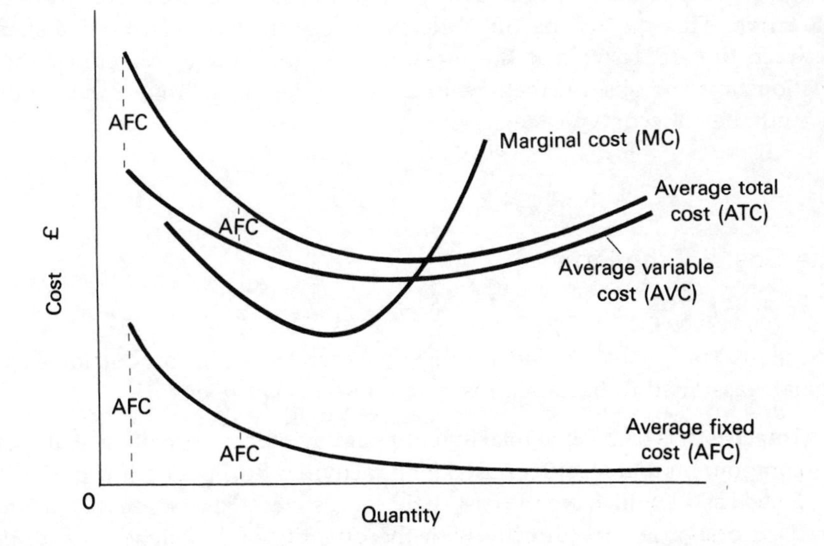

Fig. 1.10 Short-term average costs

Long-run costs

In the long run all production factors become variable and fixed costs rise in stages. As long as firms can increase **all** factors, including levels of technology and managerial skill, it may be possible to prevent marginal costs from rising above average total costs so that the U-shaped curve can be flattened. The long-run average total cost curve may thus assume a shape that is roughly similar to the average fixed cost curve in Fig. 1.10.

2 Entrepreneurship and the Structure of Business

More about the Entrepreneur

In Chapter 1 we introduced the economic concept of the **entrepreneur**, the person responsible for making business decisions about markets, products and technology and organising the factors of production. In addition, the entrepreneur is supposed to be a risk-taker in business. The production of goods and services always involves an element of risk as resources have to be committed to production and, therefore, costs incurred, before any revenues are earned. This applies in any type of commercial undertaking. At one extreme, we have already seen how companies producing electricity generating equipment started spending money on research into nuclear energy decades before this source of power started to be widely used. Oil companies have to undertake exploration for new fields many years before these can be expected to yield commercial returns given the time necessary for commercial development. Such projects are said to have very long **lead times**. At the other extreme even a window-cleaner undertakes commercial risks. Bad weather may prevent him from undertaking his rounds; customers may move and no longer require his services. Even when he is actually cleaning windows there is always the risk that the customer may not pay.

However, while it is true that every business involves some element of risk, can it be true to say that every business involves entrepreneurship? The window-cleaner is clearly an entrepreneur, putting in his own time and money, making decisions and carrying the risks himself, but where is the entrepreneur in the large firm? It is possible to point to one or two individuals who have been spectacularly successful entrepreneurs. Alan Sugar of Amstrad, Richard Branson of Virgin and Anita Roddick of Bodyshop have all built up large businesses by seizing market opportunities, developing products or services and tapping new markets. Nevertheless these tend to be the exceptions rather than the rule. Most large businesses are not headed by entrepreneurs of this kind but by managers who have worked their way through the organisation or who have been brought in from outside. Even if the businesses are successful where is the entrepreneur?

It may be true to say that every business involves **entrepreneurship** rather than an identifiable entrepreneur. In the larger business the different elements of entrepreneurship may be undertaken by different people working together. In this chapter we examine how this is achieved and some of the implications for the structure of business.

The Basis of Business

Let us begin by summarising briefly the basic elements of any business:

1 **Decision-making** This involves the fundamental questions:
 – What is to be produced? (This concerns the product.)
 – Who is it to be produced for? (This concerns the market.)
 – How is it to be produced? (This concerns resources and technology.)
2 **Resources** These relate to the labour, capital and other inputs required for the production process.
3 **Co-ordination and organisation** This is the work of bringing the resources together, i.e. to carry out the decisions that have been made.
4 **Risk taking** This is chiefly concerned with risks arising because resources have to be acquired and committed and, consequently, costs incurred, before revenues are earned.

In the small business all the activities may be carried out by one individual who decides what he or she wishes to do, puts up the capital, invests his or her own time and labour, organises the business and takes the risk. In the larger business there is likely to be an element of specialisation so that different people or groups of people undertake different activities.

Financial Capital for Business

We shall be looking in detail at the sources of business financial capital in Chapter 8. At this stage we need to distinguish between **risk capital** and other types. Consider the following example.

Bright has observed that many students who want to buy textbooks cannot afford the full price. On the other hand, many of last year's students have left on their hands textbooks that they do not want. Bright reasons that textbooks bought from last year's students could be resold to this year's at a profit. All that is required is some money to finance the operation and the willingness to take the chance of being left with a lot of unsold books.

Bright has little money so he approaches two colleagues, Shaw and Gamble. Shaw agrees to lend Bright some money for a year. At the end of that time the loan is to be repaid with the addition of some interest. Bright agrees that this repayment will be made even if the business venture is not a success. Gamble, on the other hand, agrees to put some money into Bright's venture on a profit-sharing basis. If it makes money some of this will go to Gamble and some to Bright. If it makes a loss this too will be shared. There is no obligation for Bright to repay Gamble if the venture loses money.

Gamble's investment is of **risk capital**; Shaw's is a **loan**. Each is involved in the venture in a different way. Shaw is simply providing the use of capital without taking any risk, other than failing to secure repayment of the loan from Bright. Gamble is assuming the function of providing some of the capital and is also sharing the business risk. If the money is raised from Shaw then Bright remains the sole entrepreneur. If it is raised from Gamble then the functions of entrepreneurship are shared.

Most of the money used by business in the UK is, in fact, risk capital rather than loans. This risk capital comes either from new injections of funds from the owners of the business or from other individuals, or, much more frequently, from the profits earned by the business which are thus 'ploughed back' into the organisation. Over 50 per cent of new capital for investment in business comes from these **retained profits**.

Paradoxically, if a business relies too much on borrowing rather than obtaining risk capital this, in itself, can be very risky. One of the great attractions of raising money through risk capital is that there is no obligation to make any payment unless profits are made. If, on the other hand, loans are raised, there is usually an obligation to repay or to pay interest whether or not any profit is earned to enable the obligation to be met. This by itself can cause the failure of a business venture. This issue is discussed further in Chapter 8.

Legal Liability

Unlimited Liability

In terms of sheer numbers the majority of businesses in the UK are what are termed **sole proprietorships** or **partnerships**. These are businesses established with a minimum of formality in which one person or group of people undertakes all the entrepreneurial functions. They put up the risk capital, organise the business, make all the decisions and take all the risks. If the business succeeds they take the profits. If it fails they stand all the losses. If the losses are great this could even involve the loss of their private assets and personal bankruptcy. Indeed the law recognises no basic distinction between the assets and liabilities of their business and those such as houses and mortgages that they have as private citizens.

This can be a particular problem for partnerships. In the case of Bright's book venture, business failure could mean that many business debts remained unpaid. Bright, as sole proprietor, would be responsible for paying these even if this meant the sale of personal possessions. These debts could include money borrowed from Shaw who would, himself, be a creditor of this business and would certainly have no obligations to assist Bright in meeting his other business debts. On the other hand, if Gamble had put money into the business on a profit-sharing basis, Gamble and Bright would very likely be regarded in law as partners. This would mean that Gamble would be risking not only the original amount of money he invested but also the chance of being called upon to meet all of Bright's business debts if the venture failed and if Bright had no personal assets of any value.

This unlimited liability for the debts of a partnership can obviously act as a deterrent against people putting money into risky business ventures – and all businesses, by their very nature, involve an element of risk. If you put money into a partnership other than as a genuine loan, you may be risking not only the money invested but all your other assets as well. Note too that your liability is not just limited to your share of the partnership debts but to the full amount of the debts. Any creditor can take legal action against any one of the partners for full recovery of the business debts.

This deterrent extends both to rich investors and to those of modest means. The latter will fear even fairly moderate losses over and above the original investment. For the former there is the risk that creditors will, logically, proceed against rich rather than poorer partners in greater hope of recovering their money.

One implication, therefore, of unlimited liability is that many potential investors will be deterred. The supply of capital to business will be less than it might otherwise be. Many potentially successful, but risky, ventures will not be undertaken. Innovation may be stifled.

A second implication is that, even if people invest in partnerships, they are unlikely to be content to restrict their involvement to the provision of capital. Decisions by other partners could commit them to unsustainable losses. Consequently they will probably insist on some say in running the business. They will want to take part in decision-making, at least at the most general level. This is likely to mean that quite apart from any legal restriction on the number of partners, a partnership is likely to be limited in size by the number of people who require a say in the management of the business. It would also be difficult to build up significant levels of management among the partners. After all, when someone stands to lose everything as a result of bad management it is difficult to expect that person to defer to decisions made by others if he or she disagrees with them.

There is, in fact, a provision under the Limited Partnerships Act of 1907 for the formation of **limited partnerships**. In these it is possible to invest as a **limited partner**. Such a partner stands only to lose the money invested in the business as long as:

1 no part is taken in running the business;
2 there is at least one **general partner** who accepts full, unlimited liability.

There are many limited partnerships, but for most types of business the attractions of limited company status, described in the next section, are much greater.

Some implications of unlimited liability

All this tends to mean that:

1 With few exceptions, unlimited liability organisations tend to be small. They are very numerous but collectively account for only a minor part of

total business activity. They tend to be concentrated in business sectors suited to small firms (see Chapter 4) and/or where the risks of large financial losses are also small.

2 In unlimited liability organisations the different functions of entrepreneurship – decision-making, risk-taking and management – tend to be undertaken by the same people. The nature of the personal risks they are taking usually drives such people to assume all these roles which are more easily separated where the contributors of capital enjoy limited liability.

Limited Liability

The concept of limited liability

The idea of limited liability is a simple one: it is that one's liability for an investment is limited to the amount actually invested. This and no more can be lost by the investor. It is a simple change from unlimited liability but the implications are enormous. Going back to our example of the books venture, if this were established as a limited liability operation the implications for Bright, Shaw, Gamble, customers and suppliers would all be different. Bright would know that if the business failed his personal liability would extend only to the amount risked in the business. Even if debts to suppliers or customers were run up as long as these were incurred in the course of the legitimate fortunes (or misfortunes) of business, the creditors could not look to Bright personally to make them good.

This would also apply to Gamble who has invested money on a profit and loss sharing basis. The sky might be the limit for profits but potential losses are limited to the amount invested. One might reasonably expect both Bright and Gamble to be even more prepared to take risks than previously.

The business risks, however, have not disappeared. It is sometimes said that limited liability reduces business risks. This is not true. What it does is to transfer some of the risk, often to unsuspecting people. In this example, limited liability would mean that Bright and Gamble run less risk. Consequently someone else must be running more. In fact, the extra risk is being carried by the creditors of the business. Shaw may now find that the loan is not repaid. Suppliers who have sent goods on credit, customers who have paid in advance for goods, all these may find themselves out of pocket and without redress, as long as Bright has not actually behaved fraudulently.

Put like this limited liability sometimes appears like a licence for sharp practice and, indeed, horror stories of unpaid debts left by unscrupulous people protected by limited liability are the stock-in-trade of many journalists. However, it should be pointed out that a variety of Acts of Parliament, notably the Companies Act 1985 and the Insolvency Act 1986, define the responsibilities of those running limited liability organisations in attempts to restrict the possibilities for such abuse. Nevertheless, by the very nature of business some risks remain. The object of limited liability is to reduce the risks run by those owning and operating businesses. This has to result in a corresponding increase in the risks run by other people.

Some implications of limited liability

Why has this privilege – for that is what it really is – of limited liability been created by law? Some possible answers can be suggested.

1 More people are encouraged to invest in business and a greater supply of risk capital is, thereby, made available to business. This is because:
   a investors in limited liability organisations risk only their investments and not the whole of their personal assets;
   b it follows that there is not the same need as in unlimited liability organisations to participate actively in the management and decision-making activities of the firm, investors needing to undertake only the capital providing and risk-bearing activities of entrepreneurship, leaving the remaining aspects to others.
2 With more risk capital available and with less need for investors to become involved in the details of running businesses, it becomes much easier to construct large organisations and the managerial hierarchies these require. Specialisation of management activity can occur and various economies of scale exploited to the full with a consequent reduction of unit costs and prices.
3 Many more businesses may be set up. This may be socially beneficial as competition may be increased and more employment opportunities created.
4 More innovation may be encouraged with businesses being encouraged to develop new products, technologies and markets, all of which imply an increase in risk.
5 It may make possible the development of a stock market as shareholder investors in a business are able to discharge themselves of all responsibility for it simply by selling their shares to someone else. This, in turn, makes it still easier for people to invest in business and it further encourages the supply of risk capital.

We must not, however, the negative possibilities inherent in limited liability. These include:

1 There are opportunities for the incompetent and unscrupulous to run businesses recklessly or fraudulently and run up losses which fall on other people.
2 There is a possibility that too many risky ventures will be established, implying a waste of scarce economic resources available to the community.
3 There is a further possibility that investors may take little interest in how their businesses are run. This gives rise to a separation of ownership from control. It also means that, although the investors are the legal owners of a business, the business is in fact run by managers with little, if any, ownership stake.

A note of caution

The attraction of establishing one's own business on a limited liability basis sometimes appears so great that, very often, people setting up in business for the first time feel that they must immediately make it a limited liability company. This can be a mistake. Substantial creditors, such as banks and landlords, are aware of the perils of dealing with limited liability organisations and often ask the owners of small limited liability organisations to act as guarantors for the debts of the business. This means that their limited liability for certain types of debt is taken away. In addition, the directors (this term is explained in the next section) of limited companies are personally responsible for seeing that tax money owed is paid to the Inland Revenue or to Customs and Excise authorities. The principle underlying this provision is that money becomes the taxpayers' as soon as PAYE has been stopped from employees' pay or VAT paid by customers. If company directors use this money before handing it over to the tax collecting authorities then they do so at their own personal risk.

Furthermore, in the UK, there are certain tax advantages in setting up as a sole proprietor or partnership rather than as a limited liability company. All in all, one should think long and hard before deciding whether or not to proceed on a limited liability basis.

Limited Liability Companies

Basic Structure and Types of Companies

In terms of importance in the economy by far the most important type of limited liability organisation is the limited company. Although they can be set up in a number of different ways the most common business company in Britain is the **joint stock company** which is limited by shares and which is established under one or other of the Companies Acts passed by Parliament. The joint stock is formed from the money paid to the company by **shareholders** in return for their shares. Shareholders are thus also known sometimes as **stockholders**. In law a limited company is deemed to have **corporate personality**, that is to say it is regarded in law as a person in its own right quite apart from the people who own it. The company can own assets such as buildings and machinery and incur liabilities such as debts to creditors. Quite separately from its owners it can make contracts which are legally binding agreements, and it can sue others or be sued in its own right in order to enforce contracts.

It is the legal fiction of corporate personality that makes limited liability possible for the owners of a limited company. For the debts of the firm are truly the debts of the firm only. The owners cannot be held liable in law for these debts. Indeed, if the firm, as a going concern, cannot meet all its debts and is **wound up** (ceases to exist legally as a company), then any money left over after paying all other creditors belongs to the owners who are also regarded as creditors, though ranking last in order of priority for meeting debts.

Because of the distinct privileges conferred on owners by limited liability there are more legal restrictions placed on limited companies than on unlimited liability organisations. These requirements include:

1 **Registration** All companies must be formally registered, for a fee, with the Registrar of Companies. Certain basic information must be registered. This includes the name of the firm, its registered office and the list of original shareholders. After formation a register of shareholders must be kept to show changes of share ownership.
2 **Publication of accounts** It seems only reasonable that other members of society should be able to check whether a limited liability organisation is creditworthy. To this end, all limited companies must make to the Registrar an annual return which includes a basic set of accounts for the year. These accounts are available for public scrutiny on payment of a fee.
3 **The memorandum and the articles of association** These documents are filed with the Registrar. They are supposed to set out the nature of the business the firm intends to carry on (the memorandum) and how it is supposed to be organised internally (the articles). The articles of association set out the rights held by shareholders, outline the requirements for the annual general meeting and provide for the appointment of auditors and directors, including the managing director, among many other matters relating to the legal structure of the company. In practice both the memorandum and articles are usually drawn up in a standard way laid down by regulations made under the Companies Acts.
4 **Directors and their duties** All companies must have at least one director, elected by the shareholders. Most have a group or board of directors who have overall responsibility for running the business. The various Companies Acts place obligations on the directors, for example to ensure that the annual return is made and that the company does not trade when insolvent, i.e. that it does not run up further debts when it has no chance of repaying those it already has. Although historically the directors have always been regarded as the representatives of the shareholders and, therefore, with a duty to run the company in their financial interests, modern legislation and the judgements of the courts have tended increasingly to stress that directors should also recognise that they have a wider duty to see that the company takes heed of the best interests of the community.

In Britain there are two types of companies limited by share. These are private and public limited companies.

Public limited companies, usually distinguished by the letters PLC, have to conform to certain minimum requirements. At the time of writing they have to have a share capital of at least £50 000 of which not less than £12 500 has to be fully paid and the memorandum of association must contain a statement that the company is a public company limited by shares. Companies which meet these conditions can have their shares and loan stocks freely bought and sold by members of the public, normally through a stock exchange. In 1988 there were around 6000 public limited companies.

Private limited companies, of which in 1988 there were over a million registered though many were no longer active, include all companies limited by shares which are not specifically registered as public liability companies. It is a criminal offence for a private limited company to advertise its shares or debentures for public sale or to sell them to any person knowing that this person intends to advertise them for public sale. Shares in private companies cannot, therefore, be traded through a stock exchange and are transferred privately by personal arrangements or through financial or legal agencies such as firms of accountants or solicitors. A private limited company is usually distinguished by the letters Ltd (or the word Limited or other officially approved abbreviation) at the end of its title.

Shareholders, Directors and Managers

In the limited company the various aspects of entrepreneurship are shared by different classes of people. There is nothing to stop a single person from being a member of each class, and this would be normal in the case of a very small, family company. But the larger the company the more likely is it that individuals are identified as being in one class only. The three classes are:

1 **Shareholders** A share is a clearly defined and transferable portion of the joint stock of financial capital owned by the company. In Britain, under current law, each share has a stated face or nominal value, often £1 or 50p. This, however, bears no relation to the market or exchange value of the share which depends, like any other market value, on what people are prepared to pay to obtain it. Unless stated otherwise it is assumed that a share is an **ordinary share**, i.e. that the holder of the share ranks equally with other shareholders in rights to share in profits or liability to suffer losses, to vote at shareholder meetings (normally on the basis of a vote for each share held so that voting power depends on the number of shares held), and rights to share in any remaining assets when all other creditors have been paid after the company has ceased to exist (been wound up).

   In the USA the ordinary shares are called the **common stock** and their holders the **common stockholders**. In the UK ordinary share capital is often referred to as the **equity** and ordinary shareholders as holders of the equity. These shareholders have most of the legal rights of ownership of the company but, as we have seen, enjoy limited liability in respect of some of the financial responsibilities of ownership. As shareholders, they are not required to concern themselves with the detailed management or operation of the business. Their responsibilities in this direction are delegated to a separate class of directors.

2 **Directors** These are people elected by shareholders to be responsible for the overall direction and management of the business. They tend to be major shareholders or their representatives or have special knowledge, skills or connections which are considered to be of value to the business. A director who also has specific managerial responsibilities is usually known as an **executive director**. The managing director always has an executive function and may have special powers under the articles of association.

   The main board of directors of a major public company usually consists of people with useful outside connections and influence in finance, industry, public affairs or politics (of growing importance to large business organisations as the influence of government in business affairs has itself grown). The board of a small company is more likely to be made up of specialist executive directors but will also represent the major financial interests and advisers.

Although formally elected by shareholders, in the case of large, financially successful companies the existing board normally has little difficulty in securing the election or re-election of its own nominees. Again, formally, the directors are responsible for the overall direction of operations and for making the strategic decisions which govern the direction these operations are likely to take. In reality boards of the larger companies often have little practical influence over managerial strategy and little real power to control the actions of senior management as long as it acts within its legal powers and achieves profits that satisfy the institutions of the finance markets.

3 **Managers** These are usually full-time and, in modern business, increasingly likely to be professionally trained either in the activity in which the firm operates and/or in the 'science of business management'. Managerial structures depend on the size of the company, the sector of activity in which it chiefly operates and on the company's own history and traditions. In very small and young, 'first generation' companies the senior managers are also likely to be executive directors and may also be significant shareholders either as founders of the company or under performance-related, profit-sharing schemes. In larger, older companies there is more likely to be a formal managerial hierarchy with appointments made at each level and the most senior appointments made by the board of directors or by the managing director under authority delegated by the board. There are, however, many variations and exceptions to these general tendencies. However, the main contribution required from a manager is his or her skill in the function or range of functions for which he or she is responsible.

It is the fundamental separation between the personal skill and ability of the manager from the financial risk taken by the shareholder which distinguishes the limited liability company and which really justifies the privilege of limited liability. Shareholders required to place their trust in the ability of hired managers are relieved from the limitless financial risk which engaging in a business venture would otherwise entail.

The Relationship between Shareholders, Directors and Managers

Managers are answerable to directors who, in turn, are answerable to the shareholders, though we have noted the tendency to give them wider responsibilities. Directors are required to report, in the annual general meeting (AGM), for which there is a statutory requirement, to shareholders who may then ask questions about the business and who may propose the appointment of new directors.

In practice, however, shareholders very often take little interest in the way their firms are run. They often appear interested only in the division of profits (dividends) they receive on their shares, or, in the case of public companies, what their shares are worth on the Stock Exchange. Few are likely to bother to study the expensively produced Annual Report and Accounts in any depth; fewer still turn up to the AGM or vote for directors. This is particularly true of large public companies. For example, several of the recently privatised companies, such as British Telecom and British Gas, have millions of shareholders but, in spite of the interest they have aroused because of privatisation, only a few thousand turn up at the respective AGMs.

This type of behaviour by shareholders may appear lazy, foolish or even reprehensible, but actually it is quite rational. An individual shareholder, especially in a large company, may feel powerless to achieve anything given the small size of his or her shareholding relative to those held by other people. To turn up at an AGM would simply be a waste of time and money. Most company meetings are at places and times that make attendance a matter of some difficulty and cost for the majority of small shareholders. The main power held by a disgruntled shareholder of a public company is the power to quit the company by selling shares. This, in turn, may be a much more effective discipline on directors and managers than any agitation at an AGM. If a large number of unhappy shareholders sell their holdings the value of the shares is likely to be pushed down and this provokes pressure for a change from a much more powerful group of shareholders, the **institutional shareholders**.

Institutional Investors

In the UK today the bulk of investment is not undertaken by private individuals. Notwithstanding the initial success of privatisation issues in the 1980s, most people still do not invest directly in shares. The large privatisation issues have increased the number of people holding shares but many hold relatively few shares worth a few hundred pounds and still regard building societies, life assurance policies or their pension schemes as their main channels of saving. Even among the more affluent, those with, say, upwards of around £100 000 to invest, are likely to have their **portfolios** of savings managed by a financial institution such as a bank, while those with more modest sums tend frequently to purchase unit or investment trusts which are again managed by the financial institutions.

Consequently we should not be surprised that over 80 per cent of equity investments in the United Kingdom are made by institutional investors. The fund managers of these institutions are clearly likely to take a keen interest in the efficient management of the firms in which they have invested. Paradoxically, because of the size of their holdings, they often have less power to sell their shares if they are unhappy about the quality of management. News travels very fast in the Stock Exchange. The moment it was suspected that a leading institution was sufficiently worried about a company's management to be selling its shares in that company all other institutions would start to sell and the share price would drop so much that all would suffer large losses. In fact the two-way trading (buying and selling) on which any market depends would simply break down and the shares would be untradeable. This trap in which an institutional investor can be caught was revealed in the market crash of October 1987 when the head of one major institution pointed out that his company accounted for around 2 per cent of shares quoted on the London Stock Exchange. These shares could not be sold because it would not be possible to find buyers for them.

The **positive** aspects of the role of institutional investors include the way they make available to business greater supplies of risk capital by harnessing the savings of millions of small investors and the fact that they are likely to be more knowledgeable and active than the small shareholder in supervising the activities of directors and managers in the companies whose shares they hold.

There may also be **negative** aspects. They clearly gain knowledge that is denied to less powerful investors so that, in economic terms, the stock market is a very imperfect economic market – and a very risky place for the small investor who persists in handling his or her own investments. They are also accused of exerting their influence in favour of short-term financial profits at the expense of long-term and more risky but potentially profitable industrial and technological development. It has become a common complaint among industrialists that they have become subject to the deadening hand of 'rule by accountants'. They may, of course, just be complaining that their technical ambitions have been brought under more prudent financial restraint by shareholders who have regained control over business managers.

The Structure of Enterprise

The Needs of Small and Large Firms

We began this chapter by considering the small entrepreneurial firm and have arrived at a consideration of the role of the institutional shareholder in the large public company. We have seen how the different entrepreneurial functions are carried out by different people in different types of organisation. This is reflected in the different structures of different kinds of firm.

In the smaller firm, for example, there is likely to be an **entrepreneurial** structure dominated by one or a few people who carry out a range of managerial functions as well as laying down policy for the firm and making major decisions (see Fig. 2.1). The organisation is likely to be low on formalisation. For instance, there is unlikely to be a formal, hierarchical system of communication and command while job descriptions and responsibilities are likely to be loosely defined and dependent very largely on the personalities and interests of the people involved. This type of structure does not achieve the same benefits of specialisation as are found in the larger organisations but it can be highly flexible.

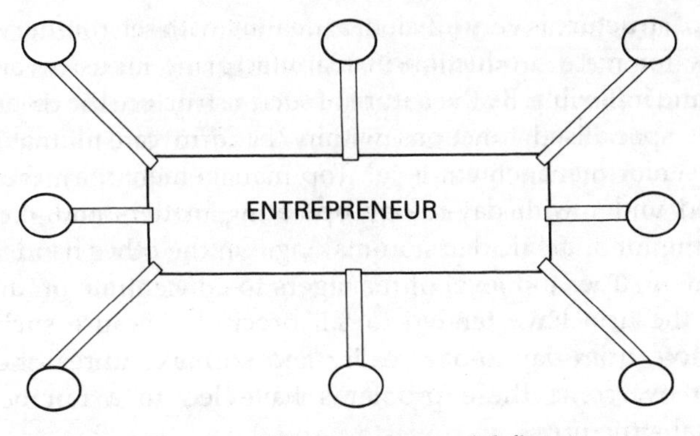

Fig. 2.1 The entrepreneurial firm

In the larger organisations the entrepreneurial structure is less appropriate. Instead of flexibility the result may be confusion with people unsure of what is expected of them and of the chain of command. In larger firms it is desirable to have clear lines of communication and authority with specific job descriptions, allowing more scope for specialisation. Such structures have been described as **bureaucratic**. The term is not here intended to be insulting but to describe a system based on distinct and clearly defined **offices**, with people chosen for their fitness to fill these positions in contrast to the entrepreneurial system where positions are modified to fit the people holding them.

The 'classical' way larger organisations have been structured is by **hierarchies** with the position of each person in each layer of the hierarchical pyramid and the responsibilities of each position clearly established (see Fig. 2.2). Each position is concerned with a part only of the firm's activity and not the whole. In many cases people's jobs are likely to revolve around specialised **functions**, such as purchasing, marketing or production control.

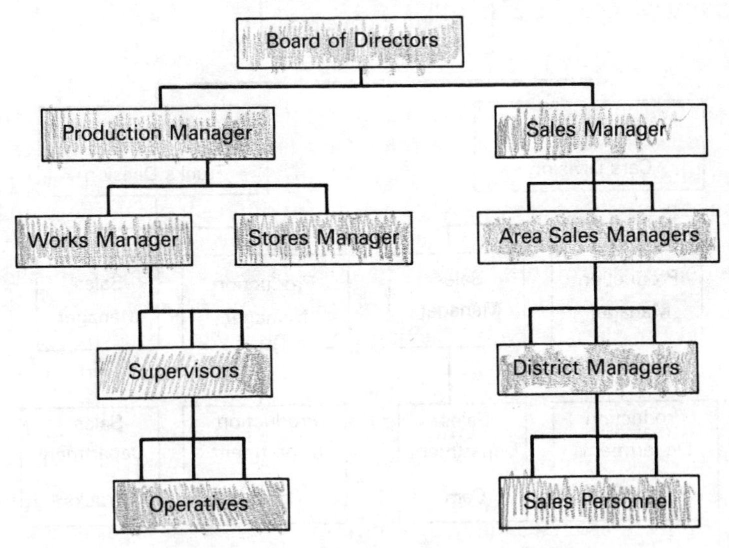

Fig. 2.2 A typical functional hierarchy

This type of structure is very efficient at dealing with set, routine work, hence its suitability for mass production in manufacturing industry, but it can be rather rigid and inflexible. By the nature of such a structure the co-ordination of the different specialised functions within the firm can ultimately only be achieved at senior management level. Top management may, therefore, find itself snowed under with day-to-day operating matters and, consequently, have little time for strategic decision-making. On the other hand, attempts to create a kind of super top level of managers to concentrate on developing a strategy for the firm have tended to fail precisely because such managers become remote from day-to-day reality and so make unrealistic decisions. Attempts to overcome these problems have led to a number of other organisational structures.

Divisionalised and Matrix Structures

In the divisionalised structure the firm is divided into a number of sections each responsible for an individual product, or territory. Functional specialisation only occurs within the divisions so that each, for example, may have its own production manager, sales manager and so on (see Fig. 2.3). Some of the benefits of specialisation are lost but, in compensation, senior management has more time to concentrate on strategic matters without being cut off from day-to-day problems. Individuals are also able to be responsible for the success of each individual product or area.

The matrix structure attempts to reap the benefits of both the previous organisational types. People are assigned to particular functional departments and activities, but each product or project is the responsibility of a project leader who draws personnel from each of the functional departments (see Fig.

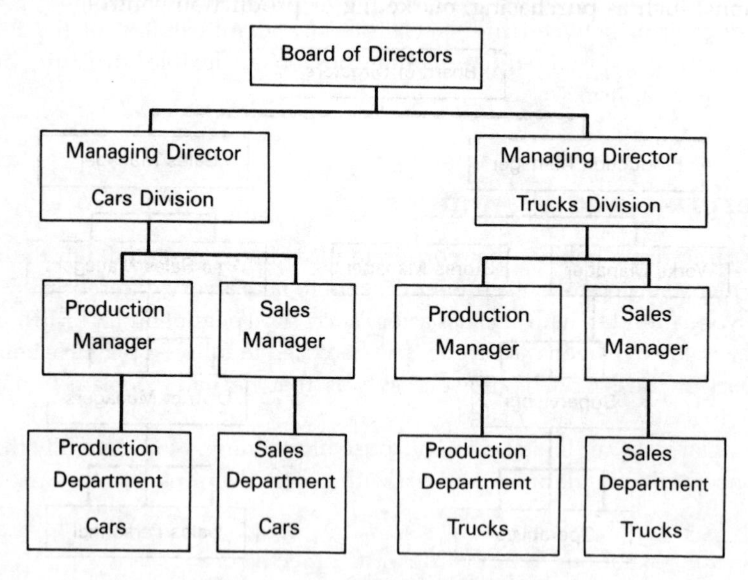

Fig. 2.3 A divisionalised firm

2.4). This type of structure has been developed in the aerospace industry. It has its advantages but one danger is that people may become confused by having more than one 'boss' – their project leader or departmental head.

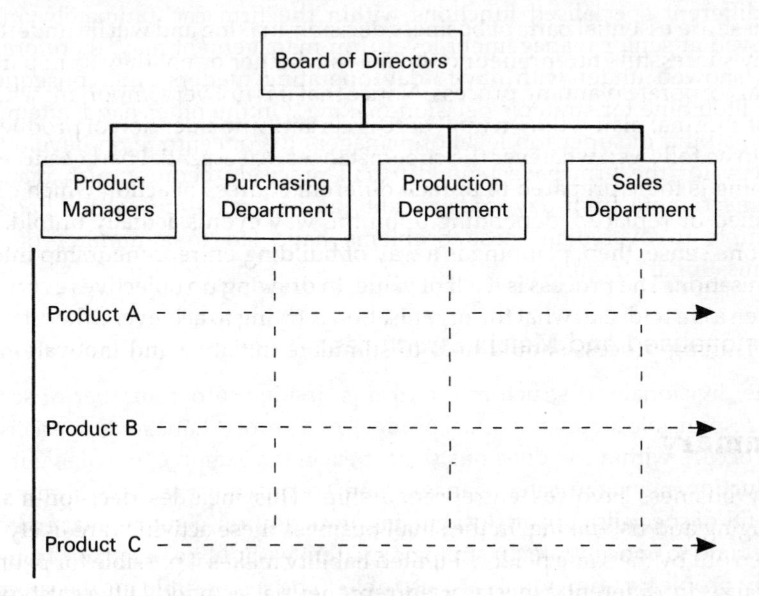

Fig. 2.4 Matrix structure

Beyond the scope of this book there are other types of structure which, for example, place emphasis on participation, the use of teams, or on **lateral communication** rather than formal **vertical communication**. All these can be seen as attempts to find a balance, appropriate for the situation of the individual firm, between the specialisation and inflexibility of the formal, functionally organised structure and the loose, flexible structure of the entrepreneurial firm.

Enterprise and Planning

Many large firms believe that corporate planning is essential. On the other hand, many successful entrepreneurs seem to take a very different view. One Hollywood film star, who also has a very successful peanut butter firm, has said that it would have been disastrous if he had tried to follow a plan. He believed that part of the secret of his success was that he had no plan. Can these conflicting views be reconciled?

They can if we understand the purpose of planning. Note carefully that we are concerned with **planning** and not with a plan. Planning involves a number of stages:

1 Deciding what one wants to do – the objective.
2 Assessing the means available and the constraints imposed on their use.

3 Devising different possible courses of action that all lead to a defined objective.
4 Assessing the risks involved with each possible course of action.

All these are essential parts of business decision-making and will be undertaken by any successful entrepreneur or business whether or not they form part of a formal corporate planning process. Notice that it is not very important whether or not a formal plan is drawn up. There is certainly no intention of producing a plan to be followed whatever the circumstances. An essential part of successful planning is to be prepared to pursue different courses of action which can be modified or replaced, depending upon the way events actually unfold.

In one sense, then, planning is a way of building entrepreneurship into the organisation. The process is itself of value. In drawing up objectives everybody is given a clear idea of what the organisation is trying to achieve. Other stages of the planning process should help to stimulate initiative and innovation.

Summary

Every business involves entrepreneurship. This includes decision-making, managing and risk-taking. In the small business these activities are likely to be carried out by the same person. Limited liability makes it possible for people to specialise in different aspects of entrepreneurial activity. Different types of organisational structure – entrepreneurial, functional, divisional and matrix – also allow different types of managerial specialisation. Corporate planning is a continuous process which helps embody entrepreneurial activity in the firm.

Discussion Questions

1 'Achievement today is essentially a team effort.' 'At the head of most successful enterprises there is usually a clearly recognisable entrepreneur.' Discuss these two statements and say how far you think they can be reconciled.
2 'Limited liability is a privilege which is too often abused by the unscrupulous.' Discuss this statement and suggest ways in which abuses could be reduced.
3 What do you think are the strengths and the weaknesses of the limited liability company as a form of business structure?
4 In what ways would you expect the structure of a service organisation to differ from that of a manufacturing firm?

Suggestions for Further Reading

Gray, J., *Business Organisations,* NCC Publications 1987.
Hudson, J., *The Limited Liability Company: Success, Failure and Future,* Royal Bank of Scotland Review No. 161, March 1989.

3

Business Objectives

The Objectives of Business Owners

At first sight it might seem that business objectives cannot be a matter for much debate. 'Of course, people are in business to make a profit,' you might say. This is true. Without profit no business can survive for long in the absence of external support. However, simply to say that people are in business for profit is really too vague to be very helpful to a student of business. 'How much profit?' 'Does the business owner pursue profit to the exclusion of other objectives?' 'Is the pursuit of profit constrained, or should it be constrained by wider issues such as care of the environment?' These are just some of the questions that arise when we start looking closely at the business pursuit of profit.

If we were to ask a hundred owners of small firms why they were running their own businesses instead of working for other employers we would get many different replies. Some might admit that joining an existing family firm was originally seen as a fairly easy path to a desired living standard and the prestige of being 'the boss'. Others would say they preferred independence and the challenge of making – and standing or falling by – decisions instead of obeying orders or fitting into a rigid bureaucratic structure. A few might have had faith in their own ideas which had been turned down by former employers so forming a business was the only practical way of finding out if the ideas were sound. One or two might be in business because the financial rewards appeared brighter than those offered by available employment – or the prospect of unemployment. In all these cases profits have to be made in order to secure an income to live on, but once this is achieved we rarely find anyone claiming to pursue profit to the exclusion of other desired rewards from business ownership.

Competitive Markets and Profit Maximisation

How then do economists take into account this range of individual motives underlying business enterprise? It must be confessed that generally they don't. The problem is evaded by assuming that most small firms operate in markets which, to a considerable degree, are regarded as **competitive**. Competition is a subject more fully analysed later in the book. At this stage we can accept that a market in which the product is supplied by large numbers of small firms which individually are too small to have a significant influence on the market price can be described as competitive. In such a market, in the long run, economists argue that firms can only achieve sufficient profit to keep them in the market. To achieve this they have to use their resources as efficiently as possible. Failure to do so in the long run will entail being forced out of the market. In the long run firms may be able to make a higher level of profit but this will attract newcomers to the market and the extra supply these bring will force down the level of profit once more.

Given these conditions the individual business has to secure the largest possible profit achievable in the circumstances. In the formal language of economics we say that, in a competitive market, **profit maximisation** is a condition for survival. In practice the strict conditions of the theoretical models of competitive markets rarely apply and there is a delayed 'time bomb' effect because some costs, such as depreciation, stay hidden for some time. Consequently firms can survive for a while even though they are really operating at a loss. Sooner or later, however, the 'bomb explodes' as essential machinery has to be replaced or a building lease expires and the firm finds it impossible to carry on.

If we accept this as an approximation of reality then we can agree that we do not need to concern ourselves too much with the objectives of small firms. They either maximise profits by skill, intuition, accident or trial and error, or they fail.

The Ownership and Control of Large Firms

When, however, we come to examine markets where a significant proportion of supply is dominated by a relatively few large firms, or in extreme cases by a single supplier, a monopolist, we face a very different situation. Profit maximisation is no longer required for survival in the market. The firm can operate at a profit within a range of output levels and prices and it becomes possible to survive in the long term even though profit is being sacrificed in the pursuit of some other goal or goals.

This possibility opens the door to a great deal of discussion as to what other goals may be pursued and why. This discussion has been a live issue among economists since researchers in the 1930s showed that large firms did not appear to be adopting the pricing and other policies needed to secure maximum profit. At the same time it was observed that shareholders could not be regarded as having any effective control over the management of the companies they legally owned.

Shareholders might be thought to be interested only in profit – and in securing the largest possible profit – but if there was an effective 'divorce' between shareholder/owners and controlling managers then it seemed reasonable to suppose that managers had gained the power to pursue goals that were in their interests rather than in those of their shareholders. Such goals might be assumed to be those likely to increase their own status and income and security, e.g. growth, elimination of competition and the use of surplus revenue to provide managerial rewards.

The problem of business goals and behaviour, therefore, cannot really be separated from the questions, 'Who controls the large company? Is it controlled by shareholders, or by managers who have secured a significant degree of independence from shareholders?' There are arguments both for and against the proposition that the large public company is managerially controlled.

Arguments for the Existence of Managerial Control

1 A glance at the published Annual Report of any major company will reveal that such a firm has far too many shareholders ever to make it practical for more than a very small fraction of them to meet, discuss and elect directors and to question them on company policy and achievements. Most individual shareholders have little awareness of the company's activities and their interest centres on the receipt of dividends (the division of profit alloted to shareholders). The ruling group of directors is usually able to keep control over new appointments and re-appointments. Some economists suggest that the senior managers are usually able to ensure that directors are appointed on the grounds of their social status combined with their ignorance of company affairs and their willingness to remain ignorant of them. Any shareholder or group of shareholders wishing to challenge the ruling group face enormous difficulties and expense both in obtaining information from within the company and in circulating information to the thousands of other shareholders. Annual General Meetings are carefully stage-managed and are normally held at times and places guaranteed to ensure that very few shareholders will attend.

2 The managers are full-time professional specialists in their various managerial skills. They have concepts of how their work should be carried out and how they should behave that result from their training and their membership of the managerial team. Their status, rewards and prospects for future advancement all depend on their ability to win the approval of other managers and generally to fit in with the attitudes and behaviour of their colleagues. Much modern management theory stresses the importance of developing shared objectives and of placing responsibility on managers at all levels. The danger is that the management team is encouraged to pursue its own interests which are not necessarily those of the shareholders.

Arguments Doubting the Divorce Between Ownership and Control

By no means all observers accept that there is any serious division between shareholders and management. Some suggest that whatever may have been the situation in the past shareholder control has now been restored. Others argue that it was never lost. Doubters of the ownership/control divorce are likely to put forward the following arguments.

1 When there are very large numbers of shareholders, few of whom attend meetings, a small, determined group with an interest and with contacts within the company can exert pressure and influence out of proportion to the total weight of its shareholding. It is thus that some families can retain effective control over large public companies. Estimates vary as to the proportion of shares a group of people needs to hold to be able to exercise effective control. These range from 20 per cent to 5 per cent. It really depends on the group's contacts within the company and its ability to secure the co-operation of other influential shareholders.
2 Estimates of the shares actually controlled by a family group are often underestimated because wealthy families are likely to have their wealth distributed in trusts for various reasons. The full number of shares that can be controlled may be substantially more than the number directly owned.
3 Some economists believe that there may well have been a gap between owners and management in the 1950s and 1960s but this closed later when the pattern of shareholding changed. The 1970s and early 1980s saw the flight of the individual investor from the stock market which became increasingly dominated by financial institutions, heavily supported by massive flows of money from company pension schemes. Small investors were discouraged from direct dealing in shares and encouraged to invest through unit trusts – another form of institutional investment. This trend continued in spite of the privatisation issues.

   These institutions are managed by professional investment managers supported by all kinds of other professionals, including accountants, lawyers and economic analysts, who tend to have access to much the same information and to come to much the same conclusions. They all, of course, watch each other's actions. When a leading institution decides to buy or sell a substantial block of shares this tends to influence others and there is an immediate impact on the share price. Consequently when such an institution suspects that the management of a particular company of which it is a shareholder is less than efficient it may not wish to sell its shares but prefer to intervene discreetly to improve the quality of management. The emergence of the institutional shareholder, therefore, has marked the return of shareholder power.

   Institutional shareholders employ specialists with the skills to obtain and analyse information formerly available only to internal management. Consequently senior managers now have to co-operate closely with leading institutions and to take their financial objectives into account in their decision-making. Some observers would argue that it also marks the imposition of short-term profit maximisation as the prime objective of business. Investment managers are judged by profit. The successful investment manager is the one who can make a given block or portfolio of shares increase its value and dividend income more than can the other managers. This will only happen if the companies whose shares the investment manager buys are more profitable than those of other companies. During some of the takeover battles in 1986–7 some predator companies were criticised on the grounds that they were interested only in making profits to the neglect of other 'desirable' objectives such as providing security of employment for workers or maintaining a reputation of service to a local community.

4 It is also possible to argue that the division between shareholders and managers is overstated. The real division may be not so much between shareholders and managers as between senior, controlling, top managers and the middle and lower ranks of management. For the most part the top managers of large public companies belong to the same socio-economic groups as the more influential individual shareholders and the top managers and directors of the large financial institutions. On the other hand many middle managers are far closer in background and socio-economic origins to the clerical workers, supervisors and skilled manual workers in the workshops. Although the senior managers may have relatively few shares in the companies for which they work they are nevertheless likely to be shareholders in other companies and they will share the same attitudes, expectations and objectives as shareholders. They can be expected to be highly motivated towards making profits and possibly to the goal of profit maximisation.

5 The development of organisational structures such as the divisionalised firm, outlined in Chapter 2, has meant that the performance of managers is directed towards the making of profits and is judged by their success in this.

The Challenge to Profit Maximisation[1]

The Requirements for Maximising Profits

It is difficult to give a conclusive answer to either of the two related questions: 'Is there a divorce between ownership and control in large public companies?' and 'Does the large public company pursue a goal of profit maximisation?' We cannot even be absolutely sure what we mean by profit maximising behaviour. The common explanation is that it means firms seeking to equate marginal cost with marginal revenue with the implied assumption that if this short-run rule is followed consistently then firms will also be maximising profits in the long run. However, this rather over simplifies a number of practical problems, including the treatment of fixed costs.

In the short run, changes in fixed costs do not affect the profit maximising output position, but this cannot be true in the long run when all costs become

[1]If you are not familiar with the requirements for profit maximisation you should refer to Chapter 1, page 15. The essential point to recognise is that, to achieve the largest possible profit, the firm should seek to produce at the level where the revenue received from the last unit produced is the same as the cost of producing that unit, i.e. MR = MC.

variable. How then do we take account of decisions to extend buildings, buy new machines or appoint new specialist managers? Clearly an attempt to achieve the largest possible profits must involve calculations more complex and extensive than simply equating marginal cost and marginal revenue. The problem becomes even more intricate when we contemplate the modern multi-product, multi-plant multinational company. Such a firm has to decide which markets to enter and when and which markets to leave and when as well as what prices to charge and how much to produce. Any one decision affects a range of others and each set of decisions involves a whole range of possible outcomes each with different profit possibilities. We have to realise that the firm operates under conditions of uncertainty regarding future developments in such areas as consumer reactions, behaviour of competitors and government policies.

Notice that we are recognising that the firm operates in a dynamic environment in which it makes decisions **now** in the expectation of certain probable outcomes in the **future**. This dynamic interpretation of the profit maximising problem, developed more fully in later chapters on market and investment appraisal, gives us an entirely different perspective from that arising out of the usual presentation of a set of static revenue and cost curves. Recognising the dynamic and uncertain environment of decision-making allows us to see that there is never just one profit-maximising solution to any given problem, but rather a series of possible solutions with no certainty as to which will lead to the best profit result in the long run.

Replacing Profit Maximisation

Do the business decision-makers then give up the direct search for maximum profit and instead choose substitute and more easily measurable goals which, they believe, do lead indirectly to the largest profit achievable in the long run? For example, do they believe that achieving market leadership gives the best chance of securing future profits? If firms can be observed pursuing policies aimed at securing and keeping market leadership how can we tell whether they are doing this because recognition as the market leader gives prestige and rewards to managers or because market leadership gives greater power to set price and ensure high profits? Another possibility is that precisely because no one can be absolutely sure that a rejected set of decisions might not have achieved higher profits than the set actually taken, and hence no one can be certain that long run profit maximisation is being achieved, senior managers prefer to pursue a goal, such as gaining a larger share of the market than any other supplier, that can be measured.

So far we have assumed that all expenditure is related more or less directly towards production and distribution, but this is not entirely true. Large firms spend money in ways that have no direct relevance to production. Some companies provide elaborate sports or leisure facilities to employees. County standard cricket grounds are not unknown! North-country mills used to vie with each other to support prize-winning brass bands. These activities might provide a limited personnel or marketing benefit but are difficult to explain in any realistic profit-enhancing terms. On the other hand, if we take the view that company behaviour and objectives can change according to the pattern of ownership and the structure of markets in which firms operate, then we would expect to see evidence of conflicting attitudes and behaviour in a period when both of these are changing. In this light the 1987 attempted takeover of Pilkingtons the glass makers produced some interesting reactions. The takeover was criticised on the grounds that the predator company appeared to place a very high priority on profit whereas the company at risk was one that had a long reputation of 'socially' directed spending on workers and the local community. This case becomes even more interesting when we realise that, in 1987, the Pilkington family retained a significant interest in the ownership and managerial control of the company.

The Managerial Theories of the Firm

There seems to be sufficient doubt about profit maximisation as the dominant business goal to justify efforts to replace or modify this assumption. There is now a considerable weight of literature to bear witness to these efforts, and we must now examine some of the most important of the modern managerial theories, so called because they are all concerned with the large public company which:

1 has a significant degree of market power, and
2 is controlled by its managers.

Sales Revenue Maximisation

One of the best known and most highly developed of the managerial theories is that based on the work of Professor Baumol who argued that managers measured business success in terms of sales revenue. He suggested, therefore, that their goal was to maximise sales revenue subject to achieving a minimum level of profit. This minimum profit was the amount needed to keep the loyalty of existing shareholders and the support of the financial institutions on which the firm depended to obtain further finance for expansion.

The consequences of this change from profit maximisation to revenue maximisation subject to a minimum profit constraint can be deduced from the graphical model given in Fig. 3.1. (See also the Appendix to this chapter and Fig. 3.4.)

The firm can make some profit at any output level between $0Q$ and $0Q_1$ but its profits are maximised at level $0Q_2$ where the cumulative profit curve reaches its peak and where marginal revenue (the slope of the total revenue curve) equals marginal cost (the slope of the total cost curve). Revenue, on the other hand is maximised at output level $0Q_3$ where the total revenue curve reaches

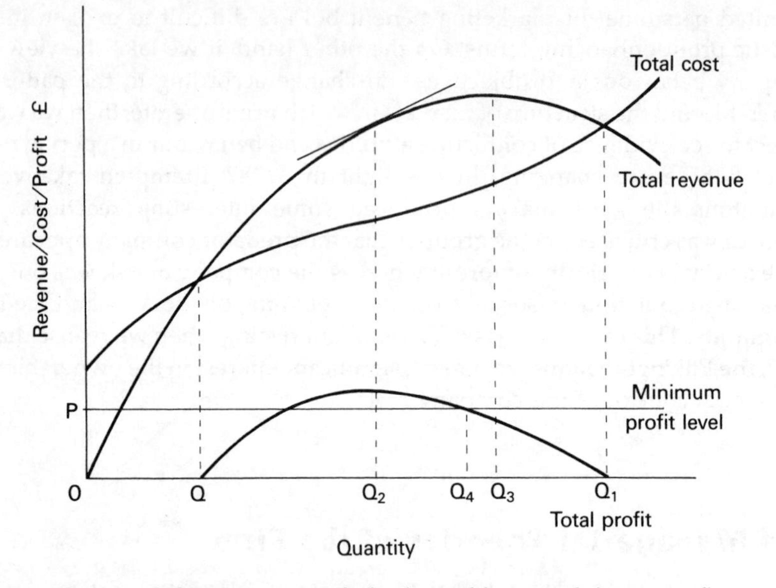

Fig. 3.1 Sales revenue maximisation subject to minimum profit

its peak and where marginal revenue equals zero. However, the firm is required to produce a minimum profit of 0P and, in Fig. 3.1, this constraint operates to limit the maximum output to $0Q_4$ below the revenue maximising output level but above that required to maximise profits.

Given that the firm which produces a significant share of total market output is facing a downward sloping demand curve this tendency to raise output above the profit maximising level will also ensure that price is below the profit maximising price and closer to the level of marginal cost. This suggests that managerial control, in comparison with owner control of the production organisation, has the desirable result for consumers in that they obtain a larger quantity of the product at a lower price and pay a price closer to the level of marginal cost, thus bringing the valuation of the product by the marginal or last buyer in the market closer to the cost of producing that product. This idea is discussed more fully in Chapter 9.

Baumol claimed that his model gave a better explanation of observed business practice than assumptions of profit maximisation. For example, observation suggested that firms tended to increase price and reduce output when faced by a rise in fixed costs. Profit maximisers would not react in this way because marginal costs are not affected. The explanation offered by the Baumol model is shown in Fig. 3.2. A rise in fixed costs reduces the profit curve from PP to P_1P_1. Assuming that the minimum profit constraint of 0P was operating the firm would need to reduce output from 0Q to $0Q_1$ and this would require an increase in price. This is explained more fully in Chapter 6.

Baumol also argued that the pursuit of revenue at the expense of profit helped to account for the tendency for large firms to advertise more than could be justified on the grounds of profit maximising behaviour. The firm seeking

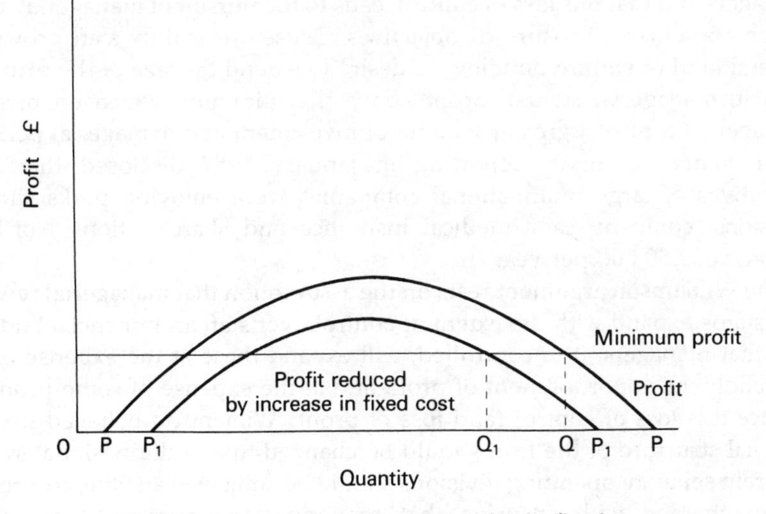

Fig. 3.2 Sales maximisation and a rise in fixed cost

sales revenue would be willing to spend money on advertising even when the net revenue gain was less than the net additional cost. This managerial preference for advertising makes it more difficult to predict the optimum prices and output levels. This helps us to recognise that, in practice, these decisions are not as precise and as clear-cut as profit maximisation assumptions would lead us to believe.

This model is an interesting attempt to bring the theory of the firm closer to observed business practice but it still leaves many difficulties unresolved. You may have noticed that it shares with traditional profit–maximising models the ambiguity between the short and the long run. Baumol's is a short-run model using short-run fixed costs and the rising marginal cost curve. The model is also one of a single product and market. If we start to apply revenue maximisation in a world of uncertainty, multiple products and multiple markets we face just as many difficulties as with profit maximisation.

Another weakness is its failure to take into account the actions of competitors. Baumol concentrates on the firm and appears to see no need to examine how industrial supply and demand would move towards equilibrium in the light of the objectives he identifies. The problem of interdependence is not really considered.

The Maximisation of Managerial Utility

We seem to come a step closer to the reality of modern firms and markets when we examine O. E. Williamson's theory of managerial utility maximisation. This accepts the view that the firm is required to achieve a minimum level of profit to satisfy shareholders and financial markets but assumes that the large firm with substantial market power has little difficulty in meeting this condition.

The Williamson model assumes that shareholders can lose control over the managers and that this loss of control leads to the pursuit of managerial utility which combines a mixture of objectives. These are mainly staff growth (a general kind of empire building – a desire to extend the size of the firm and, with it, managerial status), profit above the minimum which enables the manager to control a greater volume of investment and managerial **perks** or emoluments. A survey reporting in January 1987 disclosed that chief executives of large multinational companies were enjoying perks such as pensions, company cars, medical insurance and share options worth an average of £50 000 per year.

The Williamson argument rests on the assumption that managerial rewards and status expand with the extent of control over staff and financial budgets, and that managers, if uncontrolled, will expand these at the expense of the shareholders' apportionment of profit and at the expense of some profit. To reduce this loss of control (and loss of profit) Williamson believed that the internal structure of the firm should be changed to a multidivisional system wherein separate operating divisions should be subject to an élite, controlling group charged with ensuring that each division operates at maximum profitability.

Whatever we might think of this proposal as a technique for restoring shareholder control this argument does provide a valuable reminder that the pursuit of managerial objectives can be seen, not as a fundamental shift in business goals and behaviour, but as a problem arising out of the growth in size and complexity of the modern organisation. Such a problem can be cured or much reduced as the senior executives and influential shareholders gain increased experience of the techniques of controlling large-scale enterprise. The extension of share option plans whereby senior managers receive part of their rewards in the form of company shares at very favourable terms may be seen as providing a valuable 'perk' in a way that influences managers to share the interests and attitudes of the shareholders and so reduce the extent of loss of control.

Maximising the Rate of Growth Subject to Fear of Takeover

Most supporters of managerial theories agree that the desire to increase the size of the firm is a powerful motive of managers. There is also widespread agreement that successful managers can overcome the diseconomies of large-scale operation in order to pursue a policy of growth so that large firms continue to grow even larger. Professor Marris has commented that it is a function of management to flatten the U-shaped cost curve. He has also helped to focus attention away from size itself as an issue towards the rate or speed with which a firm is able to grow. He argues that managers will be prepared to speed up growth at the expense of the interests of their shareholders. If firms grow too fast, their share values will fall either because profits are being retained at the expense of share dividends or because too much money is being raised by new share issues so that future profits have to be divided among too many shareholders. Anything that appears to reduce the prospects of future dividends below the levels considered desirable by the powerful institutions of the capital market is likely to reduce share values on the Stock Exchange.

If share prices fall to a level where other companies can see opportunities for taking over the company and all the assets (buildings, equipment, etc.) it owns at a low cost, then takeover becomes a real possibility. A successful takeover raider is unlikely to retain the existing senior management of the acquired company. Consequently, Marris is able to imply that controlling managers fear takeover more than the power of their shareholders and this fear acts as a brake on their push for growth. Nevertheless, the growth rate of a managerially controlled company is still likely to be faster than one which is owner-managed or where shareholders continue to exercise effective control.

Behavioural Theory

So far we have implied that the firm exists as a separate entity that is, or should be, run by a managerial group in the interests of its shareholders. A rather different approach is offered by the **behavioural theorists**. *A Behavioural Theory of the Firm* was offered by R. M. Cyert and J. G. March as a fully developed alternative theory of the firm. Behavioural theory is a development of work pioneered by H. A. Simon who argued in his book *Administrative Behaviour* that managers did not seek to achieve optimum solutions but reacted to problems as they arose and sought to achieve what they perceived to be **satisfactory** solutions. Simon had thus put forward the belief that managerial behaviour was **satisficing** rather than **maximising**. He argued that, given the uncertainty of the environment in which business firms operated, it was not realistic to expect firms to pursue a maximising objective. Satisficing was the only practical policy.

Cyert and March, accepting the loss of shareholder control, saw the shareholders as but one interest group in a coalition of different interests each with different goals but coming together with the common interest in the continued survival of the firm. Each group was represented within the decision-making structure of management, e.g. shareholder interests were represented by accounts and finance managers, customers by marketing managers and so on. No one group could secure the optimisation of its interest but all had to receive partial satisfaction in order to secure the continued survival of the coalition. The people controlling the firm, therefore, had to take account of multiple goals not all of which could be pursued with equal force at the same time. The major goals actually suggested by Cyert and March were: profit, sales, market share, production and inventories (keeping a range of stock of finished product to provide service to the customer). It is, however, one of the attractions of behavioural theory that it can be adapted to any set of goals and can thus be used as a useful framework for the analysis of different kinds of organisation in different kinds of environment, e.g. for state-owned enterprise in a mixed or a command economy or a non-profit seeking organisation such as a building or co-operative society or a worker co-operative.

As the firm's management is perceived as pursuing multiple goals there can be no question of optimising anything so behavioural theory follows the satisficing tradition of Simon. Nor do Cyert and March accept the traditional classical view of the firm as operating at minimum cost. Typically the firm is seen as operating with what they call **organisational slack**, which is defined as payments to members of the coalition above the minimum required to keep them in the coalition, e.g. not using buying power to force down input supply prices to the minimum or payment of dividends higher than necessary to keep the loyalty of shareholders, nor raising product prices to the full amount that the market would bear. This slack enables the firm to adapt more smoothly to environmental shocks which would otherwise cause large fluctuations in performance, including profit. In periods when the firm is under pressure it can reduce slack and so keep a more stable level of reported profit.

At the core of behavioural theory are four concepts which are claimed to govern the way managers behave. These are:

1 **Quasi-resolution of conflict** This means that members of the coalition (or their supporters within management) are pursuing conflicting objectives which, at any given time, can only be partially achieved. For example, market share may be expanded at the expense of some profit or inventories may be expanded to please buyers, again at a sacrifice of profit.
2 **Uncertainty avoidance** This reflects the tendency of managers to try and gain control over conditions both internal and external to the firm and to form decision-making rules that enable them to react to problems as they arise. The principle of uncertainty avoidance also helps to explain the emphasis placed on gaining control over markets, even to the extent of colluding with actual or potential competitors.
3 **Problemistic search** This means that search for new solutions to a problem (defined as anything that threatens the stability of the coalition essential to the survival of the firm) only arises when a problem is encountered which is not resolved by an existing decision-making rule or precedent. Search is not then directed towards finding the best possible solution but towards finding the first or nearest satisfactory solution to the problem as it is perceived by the managers. Thus if there is a fall in demand, indicating that customers are leaving the coalition, which in the past has been checked by increasing advertising, then this will be the first remedy tried. If this does not work other solutions such as a price reduction will be sought until demand is restored. An optimising solution to the problem might have been to have abandoned the product and developed a new product in a new market, or completely re-design the product.
4 **Organisational learning** This suggests that if the search produces a new solution which resolves the problem this will pass into the managerial memory and will become part of the reaction process to similar problems in the future. In this way the organisation learns from its experiences and from managers' perception of the experiences of other firms. Goals and achievement levels will be constantly modified and adapted in the light of these experiences and perceptions.

A common criticism of behavioural theory is that it is purely descriptive. It is based on observation of how managers do behave and it makes no comment on the way we might think they ought to behave in order to increase efficiency in the use of resources or in the satisfaction of community needs. Nor does the theory account for the differing degrees of success with which firms cope with uncertain environments. It throws no light on mergers and takeovers for instance. These have become an important feature of modern industrial markets. Further, it is extremely difficult to make clear predictions in relation to such fundamental issues as price and output on the basis of the theory. In spite of the claims of its supporters and in spite of the useful insights it certainly does give into many aspects of managerial behaviour, behavioural theory is not a complete theory of the firm any more than the other theories outlined in this chapter.

Game Theory

This is not a theory of the firm but a way of analysing conflicts between people or organisations of people. It is based on the application of statistical probabilities to the options and outcomes available to the participants in a conflict which could result in winners and losers. A zero-sum game is one in which one participant's gain is another's loss, e.g. competition in a saturated market when total demand does not rise and one firm can only sell more at the expense of another. In a non-zero sum game gains need not balance losses and it is possible for all to gain something, e.g. an advertising 'war' in an expanding market where all firms increase sales revenue.

Game theory in its modern form was originally developed to assist war leaders to plan campaigns to take account of likely reactions from the enemy. Application to business competition in oligopolistic markets containing relatively few large firms seemed a natural development but predictive results proved to be disappointing. However, game theory can be applied to business simulations used in management training and development and it does give some interesting clues to managerial actions in competitive situations. It also helps to explain why competitors are frequently tempted to form – and to break – collusive agreements.

Management and Growth

You may have noticed that a recurring theme in some of these managerial theories of the firm has been that of the growth of the firm. Many observers have noted that managers often appear to have more to gain in the way of prestige, monetary and other rewards from the growth in size of the organisation than from its greater profitability. Business growth, however, is such an important issue that it forms the subject of the next chapter.

Discussion Questions

1 What do you understand by the term **entrepreneur**? Can there be entrepreneurs in **a** very large public companies, **b** organisations operating in the public sector of the economy?

2 Does it matter whether the large public company is controlled by its shareholders or by its managers?

3 Discuss the view that while an objective of profit maximisation is possible in the short term it is quite impractical in the long term.

4 What are the declared objectives of the organisation in which you are working or studying? Does your observation suggest that these are the objectives pursued by managers and other senior personnel in the organisation? How well does your observation fit the implications and predictions of the behavioural theory of the firm?

Suggestions for Further Reading

The managerial and behavioural theories of the firm outlined in this chapter are given in greater detail in a number of texts relating to microeconomics and industrial economics. These include:

Devine, P. J. *et al.*, *Industrial Economics*, George Allen and Unwin, 1985
Koutsoyiannis, A., *Modern Microeconomics*, Section E, Chapters 15–18, Macmillan, 1981

A more specialised examination of the subject is provided by:

McGuire, J. W., *Theories of Business Behaviour*, Prentice Hall, 1964

The best account of behavioural theory is contained in the first seven chapters of:

Cyert, R. M. and March, J. G., *A Behavioural Theory of the Firm*, Prentice Hall, 1963

All serious students of the business firm should read the classic:

Simon, H. A., *Administrative Behaviour*, Macmillan, 1957

Among a number of books dealing specifically with the various theories of the firm is:

Sawyer, M., *Theories of the Firm*, Weidenfeld and Nicolson, 1979

Appendix to Chapter 3

If you have already studied economics you will be familiar with the basic models of market structure. If you are not aware of these the following notes provide an outline of the two most common models, those of **perfect competition** and of **monopoly**.

Perfect Competition

The conditions assumed for this market to exist were listed in Chapter 1. In Chapter 3 we have noted that in markets approximating to perfect competition the maximisation of profit can be regarded as a survival condition. This becomes clear when you examine the graphical model for equilibrium under perfect competition as illustrated in Fig. 3.3.

Features to note from this model are:

1. The product is assumed to be homogeneous. This means that buyers do not distinguish between different makes or suppliers of the product. Buyers are indifferent between articles made by different suppliers.
2. Because the firm sells at the same price at every output level the market price is also the individual firm's average revenue and its marginal revenue. See the Appendix to Chapter 1 if you are not sure why.
3. It is assumed that cost includes an amount of **normal profit** just sufficient to keep firms in the market. Because no additional profit can be made the average cost curve is tangential to the average revenue curve (i.e. average cost = average revenue) and because this is horizontal to the quantity axis this must be at the lowest point of the U-shaped average cost curve.

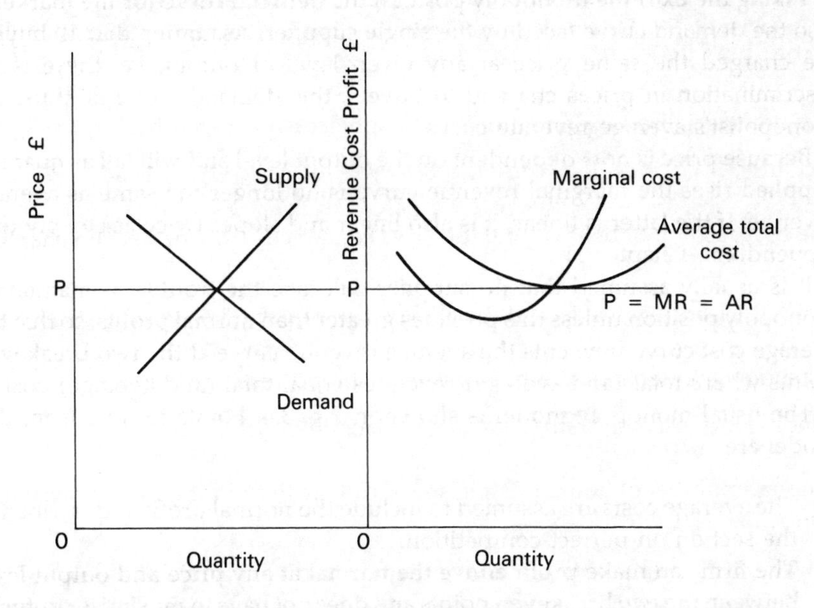

Fig. 3.3 *a* The perfectly competitive market; *b* The firm in the perfectly competitive market

If the price is higher than P the firm makes additional profits. Suppliers move into the market, the supply curve moves to the right and price falls.
If price is lower than P firms suffer losses. Suppliers leave the market, the supply curve moves to the left and price rises.
Only at P are supply and demand in equilibrium and at P no profits above normal can be earned.

4 The rising marginal cost curve cuts the U-shaped average cost curve at this lowest point (see Appendix to Chapter 1), i.e. marginal cost = average cost which also = average revenue which = marginal revenue and price.
5 These equalities occur at the profit maximising output level, i.e. where marginal cost = marginal revenue, which is the only output level where the firm can avoid a loss. To survive in the market the firm must produce at this level.
6 Market price is the value of the product's utility to the last buyer to enter the market, i.e. the marginal buyer. This is the market's marginal utility which thus = price and also = marginal cost.

Monopoly

At the other extreme from perfect competition there is the market model of **monopoly** where there is only one supplier to the market. The model, however, is also often held substantially to apply to any large firm which has a significant degree of power in the market, i.e. it supplies a proportion of market output large enough to influence price.

Taking the extreme monopoly position the demand curve for the market is also the demand curve faced by the single supplier. Assuming that all buyers are charged the same price at any given level of output, i.e. there is no discrimination in prices charged to buyers, this demand curve is, thus, the monopolist's average revenue curve.

Because price is now dependent on the output level and will fall as quantity supplied rises the marginal revenue curve is no longer the same as average revenue. If the latter is linear, it is also linear and slopes twice as steeply (see Appendix to Chapter 1).

It is usually assumed that no supplier will take the trouble to maintain a monopoly position unless this provides greater than normal profits, so that the average cost curve now cuts the average revenue curve at the two breakeven points where total (and average) revenues equal total (and average) cost.

The usual monopoly model is shown in Fig. 3.4. Points to note from this model are:

1 The average costs are assumed to include the normal profit as described in the section on perfect competition.
2 The firm can make profit **above the normal** at any price and output level between the two breakeven points and does not have to maximise profits in order to survive in the market. It may sacrifice some profit in order to pursue other objectives if it wishes.
3 We can only deduce the actual price and output levels chosen by the firm if we know its objectives. If the assumption is made that the firm is maximising profits then it will produce at the output level where marginal cost = marginal revenue (Q) and charge the market clearing price appropriate to this level (P). Different objectives will require different

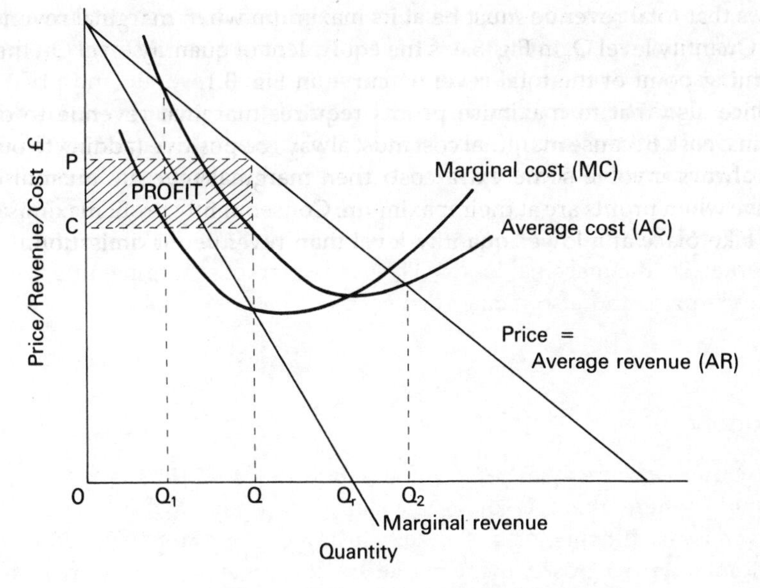

Fig. 3.4 The monopoly model
The monopolist can make a profit above normal at any quantity level between Q_1 and Q_2. Between these points AR > AC. Profit is maximised at Q.

outputs and prices. At which output levels would the firm have to produce to **a** maximise revenue or **b** maximise output subject to making a normal profit?

4 Only if the firm is maximising profit will its **above normal** profit equal the shaded rectangle. Profits will be lower if any other objective is sought.

5 Price is above marginal cost. From this it is frequently assumed that the supplier is gaining a **surplus** which is denied to the rest of the community. Economists often argue that the most desirable position from the community's point of view is for the firm to produce at the quantity level where P = MC. This point is discussed further in Chapter 9. Compare monopoly with perfect competition from this point of view.

The Maximisation of Revenue

Do not confuse revenue which is the gross income from sales, with profit which is revenue after costs have been deducted.

If you look at Fig. 3.4 you will see that marginal revenue falls as the quantity sold increases. Up to quantity level Q_r marginal revenue, though falling, is still **positive**, i.e. it is still adding to total revenue. Up to quantity level Q_r, therefore, the total revenue curve must still be rising. However, at Q_r marginal revenue is zero and at higher quantity levels it is below the horizontal axis and is thus **negative**. Thus at quantity levels above Q_r selling more **reduces** total revenue. It follows that total revenue must be at its maximum when marginal revenue is zero. Quantity level Q_r in Fig. 3.4 is the equivalent of quantity level Q_3, the top or turning point of the total revenue curve in Fig. 3.1.

Notice also that to maximise profits requires marginal revenue to equal marginal cost. Because marginal cost must always be positive (adding to output must always involve some extra cost) then marginal revenue must also be positive when profits are at their maximum. Consequently profit maximisation must take place at a lower quantity level than revenue maximisation.

4 Business Growth

The Widespread Acceptance of Growth as an Objective

The importance of growth as a managerial objective was noted in Chapter 3 and we now examine this more closely. We live in a world which contains some very large firms. Table 4.1 lists some of the largest firms in the UK economy. Nevertheless, as shown in Table 4.2, in world terms, many of these are pygmies.

It seems more than likely we shall see even bigger firms in the future. In the

Table 4.1 The 10 largest industrial groupings in the UK in 1987 (by sales turnover)

Rank	*Name*	*Main activity*	*Sales (£ million)*	*Capital (£ million)*
1	British Petroleum	Oil industry	34 932	18 477
2	'Shell' Transport & Trading	Oil industry	22 924*	14 579
3	BAT Industries	Tobacco, retailing, paper financial services	11 255	6 396
4	Imperial Chemical Industries	Petrochemicals, pharmaceuticals	11 123	6 154
5	Electricity Council	Electricity supply	11 119	38 778
6	British Telecom	Telecommunications	10 185	12 064
7	British Gas	Gas supply	7 610	7 392
8	Hanson	Consumer products	6 682	4 871
9	Shell UK	Oil industry	6 677	3 685
10	Grand Metropolitan	Hotels, milk products, brewers	5 705	3 356

*Based on 40% of Royal Dutch/Shell Group

Notes

1 The largest UK company (BP) had less than 59 per cent of the sales of the largest USA company (General Motors) and 119 per cent of the sales of the largest (non-sogo shosha) Japanese company (Nippon Steel Corporation).

2 The 10th largest UK company had roughly 32 per cent of the sales of the 10th largest USA company (EI Du Pont de Neman & Co) and under 60 per cent of the sales of the 10th largest (non-sogo shosha) Japanese company (Toyota).

Table 4.2 The world's 10 largest industrial groupings in 1987 (by sales turnover)

Rank	*Company*	*Country of headquarters*	*Main activity*	*Sales (£ million)*
1	C Itoh	Japan	Sogo shosha	64 827
2	Mitsui	Japan	Sogo shosha	64 218
3	'Shell' Transport & Trading/Royal Dutch Petroleum	UK/Netherlands	Oil industry	59 811
4	General Motors	USA	Vehicle manufacturers	59 530
5	Marubeni	Japan	Sogo shosha	58 169
6	Sumitomo	Japan	Sogo shosha	57 353
7	Mitsubishi	Japan	Sogo shosha	55 595
8	Exxon	USA	Crude oil & natural gas producers	53 587
9	Ford Motor	USA	Vehicle manufacturers	41 903
10	British Petroleum	UK	Oil industry	34 932

Notes
1 Apart from Unilever, also combined UK/Netherlands, no other UK company appeared in the world's largest 50 industrial groupings.
2 **Sogo shosha** is an 'umbrella' organisation providing integrated marketing, finance, transport and information services for member companies. This is an important feature of Japanese business organisation.

1980s we have seen mega-mergers in which firms that might have been thought too large to have been swallowed up by any others have nevertheless gone this way. The take over of Imperial Group by Hanson is just one example. In 1988 the Rover Group, the last remaining UK-owned volume car manufacturer, was taken over by British Aerospace, to form one giant engineering company.

Growth is not just an objective of large firms. Many owners of small businesses have an ambition to build their organisation into something substantial. It also seems that for firms both large and small growth is an objective valued for its own sake and not just because it may lead to increased profits. Share prices are often favourably influenced by rapid corporate growth. Where firms have formally expressed corporate objectives these often stress growth as well as profit. A Japanese subsidiary company operating in the UK was, in 1988, set a target of tripling its market share regardless of the effect on short-term profit. Company managers frequently support growth as an objective since this provides opportunities for increasing their status in the larger organisation.

Growth, however, is not always beneficial to firms. Diseconomies of scale may set in, particularly as managements struggle to keep control of overblown corporate empires. This is always likely following takeovers, particularly when organisations that do not fit together too well are linked in such a way. The 1980s have also seen a wave of **de-mergers** where larger organisations have been broken up or have shed some of their activities. For example, the ambitiously growing Asda supermarket group first acquired the MFI furniture chain but then retrenched by selling it in a **management buy-out**. (This is the term used when a subsidiary of a large group is bought by its existing managers, sometimes with financial support from the workforce as a whole and usually assisted by financial institutions such as merchant banks.) Parts of Imperial Group which did not fit the wider activities of the Hanson family of companies were sold to other companies.

Moreover, there are a number of industries where small size seems to be a positive advantage to firms. It allows greater flexibility and market familiarity and avoids some of the inflated costs of size.

It is important, therefore, to remember that, contrary to what is often maintained, it is simply not true that 'it is necessary to grow in order to survive.' Nevertheless, as so many managers and shareholders have growth as an objective we shall first consider the various attractions of size and then look at ways that firms may grow. Later we look at some of the drawbacks, some features of industries where small size may be a plus factor, and finally the trends towards de-merger and some other interesting developments born of a realisation that it is not always to a firm's best advantage to attempt to do everything.

The Cost Advantages of Size

The Minimum Efficient Scale

An increased scale of operations often means lower average cost, that is the total costs of production divided by the quantity produced. At some level of output, average costs may 'bottom out', i.e. there is no further significant reduction in average cost (AC) as output increases. AC will then be constant, or roughly constant, for further increases in output, unless the cost **disadvantages** of greater output become so great that AC actually starts to rise. This is illustrated in Fig. 4.1.

The level of output Q^* is very significant. It represents the minimum level of output required for full efficiency in costs – the **minimum efficient scale of output (MES)**. Firms operating at output level below Q^*, e.g. at Q_2, will have average costs significantly higher than those able to produce at quantity levels of Q^* or above. The smaller firms are likely to find it difficult to survive.

Some Implications of the MES

1 If MES is very large it may be very difficult for a new firm to enter the market and compete successfully. This is especially true if the MES represents a significant proportion of the total amount the market can absorb. For example, the MES for aerospace equipment probably represents more output than the whole UK market can absorb, so that aerospace firms have to be very large and operate in world markets. Few firms have the resources to do this successfully.

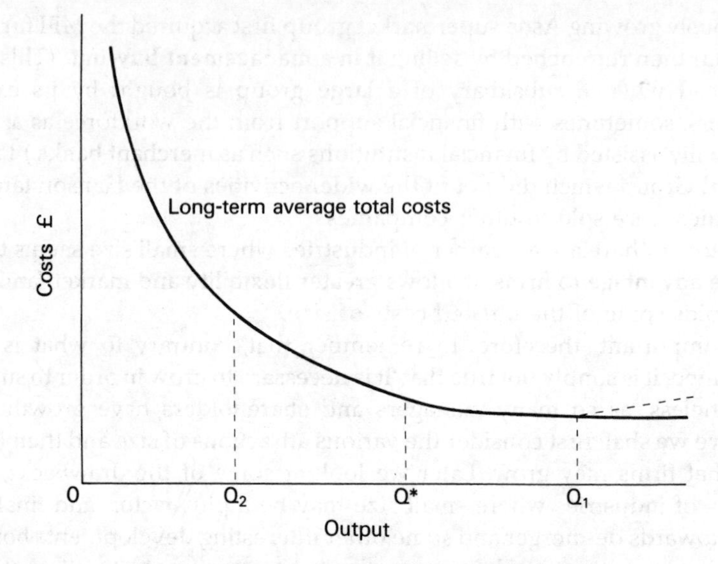

Fig. 4.1 The minimum efficient scale (MES)
For levels of output above Q* no further significant cost economies are achieved. If diseconomies outweigh economies the average cost curve could start to rise again as shown by the dotted line at Q_1. The firm able to achieve output at Q* enjoys substantially lower average total costs than the firm producing at Q_2.

2 The cost curve may have a much gentler slope than that illustrated in Fig. 4.1 so that the cost disadvantage of firms operating at less than MES may not be very great. In some cases a firm operating at half MES could have a cost disadvantage of only 1 or 2 per cent. In such industries many firms may be able to survive at well below the MES and it will be easier for new firms to enter the market and survive competition from those already established.
3 In some industries the MES is low and there is a substantial range of output where costs are constant or nearly so. In these cases we can expect to see numbers of both large and small firms operating successfully. The building industry appears to be one such example.
4 If the MES is small in relation to the total size of the market and if it is possible for small firms to enter without facing too great a cost disadvantage, as for example in many labour intensive service trades, we can expect to find large numbers of small firms. In these cases there could also be diseconomies of scale arising at relatively low levels of output so that here it is the large firms that find it difficult to compete and survive.

Plant and Organisational Economies

Most cost benefits derive from economies of scale. These may result either from technical/engineering 'facts of life' or from the advantages of operating as a larger organisation. Another way of making much the same distinction is to distinguish between cost savings derived from operating larger plants or increasing their throughput and those that arise out of operating a number of plants as part of a single firm. This is an important distinction. It was thought that the reorganisation of most of the UK vehicle industry into a single firm – then known as British Leyland – would lead to efficiency gains that would help it to compete internationally. However, as the change was largely organisational involving very few changes in operating plant size the anticipated gains were not forthcoming.

Technical Savings

Technical or plant economies of large-scale operation come about in a number of different ways:

1 **Operating larger plants** This often leads to lower unit costs than operating from small ones. Compared with small oil tankers a large tanker requires less materials in its construction, less power to propel it and fewer crew members to operate it per tonne of oil. Large blast furnaces or warehouses suffer less heat loss than smaller ones because they have a smaller surface area per unit of capacity.
2 **Obtaining a larger volume of output from existing plant** Operating a factory on a three-shift basis or a coal mine for a six- instead of a five-day week, spreads the fixed costs of operation over a greater volume of output thus reducing the average cost. It then becomes more worthwhile to buy specialised equipment. Larger volumes of output increase the predictability of breakdowns, faulty output and other problems and they can be allowed for more easily and with less cost. Maintenance teams, for example, can be kept fully employed and develop specialised skills. In addition, a production run that lasts for a longer period allows more chance 'to iron the bugs out of the system'. Experience in the aerospace industry shows that costs are continually reduced as successive batches of an aircraft are produced.

Organisational Economies of Large-scale Operation

Organisational savings can arise from some or all of the following:

The division of labour
In large organisations there is scope for people to specialise from the factory floor, through staff jobs and management to the director level. Areas of specialisation include:

1 **Selling** In terms of potential customers reached per pound of advertising expenditure national television is the cheapest and most effective medium for advertising. In its present state of development it is clearly only available for larger organisations. The full range of marketing techniques, media and outlets (see Chapter 5) are only available in practice to larger organisations. Nestlé, for example, supported its successful takeover bid

for Rowntree in 1988 by suggesting that the English company would benefit from Nestlé's marketing support with the advent of the 'single European market' in 1992.

2 **Buying** It is cheaper for suppliers to deal with single large orders than many smaller ones. In recognition of this they are often prepared to allow substantial discounts for bulk orders.

3 **Organisational structure** The great majority of larger firms now have a **multi-divisional structure**, of the kind outlined earlier. This structure cuts down the chain of communication and co-ordination between departments but it is only really feasible if the output of each product is so great that the available economies of scale in each function can be exploited within each separate division. A smaller multi-product firm might not be able to adopt this structure and so be forced either to organise inefficiently or lose the advantages of multi-product and multi-market production.

4 **Finance** Larger organisations may have access to more sources of financial funds. For example, only large public limited companies with the funds to meet the costs of meeting stock exchange requirements can raise money by selling shares to the general public. The larger public companies are also likely to be able to borrow finance at lower interest rates if they are regarded by banks and other financial institutions as low-risk organisations.

Marketing benefits

We have already noted how greater size helps reduce the costs of marketing through, for example, scale economies in advertising. There are further advantages:

1 **A well-known name** A multi-product firm may enjoy further marketing economies. For example, advertising one of the products made by Kellogg, Heinz, BP or Zanussi effectively advertises a whole range. The name is instantly recognisable. Similarly, marketing outlets and contacts built up for one product are useful for others, especially when a new product is launched. Supermarket chain buyers are ready to listen to firms which have already proved their ability to dominate their chosen markets.

2 **Market power** Market power, at its crudest, is the ability to dominate a market even to the extent of exploiting customers through excessive prices, reduction of choice or restricting after-sales services. In most industrialised countries, including the UK, there are laws and government agencies to discourage such blatant abuses of power and no firm would admit to exploiting its customers. Power, however, can be used in more subtle ways.

For example, high profits earned in one part of the business where competition is weak can be used to subsidise sales in another part enabling the large firm to set low prices that force out weaker competitors lacking a large product range. The known ability and willingness to use this strategy of 'predatory pricing' can be a powerful deterrent against new competition. It has been alleged that the larger, established airways used this practice to prevent Laker Airways from gaining an adequate share of the prized North Atlantic air routes. The Laker organisation subsequently failed.

Market power can also be used to negotiate **exclusive dealing** contracts. A retailer wishing to stock some of a firm's products may have to agree to stock others and not to stock the products of rival suppliers. A powerful seller may also seek to force the buyer to accept other conditions relating, for example, to the price charged to consumers or to services to be provided to customers. It is also possible to employ market power as a buyer large enough to dominate the market, especially when suppliers are relatively small. Large firms can exploit their purchasing power by extracting very low prices and sometimes by taking extended periods of credit – thus trading on their suppliers' finance, eroding their profits and effectively keeping them weak.

What may appear to others to be an attempt to obtain and make ruthless use of market power may, to the firm concerned, seem no more than a prudent attempt to reduce the uncertainty with which it is surrounded. It is not fashionable for a modern business manager to criticise competition which is said to be 'healthy' and to 'keep business on its toes'. Nevertheless firms often appear to go to great lengths to reduce market competition and consequently to reduce the unwelcome uncertainties that it can bring. Future planning is made simpler when firms are confident that they do not need to fear unexpected actions from a market rival. If firms are unable to reach a position of market dominance they may still try to reduce uncertainty by collusion even where this is discouraged by anti-trust or anti-monopoly laws or simply by keeping to long established market customs that avoid rousing active competition from which all suppliers stand to lose. Such behaviour can appear very reasonable and understandable but it does represent an attitude fundamentally hostile to competition. The most effective way to reduce competition is to gain dominance in the market. The desire to grow is thus seen as a way of reducing the uncertainties created by competition rather than as a means of exploiting consumers. Such exploitation becomes a temptation once market dominance has been achieved.

Further Benefits of Size

In addition to the well recognised technical and organisational economies arising from large-scale operation there are a number of less obvious but still very important benefits that are associated with very large organisations.

Security

Increased size may increase security in several ways. A multi-product or multi-market firm is more secure in that as one market declines another may compensate. Any conglomerate organisation may experience this benefit but with careful planning and foresight this can become rather more than just a 'swings and roundabouts' adjustment. A firm may analyse a currently successful product to determine what might bring about a decline in sales. For example, sales of national newspapers and their attractiveness to advertisers might be damaged by the expansion of commercial television, radio or local 'free' newspapers. Consequently many newspaper publishers have diversified successfully into these markets to gain protection from potential future threats and to be in a position to exploit opportunities as they arise.

Secure access to sources of supply and to markets are essential to the well-being of all firms. It is frustrating to lose sales because of inability to obtain an essential component or raw material or to be unable to break into markets with what appears to be a good, competitive product. Failure to obtain supplies is most likely to occur when markets are booming and when suppliers are unable to meet rapidly rising demand. Failure to find distribution outlets is most likely when markets are depressed and other, established producers seem to have all available outlets 'sewn up'. To overcome these problems it may be desirable to expand the activities of the firm by producing more of the essential inputs, perhaps taking over a component producer, or gaining control over more outlets.

Political power

Increased size tends to make it easier to influence public opinion and to gain access to people with political power. When a firm employs several thousand workers or contributes significantly to the national balance of payments any threat to the firm's fortunes becomes a potential threat to the community and a matter of public interest. Governments can use their overseas connections – and travelling cabinet ministers – to support sales efforts. The very wide discretionary powers available to the government under the Industry Acts can be used to help firms facing difficulties. Banks are also likely to react with sympathy to the needs of a single very large borrower while being considerably less sympathetic to their hundreds of small borrowers, even though collectively the small firms are just as important.

This kind of power is likely to be greater when the large firm has **multinational** status. Multinationals can be defined as firms which own and exercise direct control over production organisations in several countries. They thus have the power to switch production between countries. The negotiating power this gives in dealings with governments is very evident. They do not need to express openly an intention to move production away from a country whose policies they dislike. Ministers, civil servants and trade union leaders are well aware of this power.

The informal political influence possessed by the leaders of the giant multinationals is very great indeed. Professor Galbraith has pointed out that the Chief Executive of General Motors has an ease of access to the President of the USA denied to the leaders of all but the most powerful foreign nations. A number of the chief executives of the giant multinationals operating in the UK are members of the Athenaeum where they can meet top civil servants and politicians privately. They also meet members of the Cabinet and Shadow Cabinet socially. It should, of course, be recognised that these informal or semi-formal contacts provide two-way communication. A large multinational company has continual business contacts with people abroad that the government cannot officially recognise or be seen to be dealing with openly. These contacts can be very useful to governments from time to time.

Economic and financial benefits of multinational status

Multinational corporations have many purely economic and financial advantages. They can and do take advantage of favourable input prices and taxation conditions in different countries. For example, labour intensive activities can be concentrated in low wage countries and revenues accumulated in low tax and high valued currency areas. They can also take advantage of the fact that different products suit different national markets at different times. Low temperature washing powders, for example, were introduced into British markets later than in many other countries.

It is not difficult to appreciate the attractions for business leaders of being associated with large, and especially multinational, corporations. Some of these advantages as summarised in Fig. 4.2 – for example, those relating to sources of finance – are examined more fully in other chapters.

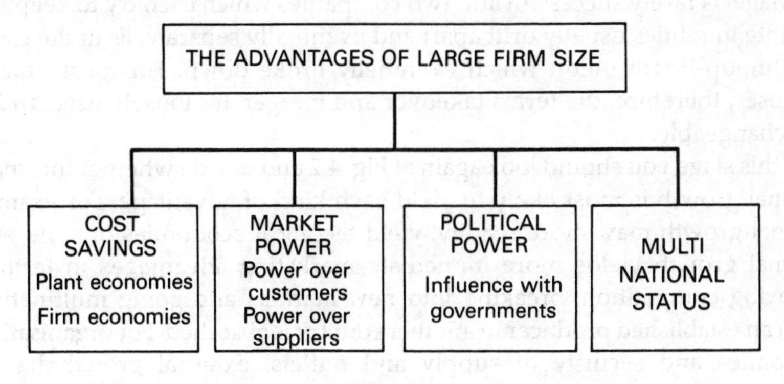

Fig. 4.2

Types of Growth

Corporate growth may take many forms. Although we propose to draw some fairly sharp distinctions between different directions of growth, in practice, a firm is likely to grow in a number of different ways at different times. The point of making distinctions is to show that different types of growth may serve different objectives and serve different corporate strategies.

Internal and External Growth

For example, if the object is to exploit technical economies of scale and thus reduce costs, then there may be no alternative to planning and building a new factory even though this is a fairly slow process. However, if the object is to exploit a perceived opportunity in a rapidly changing environment, then the acquisition of another firm with the required product and expertise may be the better route. Once again we see the importance to any firm of having clear objectives and a clear idea of the strategies that will lead towards those objectives.

These two examples have already illustrated one important distinction. This is between **internal** and **external** growth. Internal growth means the development of a firm's existing capacity and product range by processes such as building new plant, developing new products, introducing new brands and opening up new markets.

External growth means the acquisition of plant, products, technology and skilled labour by buying up other firms. Two terms are usually employed when describing this process, **takeover** and **merger**. Strictly takeover refers to the acquisition of one company by another, the company taken over losing its identity. Merger, on the other hand, refers to the fusing together of two companies to form a new, larger organisation. In practice this strict distinction is often very difficult to make. There is almost always one dominant firm in any form of company integration. Indeed, in the absence of this the business 'marriage' is rarely successful and two companies which each try to keep their separate identities usually drift apart and eventually separate, as in the case of the Dunlop-Pirelli union which eventually broke down. For most practical purposes, therefore, the terms takeover and merger are loosely used and are interchangeable.

At this stage you should look again at Fig. 4.2 and decide whether internal or external growth is most likely to yield each kind of advantage. For example, internal growth may, more readily, yield technical economies of scale while external growth yields more immediate marketing advantages in terms of removing competition, breaking into new markets and going multinational when an established producer in another country is absorbed. For organisational economies and security of supply and outlets, external growth has the advantage of speed and may also be necessary when it is not really possible to extend in the way desired by internal expansion. The French oil company Elf, for example, found that the only feasible way to develop retail outlets in the United Kingdom was to take over the independent VIP petrol retailing chain.

Horizontal Integration

Another way to classify growth is by **direction**. In Fig. 4.3 each box represents a plant or establishment – that is a factory, mill, pit, office, shop or other name given to a workplace – involved in the production process. Those towards the top of the diagram represent earlier stages of production such as the extraction of raw materials and those towards the bottom, the later stages such as shops and other distribution outlets. The bold lines separate different industries.

Horizontal integration, such as the line AB in Fig. 4.3 represents the linking of plants, i.e. the expansion of the firm within the same industry and at the same stage of production. The takeover of British Caledonian by British Airways or

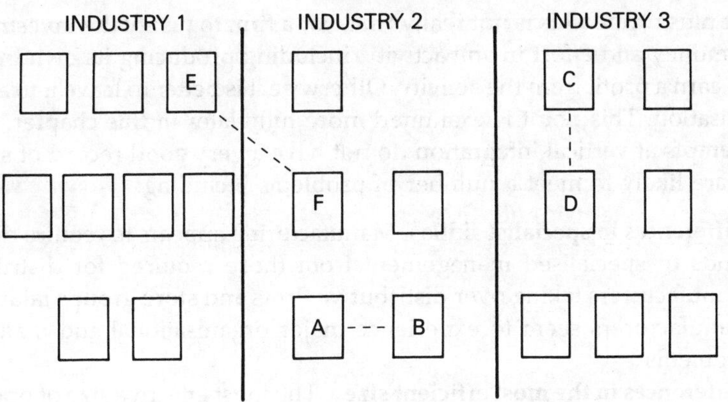

Fig. 4.3 Directions of corporate growth

of Britoil by BP were horizontal in this way. The majority of mergers and takeovers that come to the attention of the Office of Fair Trading are horizontal. A moment's reflection will show that of all types of expansion, external horizontal integration carries the biggest direct threat to competition and the concentration of market power whether or not this is actually intended by the firms involved. Other benefits, commonly claimed by firms expanding this way, include the opportunity of greater economies of scale.

Vertical Integration

Vertical integration, such as line CD in Fig. 4.3, is the linking of successive stages of production within the same industry. The Elf-VIP case, mentioned earlier, is an instance of this. Its benefits included greater security. Access to outlets could be secured by forward vertical integration, i.e. moving forwards along the chain of production towards the final customer. Backward vertical integration, i.e. moving back along the production chain to an earlier process, helps ensure supplies of essential components and raw materials. In addition, vertical integration can cut out a lot of costs. For example, if dealing with another firm for the supply of components there are contracts to be negotiated and paperwork to be completed – all these operations involve time and money.

Vertical integration does not carry the same direct threat to competition as horizontal takeover because it does not actually reduce the number of firms in competition with each other at any single stage of production. There are circumstances, however, when it can be a way of increasing market power. For example, if a firm takes over the only component supplier in an industry it would be in a position to apply pressure to its rivals, perhaps by discriminating against them in the prices they pay for inputs. Vertical integration in itself does not create this kind of market power. This is possessed by the component supplier before such a takeover. Nevertheless it does make its exploitation more likely. It is sometimes said that taking over a supplier saves money by cutting out the **middle man**, i.e. allowing inputs to be bought at cost instead of at cost plus profit. This is not really true. For a firm to justify the investment of time, money and effort in any activity, including producing its own inputs, it has to earn a profit from the activity. Otherwise it is better to leave it to another organisation. This point is examined more fully later in this chapter.

Attempts at vertical integration do not have a very good record of success. They are likely to meet a number of problems including:

1 **Differences in specialist skills** Manufacturing appears to require different kinds of specialised management from those required for distribution. Manufacturers taking over distributive firms and store groups taking over manufacturers seem to experience major organisational and managerial problems.
2 **Differences in the most efficient size** The most effective size of operation tends to be different at different stages of the production process. Rarely can an absorbed firm produce efficiently at the output level required to satisfy the requirements of its parent. Usually it has to produce more and sell to the market or produce less and leave the parent to buy some inputs from the market. It may then be found that other firms in the market are unwilling to co-operate with these requirements. Firms do not want to have to rely for essential supplies on a producer owned by a competitor, nor do they wish to market their products through a distribution channel owned by a rival.

Growth by Diversification

Growth by diversification involves the expansion of activities into another industry, such as EF in Fig. 4.3. An immediate attraction of diversification is the spreading of risks – not having 'all one's eggs in one basket' – whereas integration, both horizontal and vertical, involves a greater commitment to the same product or market. A careful corporate strategy of diversification can anticipate a downturn in a market and suggest entry to another that is likely to expand. As a population ages, for example, the demand for products aimed at younger people is likely to contract while markets directed at older age groups expands. In recent years, sportswear manufacturers skilfully developed markets among older age groups (e.g. jogging clothes) to compensate for falling numbers of young people.

Diversification is seldom a random activity bringing together collections of unconnected products produced by a single firm. There are usually threads connecting the products or markets. They may employ similar raw materials or technology (e.g. the rubber based technology of Dunlop) or have similar target markets and outlets (e.g. Zanussi with its domestic appliances). British and American tobacco companies have sought to reduce their dependence on tobacco by diversification but have generally kept to consumer products sold through distribution channels familiar to the companies from their marketing of tobacco products.

Sometimes diversification gives opportunities for exploiting economies of scale, either technically through the use of spare production capacity, or through the more efficient use of organisational capacity in such areas as marketing and finance.

Where there appear to be few obvious links between the products and the only economies of scale that are being exploited are organisational or financial, it is often said that the diversified firm is a **conglomerate**.

It has to be admitted that diversification, especially conglomerate diversification, has a poorer success record than other types of growth. The takeover of Imperial Group (formerly Imperial Tobacco) was almost certainly made possible by weaknesses caused by a period of over-ambitious diversification.

Classification in terms of growth is inevitably rather over-simplified. Growth can involve a takeover, for example, which includes elements of both horizontal and vertical integration. Nevertheless it is useful in that it indicates how different directions of growth can contribute to achieving different objectives.

Horizontal integration contributes to economies of scale and market power; vertical integration to security of supply and outlets. Diversification and conglomeration can spread risks and enable an ambitious firm to escape from the constraints of a sluggishly growing or a declining market. These benefits, however, are not inevitable and growth can bring problems.

Some Difficulties Resulting from Growth

We have already noted that certain kinds of growth, particularly vertical integration and conglomerate diversification, can bring serious managerial difficulties and many of the large-scale mergers of the 1980s have been followed by the disposal of those parts of the taken over company which do not readily fit into the mainstream activities of the dominant group. It must also be recognised that size itself, by whatever route it has been achieved, can bring its own problems.

Increased size does not always benefit the firm. Surveys have shown that, on the whole, larger firms are not more profitable than smaller ones and that where growth has taken place as a result of merger and takeover, senior managers are frequently disappointed with the results. Diversification, in particular, sometimes seems to contain an element of wishful thinking, almost as though the desire to escape from its existing problems has persuaded management that life is bound to be easier in a new market area.

An increase in size can yield scale economies but it can also bring diseconomies of scale. These tend to be organisational and managerial in origin. Managers become remote from operating decisions. There is substantial research evidence that worker morale is frequently lower in large than in small firms. It can be difficult to locate the source of decisions that affect local working conditions. The result tends to be a kind of fragmentation in which individual managers either lose interest in the organisation or interpret company policy and objectives in their own individual ways.

Loss of control in large organisations has been a major management problem for many years as technical and other factors have created larger firms. One problem is that devices to overcome control difficulties often cause others. For example, one way to keep control is to insist that subordinates respond to situations in line with company policy and file reports in standardised ways in order to reduce misunderstandings. Both of these devices increase predictability of performance but both also increase organisational bureaucracy, stifle individual initiative and lead to cynicism when standardisation fails to make adequate allowances for local differences.

Another problem with diseconomies of scale is that they are often unforeseen. Technical economies of scale and other benefits of large size can often be forecast from known data but senior managers can be reluctant to believe that organisational and control problems are just as inevitable, though more difficult to quantify. Expansion, therefore, is undertaken in the belief that the results will be entirely beneficial and without adequate attention to its problems.

Increased size can also make the firm less flexible and responsive to changing market conditions. A larger portfolio of products can help a firm to meet shifts in demand but it can make it more difficult for senior managers to concentrate on the particular problems of individual markets – though this is less likely when firms adopt a multidivisional structure. Mass production technology reduces costs but is also less adaptable. Large-scale production assembly lines cannot quickly be re-deployed to produce a completely different product. Clothing, for example, can be mass produced efficiently but in sectors subject to fashion changes it is often more satisfactory to rely on the simple, labour intensive, technology of the sewing machine. People can change their work patterns more quickly and effectively than highly complex, specialised machines.

Management techniques and attitudes in the large firm are very different from those in small organisations. On the one hand this makes it very difficult, though not, of course, impossible, for a highly successful small firm to become a giant corporation by a process of natural, organic growth, but on the other hand it can be equally difficult for a manager who has spent his or her formative years in a large company to initiate and develop a successful small, personal enterprise. The differences are not purely those of size. They involve fundamental differences of managerial style, attitude and skill.

Small Firms

Defining the Small Firm

In the UK over a quarter of the population work in what can be described as **small firms**. These produce over one-fifth of all goods and services in the economy and the proportions in most developed industrialised countries are as high and usually higher. Clearly it is not always necessary to be big to flourish in business.

What exactly is a 'small firm'? It would be rather misleading to give a single definition of this term. A manufacturing firm, for example, employing fewer than a hundred people would usually be regarded as small but few service firms, other than those in the financial services, employ more than this. In 1971, the Bolton Committee report, the most comprehensive study of small firms undertaken in the UK, proposed a definition in terms of three characteristics. This definition still holds good today. The Committee defined the small firm as one which:

1 holds only a small segment of its market;
2 is genuinely independent, i.e. is not a subsidiary of or under the effective control of a larger organisation;
3 is, for the most part, managed by its owners, in contrast to larger firms where the majority of shareholders normally take no part in running the firm.

Strengths of the Smaller Firm

It has been estimated that there are over two million small firms in Britain. Such a large number requires some explanation. First we must stress that survival of the smaller firm does not require it to be more efficient than the large firm, only as efficient. If there is no significant advantage in being large then the small organisation has a good chance of success.

There can, however, be positive benefits in being small in some industries and markets. Where this is true we find, as we would expect, that there are substantial numbers of small firms. Operating on a small scale can offer advantages in terms of costs and market conditions.

Cost Advantages of Small Firms

In some situations there are few economies of scale but many diseconomies. This is particularly true for service trades. Because these tend to be labour intensive, large-scale operation would produce very complex management–worker relations. These are avoided by small-scale operation. It is not unusual for the manufacturers of some products to avoid becoming entangled in the complexities of servicing and maintaining their products by contracting or franchising these functions to smaller firms. The motor vehicle industry is a well-known example of this.

In addition to service trades where small-scale operation is favoured because of the labour intensive nature of operations there are sectors of manufacturing – precision engineering for example – where small size offers advantages because they depend to a large extent on skilled labour. Some of the newer activities also favour small firms. One is computer software production where some fairly large marketing organisations rely heavily on self-employed programmers to write the software.

The greater efficiency of small-scale organisations derives from:

1 short lines of communication;
2 face to face contact between employer and workers;
3 a feeling of involvement by the workers in the full activities of the organisation;
4 flexibility in working patterns and practices.

Smaller plants are also less likely than large ones to be strongly unionised and industrial relations are less formalised. The reasons for this are not entirely clear and the consequences for workers are uncertain. It could be that workers feel that unions are irrelevant to their needs or that employers have less difficulty repelling unions where small numbers of workers are involved. For this to be to the employer's cost advantage it is not essential that the workers earn less than their colleagues in unionised plants but that the labour cost per unit of product should be lower. This usually means that the amount of output achieved per worker is higher in the small firm, the result perhaps of more flexible working practices or better management rather than that the employees work harder or for more hours per week.

Another cost advantage can be found in the role of the small firm's owner-manager. The typical owner-manager provides a range of essential services to the firm, as planner, manager, risk-bearer, provider of capital and financial guarantees, and often as a worker much of whose work is done outside normal working hours for no guaranteed financial reward. In many small businesses it is doubtful whether the owner's earnings really represent a financial return at all commensurate with the time and effort supplied. If it does not then the owner is, in practice, providing a substantial subsidy to the firm. At the same time the owner may also be receiving a non-financial satisfaction that is considered worthwhile.

A rather striking example of the difference between small and large firms can be found in the area of research and development (R&D). Studies in the UK and other countries suggest that in terms of innovative output per pound spent on R&D small firms are often much more productive – up to four times more efficient in one estimate. At least part of the reason for this spectacular difference lies in the fact that R&D in the large firm is carried out by employed professionals whose time is paid and accounted for whereas in small firms much 'research' is the result of unrecorded thought, reading and experiment on the part of the owner-manager who is personally committed to the success of the enterprise.

Market Based Advantages

Markets are often too small to support production on a scale large enough to generate significant cost economies. These can only arise if the product is actually sold. Superstores enjoy undisputed cost advantages over small grocery or general stores, provided the market is large enough for them to achieve their breakeven level of sales. The small unit shop, therefore, still survives in geographically isolated or limited markets such as rural villages.

Sometimes, as in the case of many garden centres, a market is regional, with customers reluctant to travel long distances to a larger but more remote seller. Sometimes, for example with musical instruments, the entire national market is small. Market size, however, can change and with it the optimum size of firm. Crossbows, until recently a historical oddity produced by a few specialist individuals, have found a demand through sport and from less reputable uses. As a result individual producers have been replaced by larger firms. The genius of Henry Ford lay not so much in realising that motor cars could be produced on assembly lines, a fact well-known to many other engineers, but in recognising that the market for cars was becoming large enough to justify mass production methods.

Small, owner-managed firms are often more flexible and resilient in the face of economic adversity. Whereas a large firm may simply close down a subsidiary if it does not meet the parent's required profit targets and make most of the workers redundant, closing down is the last option considered by the owner-manager whose wealth and income are usually dependent on the firm's survival. The owner has more to lose than the employees and will fight harder to survive.

Consequently an area with a high proportion of small, independent firms tends to weather an economic depression more successfully than one dominated by large organisations. Many factors contributed to the speed and energy with which the English West Midlands 'bounced back' from the severe depression it endured in the early 1980s but one important factor was the large number of small owner-managed firms in that region. Before the 1980s these had been heavily dependent on the motor trade and on various forms of 'metal bashing'. Although many did go under large numbers were able to turn their skills and enterprise to new activities and industries, e.g. to plastics and other consumer goods as well as to precision engineering for trades other than those catering for the motor car.

Weaknesses of Small Firms

The obvious weakness of the small firm is its inability to gain the economies of large-scale production that were outlined earlier in this chapter. In those industries and markets which can accommodate firms large enough to attain an efficient size where there are substantial reductions in unit cost, the small firm is simply inefficient and unlikely to survive unless it can identify and occupy a small, specialist corner of the larger market. Human nature is such that the very fact that most products of a given type are mass produced will itself create among those with the income to indulge their tastes a market for goods that are not made for the masses. Rising incomes and living standards can increase the size of these minority markets until they can support a substantial number of small firms. The 1980s, for example, have seen, in the UK, an increase in the demand for individually made clothes and for local, farm produced cheeses. There is, however, no place for the firm that simply offers the same product that can be produced at a significantly lower cost by large-scale production.

There is no special virtue in being a small producer for its own sake. For this reason it is difficult to justify government schemes offering blanket assistance to all small firms for these are likely to provide subsidies for inefficient producers that raise the taxes paid by the efficient.

Even when small firms are able to survive and provide satisfactory incomes to their owners and employees they present two major causes of concern. These are their vulnerability and their frequent dependence on the enterprise and work of a single owner-manager or entrepreneur. By its nature the small firm is vulnerable because of its heavy dependence on a single product, market or even customer. If its main source of revenue fails, it is unlikely to have anything else to fall back on. In many ways this problem can be made worse by business success. For many small firms that start out serving a large number of customers 'success' means achieving a single, large contract. This makes the firm dependent on a single customer for a significant proportion of its business and if that customer's support is withdrawn the small firm is in great difficulty.

In Chapter 2 we observed that entrepreneurship is present in larger firms but is effectively spread throughout the organisation. The small firm is very often dependent on one or two entrepreneurial owner-managers. This is a source of strength in that the individual entrepreneur brings to the business a great depth of commitment and, as we have seen, a substantial subsidy. However, the death, illness or sudden withdrawal of the entrepreneur has a critical impact on the firm and can lead to its swift collapse, loss of employment for its workers and financial losses to investors. Just as serious can be the failure to foresee the collapse of a market due to changing technology. Although the most vulnerable time for most small firms is their infancy – a very high proportion fail within a year of commencement – the collapse of the longer established firms is generally more serious and damaging. When a new small firm fails it is usually only the new owner who suffers financially. The failure of an older small firm is more likely to harm employees, suppliers and other investors. Large firms may not show the enterprise of some small firms but they are much less likely to depend for survival on the abilities of single individuals.

The strengths and weaknesses of the small firm are summed up in Fig. 4.4.

The Changing Nature of the Firm

The Advantages of Specialisation

Earlier in this chapter we remarked on the number of de-mergers that occurred in British industry in the 1980s. This was quite a striking development. Ten years earlier a frequently quoted reason for opposing mergers and takeover bids was that they were irreversible. If they failed to work there was no way of 'unscrambling the omelette'. This no longer seems to be a problem. As noted earlier, we now have management buy-outs supported by major financial institutions and the sale of subsidiaries from one major group to another often after a **mega-merger**.

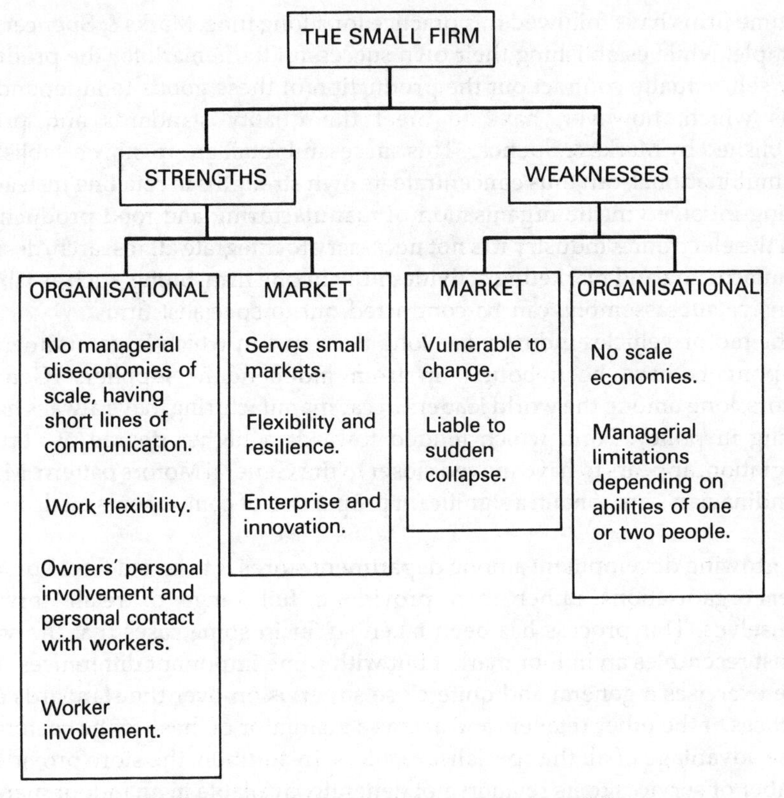

Fig. 4.4 Strengths and weaknesses of small firms

We also noted that it does not often make economic or commercial sense to try to do everything oneself in the hope of obtaining inputs at cost and removing the supplier's profit margin. After all, unless we are very interested in vegetable gardening as a hobby, few of us think it worthwhile to try to become 'self-sufficient' in potatoes or carrots, even though this might be cheaper than buying them from a greengrocer. Most of us prefer to work at something else and use our income to buy the food we need. This also gives us more flexibility. If we tire of one vegetable we can try another without wasting stocks of our own produce.

Similar principles apply in business. It is sensible for a firm to concentrate its efforts in those activities where it is most efficient and where it can earn the most profits. This helps to explain why many firms prefer to rent rather than own premises, lease rather than buy machines and vehicles. They can use finance more profitably in their main production activities instead of locking it up in expensive physical assets.

Increasingly, therefore, firms are analysing their activities to determine their strongest areas where they are most competitive and have the greatest profit potential. They can then concentrate on these by divesting themselves of subsidiaries that do not fit their mainstream production effort and buying in goods and services as required.

Some firms have followed this practice for a long time. Marks & Spencer, for example, while establishing their own successful trade mark for the products they sell, actually contract out the production of these goods to independent firms which, however, have to meet the quality standards and prices established by Marks & Spencer. This successful retail group, now established as a multinational, can thus concentrate its own strengths in retailing instead of getting involved in the organisation of manufacturing and food production.

In the electronics industry it is not necessary to integrate all research, design, manufacturing and marketing activities fully in one firm. Some, such as labour intensive sub-assembly, can be contracted out to specialist firms.

The motor vehicles industry has long been one in which large numbers of components have been bought in from independent suppliers. General Motors, long among the world leaders in car manufacturing, have always had a buying in policy. Ford, which tended towards a higher degree of vertical integration, appears to have moved closer to the General Motors pattern. Many 'Scandinavian' cars contain a significant proportion of components made in the UK.

A growing development among department stores is to let out floor space to other organisations rather than provide a full range of retail services themselves. This process has been taken so far in some cases that the store almost resembles an indoor market but with some important differences. The store exercises a general and quite close supervision over the standards and practices of the other retailers and acts as a guarantor of these to the customer, to the advantage of all the specialist retailers. In addition, the store provides a number of services to its retailers not generally available in an indoor market. These include advertising and a store charge card service. The department store thus concentrates on its own areas of expertise and leaves the merchandising to the product specialists.

The Growth of Contracting Out

UK government policy in the 1980s has been to encourage contracting out in public enterprise. All kinds of activities previously provided by 'in-house' departments of hospitals, schools and local authorities have been contracted out to independent suppliers in the private sector. Street and building cleaning and maintenance, laundry and meals services and the management of dockyards and sports centres have all been contracted out by various public sector institutions. Similar trends can also be observed in large private-sector organisations.

It has to be stressed that this does not mean that the people previously operating the contracted out activity, whether in the public or the private sector, were inefficient. Often the contracts have been gained by organisations formed by groups of managers and workers which had previously formed the 'in-house' operation. 'Management buy-outs', encouraged by this tendency and supported by financial institutions which have themselves become specialists in the field, can bring benefits to both the employing group and the contractors.

This apparent paradox is easily explained. The firm or government department divesting itself of the activity is freed from the problems of managing it, either strategically or on a day-to-day basis. If it continues to buy the service, it feels it will be supplied at a competitive rate as any supplier must be ready to face competition. On the other hand the management of the newly independent supply organisation is freed to pursue its own business plans without having to conform to wider corporate requirements. Innovation may be introduced more readily. Decision-making is simplified and organisational diseconomies of scale with their costs can be reduced.

The economist Alfred Marshall once wrote that it was possible to conceive of a remorseless process of amalgamation of firms until the output of the whole world was concentrated in one company. He had in mind the continued effects of competition and economies of scale. In the light of this section it is possible to conceive an opposite process of specialisation and contracting out continuing until everybody became a sole proprietor, with all firms consisting of just a single person doing what he or she did best and buying in everything else.

This, of course, is an impossible exaggeration, as was Marshall's vision (or nightmare!). Just as diseconomies of scale limit the growth of firms so there is a point at which the costs of continually going to the market to contract out do not justify any benefits gained. These costs include those of purchasing, selling, arranging contracts, invoicing, recording, chasing payments and general administration. Nevertheless there does seem to be a trend for firms to take stock of their activities and to concentrate where they are most efficient and profitable rather than risk the weakness of growth in areas and activities that contribute little to profits.

This trend has affected and benefited small as well as large firms. For example, one of the problems of the small firm has always been that the efforts of the entrepreneur can rapidly become deflected from his or her main activities. The manufacturer of wimwams can too easily become the administrator of a wimwam-making organisation. The time and cost of administration detract from the quality of manufacturing. Increasingly, however, such a firm may find it possible to set up in a purpose-built complex that offers not just accommodation but also a range of office services such as typing, filing, bookkeeping, telephone answering and security. A similar concept may be found in purpose-built office complexes, offering a range of services to small firms requiring simple office accommodation as a base, say for a service trade or a small haulage business.

It is interesting to note that one of the most modern business activities, that of computer software production, is often organised in a way that would have been familiar to an eighteenth-century cloth merchant. A marketing business obtains orders for software and commissions its actual production to specialist, self-employed writers who operate from their own homes. This is much the same structure as the cloth merchant who marketed the production of independent weavers working at home. Today, as in the eighteenth century, it is marketing which requires the resources of the large organisation while the actual production of goods and services can increasingly be carried out by much smaller firms.

A Note of Caution

It needs to be stressed that there are dangers in going too far down the road of specialisation, divestment and contracting out. We have already seen how even a large firm can become overdependent on a single market, product, supplier or customer. There are other, less obvious, hazards. For example, when a service is provided in-house a firm may feel that it has greater control over quality and is in a stronger position to influence specifications and schedules than when it is dealing with an outside contractor. It may be felt that there is a stronger commitment to the firm's welfare from its own employees than from outsiders concerned chiefly for their own profits. There is a further advantage in supplying at least some of one's own requirements. To have specialists operating in-house provides a guide to the costs of particular operations and consequently to the amount that should be paid when buying them in the open market.

Similarly, it cannot be forgotten that many activities still require enormous financial investment before they can be undertaken at all and can, therefore, only be carried out by large firms supported by major financial institutions. Oil exploration and drilling is never going to be an individually owned operation. The modern chemical industry is also only really open to very large firms. So great are the basic costs of setting up volume car assembly plant that it is doubtful whether Western Europe can for long support all those operating in this industry in the late 1980s.

What does seem to be emerging is a complex pattern of small and large firms many of which depend heavily on each other's specialist skills and strengths. There is also ample scope for the person of enterprise who can detect market opportunities and who is prepared to take financial risks to exploit them. All in all it is a much more interesting and exciting business environment than the one that seemed to be developing in the 1960s when growth was being pursued for its own sake and when the most basic of all economic principles, that of specialisation, appeared to have been forgotten.

Discussion Questions

1. Discuss the advantages and disadvantages of vertical, horizontal and conglomerate integration or merger from the point of view of **a** the firm's shareholders and **b** the community as a whole.
2. Suggest reasons why conglomerate mergers have often tended to be less successful and long lasting than other kinds of mergers.

3 Why do you think that a significant number of companies that have been the subject of **management buy-outs** have been able to improve their profits substantially? Does this mean that there are no real economies of scale in modern industry?

4 What are the strengths of **a** small firms and **b** large firms? In what ways have efforts been made in recent years to combine the strengths of both small and large firms?

5 What is meant by **bureaucracy** in relation to business management? Why is it an inevitable feature of many firms? What are its dangers?

Suggestions for Further Reading

Most studies of industrial economics contain an examination of business growth. Most see it in terms of limiting competition and increasing monopoly power. A more detailed examination of economic theories of growth is contained in:

Devine, P. J. *et al., Industrial Economics*, Allen & Unwin, 1985

and a more conventional analysis of the various types of integration can be found in:

Clarke, R., *Industrial Economics*, Blackwell, 1985

Professor J. K. Galbraith has written extensively about the power and influence of large firms. See particularly:

Galbraith, J. K., *The New Industrial State*, Deutsch, 1972

A major contribution to our understanding of the growth process is provided by:

Penrose, E., *The Theory of the Growth of the Firm*, Blackwell, 1980

5 The Firm and the Market

The Importance of Marketing

Ralph Waldo Emerson is reported to have said: 'If a man make a better mousetrap than his neighbour, tho' he build his house in the woods, the world will make a beaten path to his door.' Emerson was a brilliant essayist but not a notable businessman. His comment may sound profound but, unfortunately, it is almost certainly wrong. Many business people who have failed to make a success of good, well priced, quality products would bear this out. On the other hand it is undeniable that great success has been had with inferior products brilliantly marketed.

The point that must be emphasised again and again is that **nothing sells itself**. It helps, of course, to have a product in which the seller feels confident in terms of quality, price and so on, but it still has to be sold. Any people contemplating going into business for themselves for the first time need to keep this firmly in mind. No matter how good a product or service you can provide you still have to find customers. Even large firms have this problem, especially when introducing a new product or entering a new market.

In a way, Emerson begged the question when he spoke of a 'better' mousetrap. What does 'better' mean? Cheaper? Kills more than one mouse? Doesn't wear out? More humane? This question is answerable only by the customer in terms of what he or she actually wants.

Take any type of product, motor cars for example, or newspapers. In one sense a Jaguar is clearly a 'better' car than a Ford Escort but the latter will sell in far greater numbers. Here it might be that the price is all important, though it would be rash to assume that all Escort owners would purchase a Jaguar if they were rich enough. Among newspapers the price differential between so called 'quality' and 'popular' newspapers is much less marked. Nevertheless the *Sun* and the *Daily Mirror* outsell all the quality newspapers combined. It is also hard to believe that large numbers of *Sun* readers would switch to the *Daily Telegraph* if the price differential were reversed.

None of these successful products were devised without careful analysis of what customers would buy. **Marketing** has acquired a rather unfortunate connotation in some quarters: that it means foisting on people something that they would not otherwise buy. Not only is this untrue but, commercially, it would be a very inefficient way of carrying on. It is much better to **analyse** the wants of the customers, **design** the product accordingly and then **promote** it in a way that demonstrates how it meets these wants. In most businesses there is too much at stake to design and produce a product without adequate investigation of the market and then to try and persuade people to buy it.

A very successful and popular novelist has been a spectacular success by carefully analysing the type of thrillers that sell well, writing accordingly and then ensuring that likely buyers are aware of new publications by well targeted promotions. One ingenious method is to sell television serialisation rights at very cheap rates as long as transmission at peak times is guaranteed to coincide with the launch dates of the books.

What is Marketing?

Marketing is a process in which customer wants are analysed, identified and anticipated, and products developed, distributed and promoted accordingly. It needs to be carefully integrated with the design and production processes. Difficulties for the firm can be created if this is not achieved and the firm goes too far down the road of being either **market orientated**, that is geared towards giving the customers what they want, or **production orientated**, that is geared towards trying to sell the product that the firm wants to produce.

While every firm must be market orientated to a degree – there being no point in producing something people simply will not buy – this can go too far if, for example, sales people promise customers something the firm simply cannot deliver. Few things ensure greater customer disenchantment than promises of delivery dates that are not met. On the other hand, even skilled marketing cannot sell something the firm may want to make but customers do not want to buy. It was found impossible to sell the Concorde to any airline other than the state-owned companies of France and the UK; cigarettes containing 'new smoking materials' proved virtually unsellable in the 1970s; the *News on Sunday*, a newspaper specifically designed to be a quality paper inclined to the left wing of politics, failed to generate sufficient circulation to survive.

The Marketing Mix

Successful marketing is a balance between attention to product, attention to price and attention to promotion. One way of looking at this is to envisage a **marketing mix**, in which success depends on finding the right balance between all these elements. Each is important in its own right; each influences the others (see Fig. 5.1).

How can a firm be sure that it has a mix that, if not the best – rarely can we be certain what this is – it is at least a reasonably efficient one? The starting point has to be an analysis of:

1 **The firm's marketing purpose** For example, a newspaper firm may question whether it is in the business simply of producing newspapers or

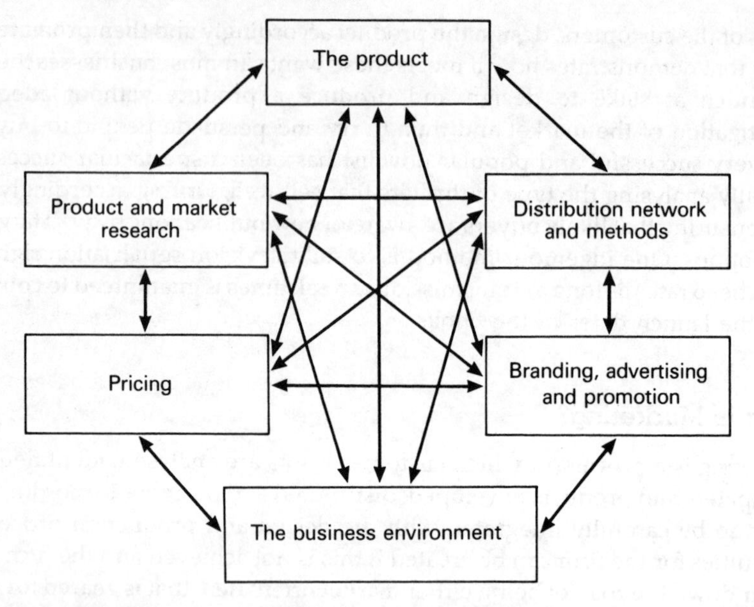

Fig. 5.1 The marketing mix
Every element of the mix interacts with every other.

whether it is a supplier of communications. The answer will help it to define the nature of the market to be analysed and developed.

2 **The firm's market environment** The firm needs to question who its customers are and what are their wants. What do they actually get from the firm's products?[1] Who are its competitors and how is the market likely to develop?

In answering these questions it is important to recognise that the market is unlikely to stand still. A product that suits the firm's marketing purpose now is unlikely to do so in ten years' time. Customers' needs and wants are likely to change over time. New technology is likely to provide new ways of meeting customer wants. The process of analysis, therefore, should be a continuous one.

Techniques of Market Analysis

Let us assume that a firm has undertaken the first stage so that it knows what it is trying to do and what product or service it is trying to provide. How then does it analyse its environment?

There are a number of techniques of varying sophistication. Some may be

[1]It is important to recognise that this is not the same question as 'What do we think we are selling them?' A security firm, with mobile patrols visiting clients' premises intermittently throughout hours of darkness, may think it is selling increased security. The customer, on the other hand, may be fatalistically convinced that intruders will simply break in when the patrols are absent but is willing to hire professional security services in order to reduce insurance premiums.

suited only to larger firms. Some at least can be attempted by firms of any size. One important point, however, common to them all, is that none is a substitute for careful thinking about the firm's situation. Every business person, however practical, has to conduct analysis and make decisions on the basis of some theory. For example, one technique that may be used is to conduct a pilot run of a product by way of a market test before committing the firm to full production. How we interpret the results of such a test, however, depends upon how we believe markets behave. For example, there may be considerable customer resistance to a new product in its early days. If we believe this to be the case then fairly modest sales in the first stages of a launch may be taken as an indication that higher sales levels will follow if the product is given a longer run. On the other hand other products, children's comics for example, have a high novelty value and unless sales are promising almost immediately there is little prospect of a successful future.

Direct Market Tests and Experiments

Ideally, before committing the firm to a new product, its marketability would be **laboratory tested** in the way that technical aspects of, for example, a new car can. The only way to be sure what the effects of a national advertising or price-cutting campaign would be is to carry it out, and that is not really an experiment but the real thing. In practice, firms that could afford a national campaign would be advised by market research organisations and advertising agencies and these specialists would have a great deal of experience of past campaigns.

An alternative is to run a test in a selected area and then attempt to conclude from this what the national reactions would be. This procedure, for example, has been used in attempts to measure the market for such products as confectionery and to test advertising slogans. There are a number of problems when it comes to interpreting the results. For instance, no single area is typical in all respects of the country as a whole. Tests can usually only be conducted for relatively short periods and the results projected into the future. There is, of course, no guarantee that these projections will be accurate. Allowance has to be made for the 'novelty effect' already mentioned or for initial consumer resistance.

Although this form of **test marketing** can appear to be the most expensive way to predict future sales, in practice it may be the only method available to the smaller firm. Lacking the resources or expertise for other techniques such firms may have little alternative to introducing a new product or service and seeing what result it brings. There is then the danger that, having committed resources to the product, managers will feel that they must persevere with it even when the initial market response is unfavourable. This often involves throwing good money after bad. One strength of the smaller firm, noted in the previous chapter, is its flexibility. An important aspect of flexibility is the ability to adapt marketing intentions in the light of information received about the state of the market.

Another possibility is to experiment with a panel chosen to represent typical customers. This is cheaper and is easier for the researcher to control but can be hazardous in that the psychology of the panel may be quite different from that of customers in the actual marketplace. Panelists, for example, may be over concerned to demonstrate how rational they are in their responses to changes in price or packaging whereas there is much evidence that buying habits are formed in less rational ways, e.g. by the imitation of other people's behaviour or by assuming that price is a reliable indicator of quality.

Questionnaire Surveys and Interviews

On the face of it, the most direct method of finding out how people are likely to respond to a product or to its price and packaging and other features is to ask them.

Once again, however, there is the problem of knowing whether the answers would be truthful and reliable or whether they would simply reflect what those questioned felt they ought to say or what they thought the questioner wanted to hear. There is a very well recognised tendency for people responding to surveys to understate their consumption of products such as alcohol and tobacco where there is an element of social disapproval. Most people also prefer to give positive rather than negative answers. They may not want others to think that they are not aware of well advertised products or that they are unwilling to buy a new product.

Skilled interviewing or questionnaire construction can reduce such bias and distortion. In one survey, for example, interviewees were asked a large number of questions about their consumption habits, lifestyles, incomes and so on. **Outside** the interview the interviewer offered them, as a reward for co-operation, a bottle of spirits of their choice. In this way it was possible to construct a picture of the typical potential customer of different types of alcohol.

Nevertheless, there remains the problem of how closely those interviewed represent the totality of the potential consumers of a product. It is actually quite difficult to put together a true random sample of the target population. Interviews conducted at home during working hours, for example, will produce an over-representation of housewives, elderly people, the housebound and unemployed. The researcher needs to know precisely what the target population actually is. If it has already been established that the most likely customers for a product are middle-aged men then the sample must reflect this. If the target population is, say, female golf players then the sample should reflect that fact.

Another point, of special importance here but also crucial throughout all marketing activities, is to remember that the **consumer is not necessarily the customer**. Manufacturers who distribute exclusively through other firms need to remember that they do not sell their products to the final consumer but to an intermediary. Of course, a product's attractions to the final consumer are important in persuading the buyers of other firms to place orders but purchasing decisions are also influenced by other factors such as profitability or reliability of delivery dates.

Even when looking for responses from the potential retail customer we should be careful not to confuse consumer with customer. Educational textbooks are used by students but buying orders or places on a reading list originate with teachers! Within the household it is important to know who actually does the buying. Many men's toiletries and clothes and children's toys are not bought by the final consumer. It is also believed that the final decision on choice of family car is often made by a woman rather than by a man and this influences the marketing approach of motor vehicle makers – who are also well aware that, in the UK, a very high proportion of all new cars sold are purchased by employers under car fleet arrangements.

However simple it may appear, there are clearly many facets to market research and the choice of marketing technique, and these are matters for specialists.

Estimating Trends

A firm may try to deduce future movements in markets from the way they have behaved in the past. All business people do this, even unconsciously, when they try to 'learn from experience'. The use of formalised techniques is simply an attempt to ensure that experience is analysed and interpreted correctly.

The material for such estimates can be derived from a number of sources. The **firm's own records** of sales, profits, etc., are a valuable resource. So too are **officially published data** on such matters as the age structure or income distribution of the population, as is material published by **trade associations** and in **trade journals**. In some cases it is possible to 'see the future today' by examining **market developments abroad**, on the assumption that these may be repeated at home. Some shrewd business people, for example, saw the success of Space Invader machines in Japan when they were still unknown in Britain.

This last example, however, shows one of the hazards of forecasting trends from experience in other countries. Few people would wish to deny that, in the past few decades, British food has been greatly influenced by exposure to foreign influence both through immigration and through packaged holidays. Nevertheless even fewer people would give a firm prediction that future British eating habits are likely to follow the Japanese taste for raw fish, or the French taste for almost raw meat. Trends and influences need to be interpreted against the background of **a theory** of the way the market environment is likely to behave.

We can illustrate this dependence on a foundation of theory by referring to a concept widely used in marketing, that of the **product life cycle**. The product life cycle theory – and it is only a **theory** of market behaviour – suggests that a new product will experience fairly low sales growth in its initial period. If and as the product becomes established sales growth will accelerate and then fall back until a market saturation level is reached. The volume of sales will remain at this level for a period, which may be short or long depending on the

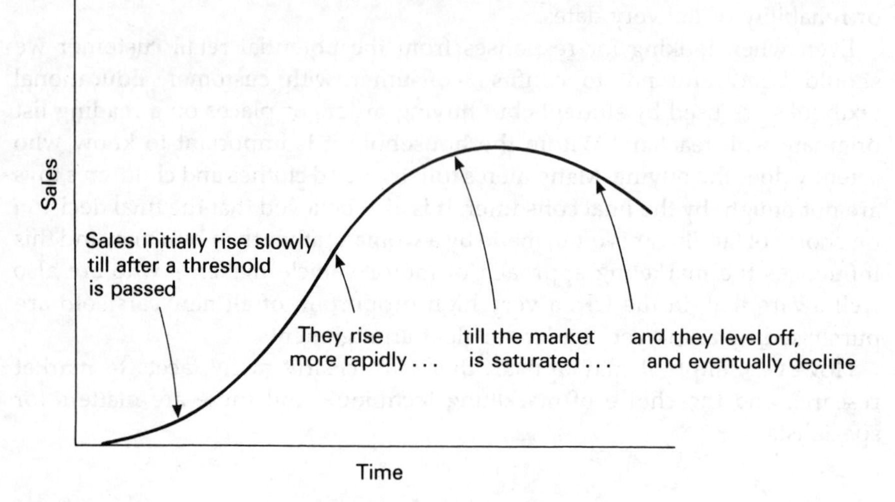

Fig. 5.2 The product life cycle

product and market. Eventually and inevitably sales will decline as the product is replaced by others.

One of the criticisms of this theory is that it has almost nothing to say to the firm about the probable timescale of each stage in the cycle, but if firms believe that it is an accurate reflection of the way markets behave then they can modify their marketing strategy according to the stage they think a product has reached in the cycle. Suppose the sales figures for a product are as shown in Table 5.1. Forecasts of future sales depend on where the firm considers the product to be on the life cycle and these will suggest different marketing decisions. For example, a product thought to be in the growth stage will be priced differently from one suspected of reaching saturation. Actual pricing policies are examined more closely in the next chapter.

The techniques used in estimating trends involve statistical analysis which is outside the scope of this book. However, it is desirable to be aware in general terms of some of the most common techniques and to recognise a number of pitfalls.

Look at the sales figures for the product **boggins** shown in Table 5.1. One way of estimating a trend here would be to draw a **line of best fit** through these

Table 5.1 Sales figures for boggins, 1991 (000s)

January	20	July	30
February	34	August	52
March	22	September	50
April	38	October	58
May	34	November	54
June	42	December	66

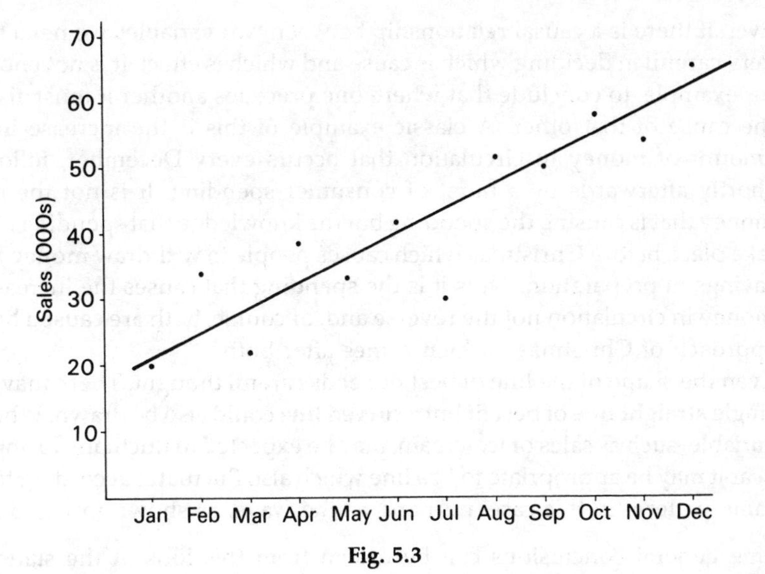

Fig. 5.3

observations.[1] One such line is shown in Fig. 5.3. This might be interpreted as indicating a steady increase in the sale of boggins over time.

However, before rushing to this conclusion and interpreting it in the light, say, of product life cycle analysis, a number of questions, such as the following, need to be asked.

1 Is the relationship between sales and time **significant**, i.e. is there a real trend present at all? It is always possible to draw a line of best fit through any set of observations but that does not mean that there is any real connection between the two variables, here time and sales. Estimation of the trend needs to be supported with statistical significance tests to show if there is any genuine relationship or whether the variation in sales is simply a random one.

2 Even if it is established by such tests that there is a statistically significant relationship this does not prove a causal connection. We cannot be sure that a change in one variable, in this case the passage of time, actually causes the other (here, a change in sales). It is quite possible for two variables to appear to be very closely related without one causing the other. For example, some of the heaviest road traffic occurs shortly after the peak period in the day for the consumption of breakfast cereals. All this means is that the morning rush hour occurs shortly after breakfast. It does not mean that eating a breakfast cereal causes people to drive to work, nor does it mean that we could reduce traffic congestion by persuading people to eat less cornflakes. Both variables result from a third – time. Simply to look at the statistical relationship between traffic volume and cereal consumption could lead to absurd conclusions.

[1] Strictly, this is the line which minimises the sum of the squares of deviations of observations from this line.

3 Even if there is a causal relationship between two variables we need to be very careful in deciding which is cause and which is effect. It is not enough, for example, to conclude that where one precedes another it must also be the cause of that other. A classic example of this is the increase in the amount of money in circulation that occurs every December, followed shortly afterwards by a burst of consumer spending. It is not the extra money that is causing the spending but the knowledge that spending has to take place before Christmas which causes people to withdraw money from savings in preparation. Thus it is the spending that causes the increase in money in circulation not the reverse and, of course, both are caused by the approach of Christmas – which comes after both.

4 Even the shape of the line of best fit needs careful thought. There may be a single **straight line** of best fit but a **curved line** could also be drawn. Where a variable, such as sales of ice-cream, may be expected to fluctuate during the year it may be appropriate to fit a line which also fluctuates according to the same pattern, in this case, perhaps, a sine wave, as shown in Fig. 5.4.

Some general conclusions can be drawn from this look at the statistical analysis of trends. In the first place, without a considerable degree of statistical knowledge it is possible to make serious errors in the estimation and interpretation of trends.

Then, it cannot be emphasised too strongly that it is a serious mistake to believe in statistics that 'the figures speak for themselves'. It is essential for statistics to be interpreted against the background of a **theory** or **model** of what is being examined. This is where economic analysis can help. By identifying the way a relationship is likely to work and the most important variables likely to be found it assists us to determine the relevant statistics and identify the relevant relationships.

In Chapter 1, for example, we gave a list of the factors that were believed to affect demand. In analysing the market for a product it is as well to start with a list so that we can look for answers to such questions as: 'How important is price?' 'How important is consumer income?' 'What are the main competing products?' and so on.

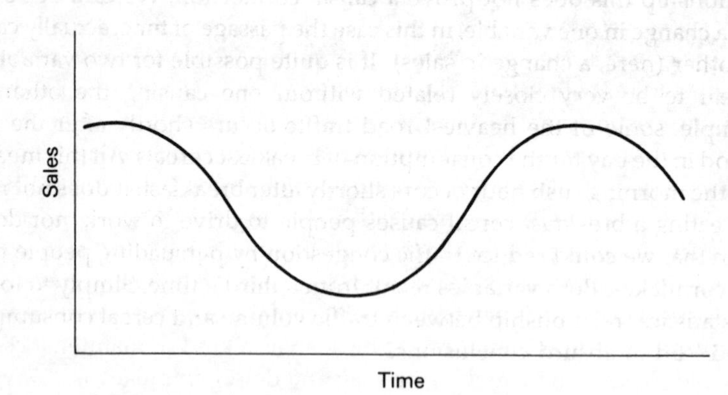

Fig. 5.4 A linear trend: the line of best fit

At the start of this section we supposed that a firm knew its marketing purpose and was using techniques to investigate its environment. This, we suggested, implied that it knew the product or service it was trying to provide. This, however, it should now be clear, would only be true in the broadest sense. For example, a firm could believe that it was in the business of providing transport or communications or domestic appliances. The details of the actual products produced for sale would normally be strongly influenced by the results of market research. Thus the first element in the marketing mix that is likely to be strongly influenced by market research is the **product**. We now consider other elements in this mix.

Price

The simplest way of setting a price is to calculate costs and then to add a mark up. However, not only is this a not very efficient way of setting price (for example, there is no guarantee that customers will pay this price) but it should be clear from the discussion earlier in this chapter that different prices might be appropriate under different market conditions. The price charged when trying to establish a new product is often lower than that charged for the same product at a later stage in its product life cycle.

The whole question of pricing is examined in greater depth in the next chapter.

Advertising

Total advertising expenditure in the UK in 1985 was £4441 million[1], of which the greatest proportion (63 per cent) took place in the press, while 31 per cent went to television, 3.7 per cent to billboards, 1.8 per cent to radio and 0.4 per cent to the cinema. Advertising may serve a variety of functions for the firm and successful advertising depends to a large extent on determining its precise objectives in terms both of **strategy** and the **audience** involved.

Strategy

Recall the earlier comments concerning the product life cycle. Advertising can have many different objectives. The aim may be to introduce a new product, to promote an existing one, to change the public's perception of an existing product or to counter the advertising and other marketing efforts of competitors. Another aim may be to build up such strong brand loyalty that the firm's existing market share is protected.

It is sometimes observed that high levels of advertising effort and expense do not seem to correspond with increased sales so that advertising is accused of being a waste of money. However, if the object of the exercise was to protect an existing market position then it might be seen as a kind of maintenance cost. For example, Procter and Gamble, the soap and detergents giant, is always one

[1]Source *Britain 1987: An Official Handbook*, HMSO

of the heaviest advertisers in the UK. One of the major reasons is the intense rivalry that exists between this firm and Unilever. This rivalry shows itself in heavy promotion of the washing powder brands sold by each. Neither expects the heavy spending to produce any significant increase in sales in any one year but both believe the advertising to be necessary to protect their existing market shares against inroads by the rival producer.

A firm's strategy will also reflect the firm's **marketing purpose** referred to earlier in this chapter. Advertising represents the most public statement and demonstration of what the firm itself believes to be the nature of the product it is producing and the markets it is serving.

The firm's advertising strategy must always influence both the type of advertising undertaken and the media used. It is unlikely that machine tools, very expensive cars or books would be advertised by cartoon commercials at peak hour viewing time on a national network. Nor would we expect to see display advertisements for holiday camps or children's toys in *The Financial Times*.

Audience

Careful investigation of the actual and potential customers for a product may demonstrate that one particular medium is far more effective for reaching a specific group of people than another. For example, there are publications which are aimed at a particular interest group, or people of a particular age or sex. Similarly the extent to which people watch television and their choice of programmes varies between groups. Billboards and other forms of poster advertising are likely to be noticed by motorists and commuters. It is not enough simply to ensure that advertising is seen by large numbers of people. It is more effective for it to reach the people most likely to be influenced by it. The introduction of specialised television channels via cable or satellite dish is also likely to increase advertising targeted on people with specific interests.

The Advertising Budget

How much should a firm spend on advertising? It has to be admitted that, at least in the past, this has tended to be one of the least scientific decisions that many firms have made. Very often the advertising budget has been set as a fraction of the projected sales revenue so that it is possible for increased advertising to be generated by increased sales instead of the reverse. Similarly when sales have been sluggish and the firm might be expected to increase its marketing effort it has actually appeared to reduce this effort.

Economic analysis has not always been of very great assistance to firms. It is possible to show that the profit maximising level of advertising can be expected to be that level where the ratios of the product's advertising and price elasticities of demand are equal to the ratios of the advertising spending and total sales revenue. However, the concept of advertising elasticity of demand is not always easy to apply in practice. It assumes that a pound spent on advertising will result in a predetermined increase in sales and ignores differences in the quality of advertising and the skill with which different firms are able to identify and target a specific audience. In practice firms pay considerable attention to quality and, as we have seen, to the identification of their relevant audience. There is considerable competition among advertising agents for the business of the big advertising spenders.

It is probably fair to admit that neither theory nor the study of business practices has produced a completely satisfactory model where an optimum level of advertising can be linked to particular determinants. The search for a more scientific guide to effective advertising expenditure has not been helped by the very great practical difficulty of linking sales to precise advertising efforts. We often have little idea of the precise influence that turned interest in a product into a definite decision to purchase. An advertising campaign for a new car model, for instance, may bring large numbers of people into distributors' showrooms but it may well be that what goes on inside the showroom and the service experienced by the interested motorist will have a considerable influence on the number of people who actually purchase the model. Given this kind of uncertainty then the patently unscientific rule of thumb linking advertising spending to actual or estimated sales is easier to understand. It does have the merit of keeping the advertising budget within the boundaries of what the firm can afford to spend.

However, no one suggests that firms should be content to operate in the dark and throw money into advertising with little idea what, if anything, it will add to sales and profits. On the contrary scientific investigation of such matters as the behaviour of consumers and the audience for various media has meant that advertising can be targeted much more accurately than in the past and that, with expert advice, a firm can be rather more confident of the results of its advertising expenditure.

Marketing Databases and Direct Marketing

One major development which has assisted the increasing accuracy of the targeting of advertising and marketing efforts generally has been the preparation of computer database packages in which computer lists of potential customers can be purchased and incorporated into electronically prepared mail shots or used for other forms of selling such as telephone canvassing. Consequently anyone who has subscribed to a book club, purchased shares, has a small mortgage or growing children may become the target of an attempt to sell products in which some degree of interest might reasonably be assumed.

It is the proliferation of computer lists and the increasing sophistication with which they can be used in modern software packages that has led many firms to employ **direct marketing** as either an adjunct or an alternative to conventional advertising. This, of course, helps to explain the amount of 'junk mail' that many of us receive! The operators of some databases believe that in a very few years, if not already, they will effectively know what particular consumers are likely to want before they realise it themselves.

Other Forms of Sales Promotion

Above the Line

Marketing people refer to **above the line** and **below the line** sales promotion. In the former, the firm is quite clearly promoting its products and advertising is clearly one such device. Others include, for example, trade fairs and other exhibitions and free samples. As with advertising the audiences for these promotional activities can be carefully investigated and analysed.

Below the Line

Promotional activities of this kind are less direct. Much public relations (PR) work or sponsorship of the arts, sport and so on come into this category. The link between the marketing effort and expenditure and the particular product may be much less direct. Sometimes all that can be hoped for is a greater public awareness of the firm's name. On the other hand, it can sometimes represent very good value for money. Cornhill Insurance, for example, were able to enhance very significantly their public image by their sponsorship of test cricket. Although this sponsorship could tell potential customers nothing about their capabilities as an insurance company nor anything about the insurance policies they offered nevertheless it achieved the major benefit of establishing Cornhill in the public perception as a major insurance company and raised their general standing relative to other insurance offices. Below the line activities may, therefore, be particularly worth considering when a promotional budget is limited or where **market penetration** is a key objective.

The Changing Market

The marketing mix for a firm is unlikely to remain the same for any great length of time. Products age, advertising campaigns lose their impact and the tastes, incomes and other characteristics of customers change. All the elements of the mix should be subject to continual scrutiny, and, where possible, the firm must anticipate future market changes and prepare appropriate responses.

Once again a clear vision of the firm's marketing purpose and environment is invaluable. For example, if the purpose is to be a leading firm in the communications or home furnishings industry what are these industries likely to look like in five, ten or twenty years' time? Looking this far ahead may be necessary if the time to develop new products is also likely to be lengthy. If it is, then even as new products are being introduced, firms may be developing their successors. For example, even as compact discs were first becoming widely marketed the firms concerned were developing the technology of digital audio tape (DAT), a product that could well succeed the CD or even make it obsolete.

Discussion Questions

1. 'You can sell anything with clever advertising.' Can you?
2. During the mid 1980s market research began to indicate that it was the woman of the household who tended to make the final decision on the choice of the family car instead of the man as had previously been assumed. On the other hand, it also indicated that more men were choosing their own shirts instead of leaving this purchase to a woman. Discuss the changes that these discoveries were likely to make to producers' marketing techniques and their marketing mix.
3. Which products are mostly heavily advertised on national television networks and why?
4. There are substantial economies of scale in advertising. A large multinational consumer product manufacturing company can make a single film and with relatively little extra expense show the same film on three or more continents so that the **exposure cost**, i.e. the cost per potential buyer, is very small. Discuss the implications of this for competition in modern consumer product markets and for the survival of small firms.
5. 'Marketing is something that affects every activity of the firm and not just its sales methods.' Discuss the meaning and implications of this statement.
6. Some products appear to have very long product life cycles. Suggest three such products and suggest possible reasons for their long life. Does this mean that their producers do not need to introduce new products?
7. What controls, if any, do you think a government should impose on advertising? Consider advertising expenditure, products advertised and advertising methods.

Suggestions for Further Reading

Most managerial economics texts contain a section on marketing. Most concentrate on the techniques rather than the role of the marketing function within the organisation. One widely used text is:

Reekie, W. D. and Crook, J. N., *Managerial Economics*, Philip Allan, 1982

From a range of specialised books suitable for providing a wider introduction to this subject, especially for students intending to pursue marketing studies in more detail at a later stage, the following are suggested:

Baker, M., *Marketing: An Introductory Text*, Macmillan, 1985
Christopher, M. G., *Introducing Marketing*, Pan, 1980
Lancaster, G. A. & Massingham, L. C., *Essentials of Marketing: Text and Cases*, McGraw-Hill, 1988
Wilmshurst, J., *The Fundamentals and Practice of Marketing*, Heinemann, 1978

For a detailed study of the economics of advertising see:

Comanor, W. S. and Wilson, T. A., *Advertising and Market Power*, Harvard University Press, 1974

6

Pricing in Practice

Pricing in Theory and Practice

In Chapter 1 we saw how the use of **marginal analysis** might help in setting prices. A firm needed to obtain a price so that the **marginal revenue** from sales – the extra revenue from increased sales – was sufficient to cover the **marginal cost** – the additional cost of producing that extra output for sale. If you are unsure of this proposition you should revise the section on p. 15 of Chapter 1 and the Appendix to that chapter.

In practice it has to be said that many firms do not use this type of marginal analysis in setting prices, or in deciding whether to accept orders. Instead they very often use a 'formula price', for example adding together various standard charges for labour and materials and a margin to allow for overheads and profits. Sometimes these charges are built into the labour and material costs so that the customer is presented with a bill something like Fig. 6.1. Bills of this

WOGGLEWORTH MOTOR REPAIRS LTD

Invoice to: L Driver
13 Unleaded Street
Carsby Newtown

To: Supply and fit cam belt

Labour	£18.00
Parts	£6.50
Sub total	£24.50
VAT @ 15%	£3.68
Total	£28.18

Fig. 6.1 Outline of a common type of repair bill

type are all too familiar to householders and car owners! They appear to show little evidence of marginal analysis.

In this chapter we shall look more deeply at both the marginalist approach to setting prices and also at some of the formulae commonly employed for price setting. As in Chapter 1, we shall show how approaches to pricing that might appear very theoretical, in fact, provoke some very practical analysis of the pricing decision. Furthermore, simply because a 'formula approach' is widely used does not make it correct.

Economic Theory and Pricing

Economists' theories of pricing usually combine two variables in order to make a prediction about the price that a firm will charge. These are:

1. the market structure, or the **business environment** within which the firm operates;
2. the objectives of the firm.

The Pricing Environment

Any firm must, when it sets price, take into account several factors. These include:

1. Its own costs.
2. Its market, in terms of what customers want and how much they are prepared to pay.
3. The behaviour of other firms. Economists talk about **market structure** – a phrase which, among other things, describes the number of firms in the market, their relative sizes and the likelihood of new firms entering the market. In economics there are models and theories of a large number of different types of market structure. Three of the most interesting for our purposes are perfect competition, monopoly and oligopoly. The main features of these market structures are discussed in the Appendix to Chapter 3, in Chapter 9 and in the Appendix to that chapter. However, the main characteristics of these markets as they affect prices are outlined here.
   - a Under **perfect competition** a firm is in a position where there is a going market price for the product and it has no option but to abide by this. Situations of this kind are fairly common in business although the markets in which they occur do not always meet the conditions required by economists to be recognised as **perfectly competitive**. Conditions where firms are market price takers usually arise when there is a considerable number of other sellers and where all sellers and buyers have good information about the products on offer from the suppliers and their prices. This effectively makes it impossible for one firm to charge a price higher than that of its competitors without losing most of its customers.

b Under **monopoly** a firm is the sole supplier of a particular commodity and can then fix the price without worrying about competitors' prices. This, of course, does not give it complete freedom to charge what it likes. Any increase in price is likely to result in some customers deciding not to buy and to spend their money on something else.

c Under **oligopoly** there are a number of competing firms and these must take each other's behaviour into account when decisions are made on pricing and advertising. Some of the price implications of oligopolistic markets are examined more fully in Chapter 9. At this stage it is simply necessary to note that individual firms cannot act alone on prices without recognising that competitors will seek to take advantage of their actions if at all possible, e.g. by not following an individual price rise. It is partly to avoid the consequences of this kind of rivalry that oligopolistic firms have a strong tendency to collude, i.e. to conduct their competition according to formally or informally agreed rules. However, as shown in Chapter 9, there is always an incentive to cheat so that oligopolistic 'price rings' are never entirely stable unless they can be 'policed' by a dominant firm. Consequently oligopolistic markets tend to be marked by long, uneasy periods of tacit, or secret, collusion, followed by intense bursts of fierce rivalry. As explained in Chapter 5, it must also be recognised that price is only one of a number of elements in the marketing mix and while firms often avoid uncontrolled price competition because the dangers of general financial loss are only too clear, there is less incentive to refrain from other strategies designed to increase market share. For example, firms are constantly examining the quality of their advertising programmes and are keen to obtain the benefits of the best advertising agencies. The evident futility of price competition thus leads to an emphasis on non-price competition with the ever present danger this too can lead to damaging 'wars' in which no firm is able to gain a significant long-term advantage. Interdependence is thus the essential feature of oligopoly and indeed of many other markets which could not be strictly classed as oligopolies. Very many business managers have to take into account probable reactions from competitors when they make pricing and other important marketing decisions.

Pricing to Maximise Profit or to Maximise Revenue

Where business managers are able to set prices they do so in order to further the overall objectives of the firm. These were discussed in Chapter 3 and a number of possible objectives were outlined. The starting point of any consideration of business objectives is almost always that of **profit maximisation**. This does not imply a constant, single-minded devotion to making the last possible penny from every transaction regardless of all other considerations. It does, however, suggest that when decisions, such as those on pricing, are made and when there is a choice between possible courses of action, the business

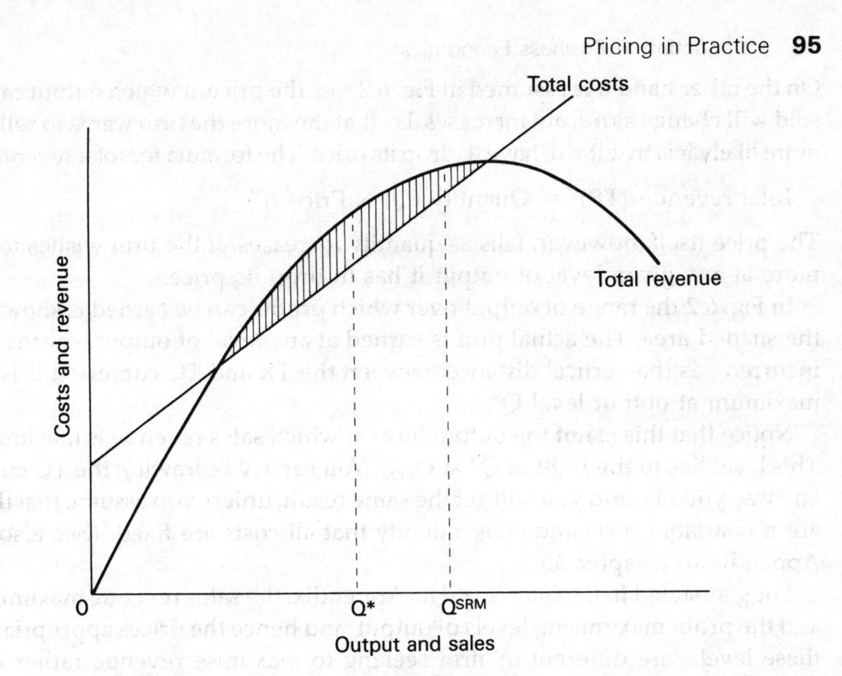

Fig. 6.2 The total revenue and total cost curves
The shaded area represents profit (TR – TC).

manager will tend towards the option that offers the greatest profit. This behaviour allows us to apply the mathematically convenient rules of maximisation to the analysis of most of the major areas of business decision-making.

As recognised in Chapter 3, managers may have other objectives which may modify their pursuit of profit maximisation. One possibility identified in that chapter was **revenue maximisation** provided that a minimum level of profit had been obtained. Some implications of pursuing that objective were examined in Chapter 3. At this stage we can examine the model a little further to see how it affects the pricing policy of the firm.

A simplified diagram to show possible total cost and revenue curves for a firm is given in Fig. 6.2. This shows how the total costs and total revenues might look for a firm selling a single product. The total cost curve is drawn on the assumption that there are certain **fixed costs** such as rent, depreciation of machines, managerial salaries and so on, which are incurred regardless of short-run changes in the level of production. In the short run these do not vary with the quantity produced. In addition to the fixed costs there are **variable costs** such as materials and fuel, which do change in line with the level of output. In Fig. 6.2 it is assumed that these variable costs are at a constant rate per unit of output. In other words the **average** variable cost does not change with output.

Total costs, therefore, are given by the formula:

Total cost (TC) = Fixed cost (FC) + (Quantity (Q) × Average variable cost (AVC))

On the other hand it **is** assumed in Fig. 6.2 that the price at which output can be sold **will** change as output increases, i.e. that the more the firm wants to sell, the more likely it is that it will have to drop its price. The formula for total revenue is:

Total revenue (TR) = Quantity (Q) × Price (P)

The price itself, however, falls as quantity increases. If the firm wishes to sell more at any given level of output it has to drop its price.

In Fig. 6.2 the range of output over which profits can be earned is shown by the shaded area. The actual profits earned at any level of output – or the loss incurred – is the vertical distance between the TR and TC curves. This is at a maximum at output level Q*.

Notice that this is **not** the output level at which sales revenue is maximised. This level lies to the right of Q* at Q_{SRM}. You can try redrawing the TC curves any way you like and you will get the same result, unless you assume that there are no variable costs and consequently that all costs are fixed. (See also the Appendix to Chapter 3.)

Thus, as stated in Chapter 3 and its Appendix, the sales revenue maximising and the profit maximising levels of output, and hence the prices appropriate to these levels, are different. A firm seeking to maximise revenue rather than profit will try to sell more and at a lower price than a profit maximising firm.

This is what most people would expect but Figs 6.2 and 6.3 also support another conclusion which was arrived at in the explanation of the Baumol model in Chapter 3. This is the reaction to a change in fixed costs. Suppose fixed costs were to rise as shown in Fig. 6.3. This would cause the whole TC curve to shift upwards to produce a new TC curve parallel to the old one.

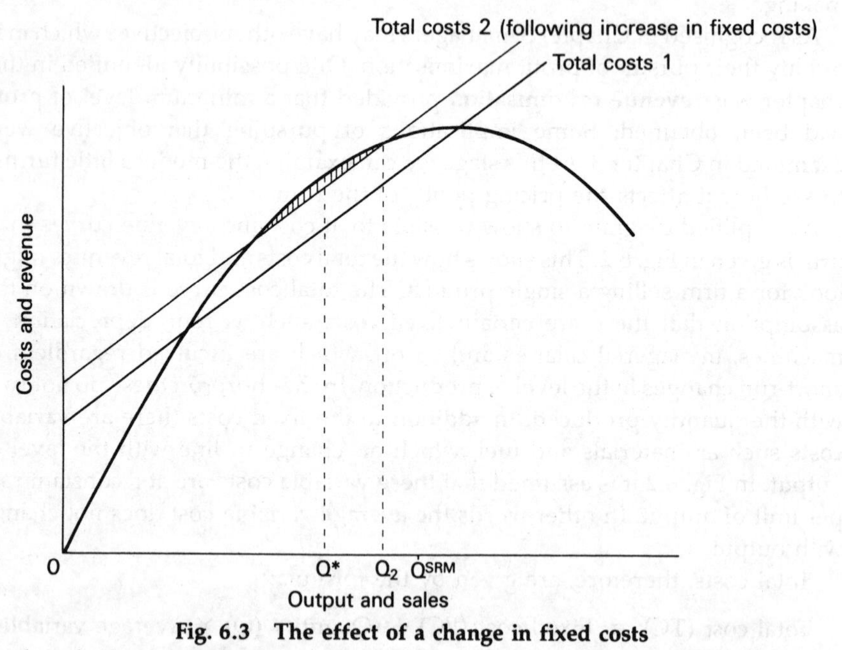

Fig. 6.3 The effect of a change in fixed costs

Total profit changes but not the quantity level at which profits are maximised (Q*).

At the new level of fixed costs production at the level of Q_{SRM} would mean incurring a loss. Assuming that the firm cannot run at a loss and must, at least, break even (ensure that TR at least = TC) it is obliged to reduce output to the level Q_2 at most. The sales revenue maximising firm is thus likely to respond to an increase in fixed costs by cutting back output and raising price. Contrast this with the profit maximising position shown in Fig. 6.3. This is still unchanged, at Q*. The profits are lower than in Fig. 6.2 but neither output nor price has changed.

This may seem a surprising result but remember that Q* represents the profit maximising output position in the first place. Given that demand conditions have not changed, i.e. the amount customers are willing and able to buy at any given price is unchanged and the variable costs of producing extra items of output are unchanged, it is not really surprising that it is not worthwhile trying to produce or sell more or less to change price. The profit maximising firm cannot pass on changes in fixed costs to its customers. If it could then it could not have been maximising profit before the change. This leads to the conclusion that any pricing formula designed, say, to provide a given level of profit or to ensure that price is above average cost, and which results in a price increase following a rise in fixed costs, is not allowing the firm to make as much profit as it could, at least in the short run.

It would, however, be wrong to think that managers were failing to profit maximise out of ignorance, though this may be true in some cases. They may, and do, consciously adopt a price that is not a short-run, profit-maximising one for a particular product because they have some other objective.

Further Pricing Objectives

Among the objectives that managers may be pursuing through their pricing decisions are the following.

1 Price may be set to maintain or improve a share of the market. This may be particularly important when a **new product** is being launched or to maintain a market share in the face of intense competition from an oligopolistic rival, perhaps as part of a 'price war' as described in Chapter 5.
2 A particular price may be set as part of an overall marketing mix. Recall from the last chapter that there are various elements to this, including the product itself, advertising and promotions and distribution. Among other things, marketing may aim to convey to the consumer a particular message about the product, for example that it is of high quality or a bargain. The chosen price may be intended to reinforce that message.
3 A price may be set with a view, not to meet existing competition, but to deter potential rivals. A profit-maximising price in the short run may attract to the markets entrants whose production will erode long-run profits. Whether or not a lower **limit price** or **entry forestalling price** is set depends on a number of factors such as:

a the ease with which new firms can enter the market, or, once in, get out again. If entry and exit are very easy the limit price would have to be very low and probably not a practical proposition;

b the size of potential short-run profits. Firms may be tempted to exploit a very favourable market position as much as they can, believing it to be temporary, even if high prices and profits do encourage entry of competitors.

Limit prices in oligopolistic markets are looked at further in Chapter 9.

4 A multi-product firm may attempt to **segment** its market between products. Different prices for different products is another way to try and influence consumers to view products differently and to build separate markets for the firm's various lines. Market segmentation is also examined in Chapter 9.

5 For multi-product firms the price of one product may only make sense when seen in the context of its overall pricing policy. For example, consider a car firm. It will be aware that its product is of greater value to some customers than others but it cannot charge them different prices even if it could identify which customers are which. What it **can** do is to offer a 'basic' model at a price close to the cost of production. This will appeal to customers who, for whatever reason, low income say, or no strong need, are only just prepared to buy. Other models with greater refinements of performance, appearance or comfort may be offered to customers who are keener to buy, who economists would describe as having a higher marginal utility for the car. The price differential charged to these customers is likely to be greater than the production cost differences but would reflect their greater willingness to buy. Another pricing option is to offer a product such as a car or piece of office equipment at a price close to cost but to ensure that parts needed for repairs, or even for normal operation, are sold at inflated prices. Customers who do not use the car or equipment very much pay, in effect, a lower total price than those whose use is greater and, therefore, we may assume, whose marginal utility is greater. Buyers whose utilities are greatest contribute the most to the producer's profits.

6 Prices may sometimes be set with an eye to tax conditions. This may be particularly true in the case of a multinational firm moving semi-finished products between plants in different countries. The **transfer price** fixed for goods moved in this way may be set to ensure that government export incentives are maximised, customs duties minimised and profits made in areas of lower corporate taxation. Similarly earnings can be concentrated in countries with **hard** currencies (currencies attractive to international traders).

Although considerations such as these make pricing decisions much more complex, the fundamental truths of marginal analysis developed by economists are still very relevant. Although simple profit-maximising rules of equating marginal cost and marginal revenue for a single product may now seem inappropriate to the needs of the modern multi-product, multinational firm, the underlying approach remains sound. When considering a proposed price change the firm should calculate the **overall incremental** effect on the company. The change should only be made if, **in the long run**, the overall effect over the whole product range is likely to bring increased benefits. Incremental refers to an addition.

The incremental approach to pricing can be summarised in the following form. For a proposed price change:

1 Estimate the likely change in sales volume.
2 Estimate the likely change in sales revenue (price × sales volume).
3 Calculate the likely effect of the change in volume on **all** costs (fixed and variable, overhead and direct).
4 Subtract the change in costs from the change in revenues.
5 If the result of **4** is positive make the price change subject to **6**.
6 Check for 'knock-on' effects such as the effect on other products the firm sells and the long-term effects on the market.

Before attempting to judge whether this is a practical approach to pricing we need to look at other ways of setting price.

Formula Pricing

There are a number of 'formulae' that can be used to fix a price. Most involve a calculation of the variable or direct costs involved in production, such as the direct labour or materials costs, and then adding a margin to allow for fixed costs such as overheads and profit.

Formula Pricing Example

Sometimes it is not at all obvious that this is what is happening. Look again at the customer's bill of Fig. 6.1. The price appears to be entirely made up of labour, parts and tax, with no provision for fixed cost and profits. The job, however, may only have taken an hour of labour time. If so, and if we assume a 40-hour working week, this would suggest wage rates of over £700 per week!

What is actually happening here is that the 'labour' costs are, in fact, calculated to cover not only the wages of the direct labour involved but also the firm's fixed costs and something to provide a profit margin. Even allowing for employers' national insurance contributions and other unavoidable costs of employing workers, the direct cost of labour (at the time of writing) is unlikely to be greater than around £6 per hour. In other words the cost of labour is being 'marked-up' by nearly 200 per cent.

How has this figure been arrived at? In the case of the motor repair company, the logic is likely to run along these lines:

	£ per week
Direct labour costs (3 mechanics)	720
Office staff	350
Vehicles	100
Rent	100
Rates	50
Post/telephone	25
Lighting/heating	40
Total	1 385

If the company is aiming for a 30 per cent profit mark-up on costs this will amount to another £415 per week, making a grand total of £1800 per week.

If it is calculated that, out of the 120 hours of direct labour time nominally available (3 man-weeks of 40 hours), 100 are likely to be directly used for doing repairs, after allowing for inevitable idle time between jobs and so on, this gives us a formula **labour price** of £1800 divided by 100 = £18 per hour.

This means that if jobs are carefully costed and priced and allocated the appropriate labour time then the firm would expect to earn a 30 per cent profit margin, i.e. £415 profit, in a normal week. In addition, parts provided in repairs are also likely to be priced so as to provide an additional profit margin. However, by far the major contribution will be made by labour costs.

The logic of this is that the provision of labour for repairs is the major activity of this firm and the number of man-hours devoted to any one job is a fair reflection of the demands that the job places on the firm's resources. It is this element, labour, which is, therefore, used as the vehicle through which to charge for, and recover, the firm's fixed costs and achieve its profits. In another activity it would probably be another item which would be subject to this mark-up. For example, a retailer would endeavour to recover fixed costs and labour costs and achieve profit through a mark-up on goods traded.

Some Variants of Formula Pricing

The type of pricing used in the motor repair example is really **full-cost** pricing which, as it implies, seeks to recover, through the price, all costs, including variable costs plus an appropriate proportion of full costs, plus a profit margin. The fraction of full cost to be built into the price is related to the significance of a particular sale.

For example, suppose a boggin manufacturer calculates that variable costs per boggin are £1 and that 100 000 boggins are to be produced and sold per year. Overhead costs are £50 000. Each boggin must, therefore, recover £50 000/100 000 = 50p towards total fixed costs.

So the formula becomes:

(Variable cost + Fixed cost per unit) + profit margin = price

If, in the boggins case, the desired profit margin is 20 per cent the price will be:

(£1 + 50p) × 120% = £1.80

A question that may occur to you is 'What is the appropriate profit margin?' In the motor repair case we used 30 per cent, in the manufacturing case 20 per cent. A general rule is that the more intensive the use of the firm makes of its capital (i.e. the more rapidly it turns it over) the lower need be the profit margin on sales. For example, if the required rate of return on capital employed is 15 per cent then:

1 A retailer with a capital employed of £1 million and sales of £10 million needs a profit margin on sales of 1 million/10 million × 15 per cent = 1.5 per cent.
2 A manufacturer with a capital employed of £50 million and sales of £30 million needs a sales profit margin of 50 million/30 million × 15 per cent = 25 per cent.

Use of this type of formula is described as **rate of return** pricing. We shall return to the consideration of the return on capital employed in the next chapter.

The Attractions of Formula Pricing

The widespread use of formula, especially full-cost, pricing suggests that they have a number of advantages and attractions.

1 Formula pricing is easy to understand and easy to implement. As costs change, the price can be adjusted.
2 The formula appears to guarantee that a firm will recover its overheads and also make a profit.
3 Formulae such as full-cost pricing ensure that every activity of the firm makes an appropriate **contribution** towards the firm's overheads and profits. The more of the firm's resources it absorbs, the greater the contribution an activity is required to make.

Criticisms of Formula Pricing

Critics of formula pricing argue that its apparent attraction rests on a number of fallacies and errors of which the first is possibly the crucial one:

1 It ignores the relationship between price and demand. In the last chapter we looked at various ways in which demand could be estimated. What is virtually indisputable is that there is some relationship between the price that is charged and the sales volume that the firm expects. It cannot be stressed enough that you cannot charge a price greater than the customer

will pay. However reasonable may seem the formula employed, however 'fair' the resultant price, the acid test remains, 'Will the customer pay it?' The underlying point here is that if the price/demand relationship **is** to be estimated then it would be better to start the pricing process from this estimate rather than a formula applied to costs. If such an estimate is **not** undertaken, then there is no guarantee that the formula will produce a price that the market will be prepared to pay.

2 A related point is that the costs built into the formula are themselves likely to depend upon the sales volume:

  a Variable costs such as labour and materials may decline – or increase – per unit as sales volume increases, under the influence of economies – or diseconomies – of scale.

  b The fixed cost per unit, because it is calculated as the total fixed cost divided by output, will clearly decline as output increases.

  As sales volume is likely to be related to price, there is the likelihood of a circular calculation here. The variable and fixed costs built into the formula make implicit assumptions about sales volume, which in turn will be affected by the price fixed by a formula which depends upon assumptions about costs and sales volume.

3 It follows from the above that it simply is not true that the formula price guarantees that every product will make an appropriate or significant contribution to overheads and profits. It will only do this if the forecast sales are achieved and this, of course, depends in large part on the price that is set.

4 It is not always the case that every product 'should' make a pro rata contribution to overheads and profits decided by the proportion of the firm's total activities which it represents. Some products may sell in very competitive markets, where margins are under heavy pressure, others in markets where it is possible to make a more comfortable margin, and this latter possibility should be exploited if the objective is profitability. A new product launched into a competitive market is likely to require a very heavy commitment from the firm's marketing and distribution resources. If a 'fair' charge were allocated to such a product the resulting price would most likely guarantee market failure. In practice firms frequently subsidise new products by over-allocation of marketing costs to well established products requiring comparatively little marketing effort.

5 In a firm which produces a range of goods and services it is very often difficult to allocate accurately between products the variable costs, leave alone fixed cost overheads. If costs are arbitrarily attributed to a product and the resulting formula price is so high that profitable sales are unlikely the mistaken conclusion may be drawn that it is not worthwhile producing. An **incremental approach** might lead to a different and more profitable conclusion.

Look again at our motor repair company example. Suppose the proprietor were asked if the firm could undertake a special repair over the weekend, when labour would normally be priced at time and a half. If it is assumed that the repair time is estimated at 15 hours and that there are no significant material costs then the formula price, excluding VAT, would be:

(15 × 1.5) × £18 = £405

As the proprietor normally expects a 30 per cent profit mark-up on costs this would be calculated as 30/130 × £405 = approximately £93.50. Suppose, however, that the client offers only £300 for the job. It appears that, instead of offering a profit, the job, if accepted at that price, would be carried out at a loss.

But reflect for a moment. The major costs that would be incurred are 15 man-hours at £9 per hour (the normal £6 + 50 per cent, i.e. time and a half). This amounts to £135. A price of £300 would make a contribution of £165 towards overheads – which remain unchanged whether the job is accepted or not – and profit. Other costs are unlikely to consume more than a small part of the £165 so that most of the £165 is an addition to profit.

Here the incremental approach would save the firm from making a serious error. Indeed it is not too strong to say that, as a general rule, **wherever formula prices give the 'right' (more profitable) answer, so too will the incremental approach, and the incremental approach often gives the right answer when the formula price does not.**

6 The formula price cannot guarantee profitability and neither can it be relied on to further any other objectives likely to be pursued by the firm. For example, it does not take into account the effect the price might have on encouraging or discouraging new entrants to the market nor does it take into account the reactions of rival firms.

Formula Pricing: A Riposte

Is there nothing to be said in favour of formula pricing in spite of its widespread use which we have already noted?

Oddly, part of its attraction is precisely this widespread use. For example, suppose an appropriate price has already been set, whether by luck, judgement or whatever. If costs change, the question arises whether and by how much to change price. There is a danger that, if price is increased while competitors keep their prices unchanged, then sales and market share will be lost.

If, however, all firms in that market are using a similar formula and facing similar costs, then all are likely to adjust to cost changes in a similar way. An individual firm may thus feel reassured that its price increase is unlikely to be out of line with that of its competitors.

Similarly, if costs are reduced, then all firms are likely to respond with a similar price cut. This could be very important under the **oligopolistic** conditions that were described earlier. Where there are only a few competitors in the market there is a danger of a price cut being seen as an aggressive act and sparking a price war. If, however, a price cut is clearly seen to be a formula response to a reduction in costs, there is less danger of its being misinterpreted as a conscious attempt to undercut the rest of the market.

Nevertheless, there remains the general criticism that formula pricing methods cannot deliver all, or perhaps any, of what is claimed for them, because they take no specific account of the various objectives that the firm might have and, crucially, because they involve no explicit calculation of the relationship between the price set and the quantity sold.

The Price-Demand Relationship

Price Elasticity of Demand

In Chapter 5 we looked at various techniques that can be used to estimate the relationship between sales volume and various determining factors, of which price may be one, though not necessarily the most important one. Economists have tended to stress the pricing decision, sometimes to the almost total exclusion of other variables, but surveys of firms have suggested that, rightly or wrongly, they do not always share this view of the importance of price. Other factors such as

1 product research and development;
2 management;
3 training of personnel;
4 advertising and sales promotion;
5 after-sales service

are as frequently, if not more frequently, quoted as elements contributing to marketing success.

Nevertheless it seems reasonable to suppose that price is a key factor in influencing the customer's decision whether or not to buy, and, as we have seen, the relationship between price and demand is a key consideration in every pricing process, whether an incremental or formula approach is adopted.

The economist's conventional way of showing the price-demand relationship is through a **demand curve** in which it is normally assumed that a higher price is associated with a lower volume of demand and vice versa. A number of different demand curves were introduced in Chapter 1 and you should make sure you have a thorough understanding of these curves.

For practical pricing decisions we do not need to know the shape of the whole demand curve but only the relationship around the current price. In particular what we are interested in for pricing decisions is how the total sales revenue is likely to be affected by an increase or decrease in price. In technical terms, this means the **elasticity of demand**, which was also introduced and defined in Chapter 1. Recall that for a given product:

$$\text{Price elasticity of demand} = \frac{\text{The proportional change in quantity demanded}}{\text{The proportional change in price}}$$

Note again the importance of **proportional** changes. A 20 pence change in price would be trifling in the case of a video recorder but could be very significant for a daily newspaper.

The significance of price elasticity of demand for business firms is that if the demand for their product is highly elastic then a relatively small increase in price will result in a very substantial reduction in sales revenue as the benefits of a higher unit price are swamped by a serious reduction in sales. Similarly a price cut could bring such an increase in sales volume that total revenue is markedly increased. If demand is price inelastic then an increase in price will not reduce sales by very much so that sales revenue will rise. A price cut will fail to stimulate sales by much so sales will be reduced. These implications are set out in Fig. 6.4.

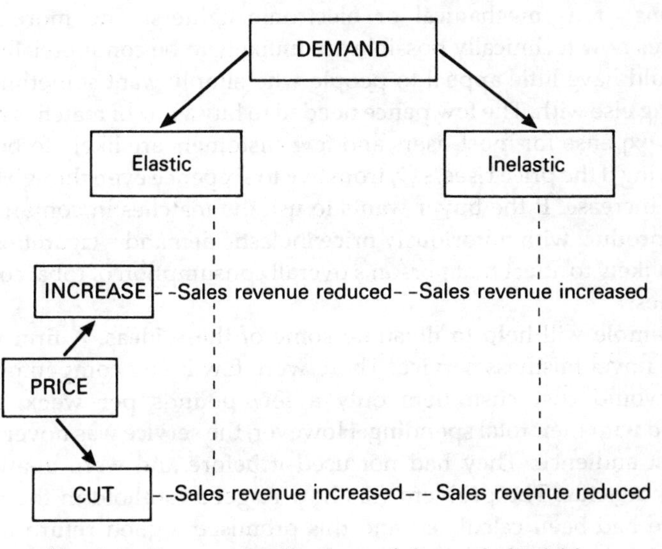

Fig. 6.4 Revenue implications of demand elasticities

Knowledge of whether demand is likely to prove elastic or inelastic can thus be decisive in deciding whether price changes have a significant part to play in a firm's marketing strategy. The techniques of statistical analysis and market research outlined in Chapter 5 can be harnessed to this end although it must be pointed out that there are certain statistical problems involved in estimating the price-demand relationship. For example, although both price and demand may be observed to fluctuate over time one cannot simply be related directly to the other. Although quantity demanded may have increased, this may have little to do with price changes. In the late 1980s there was a marked upsurge in the demand for skateboards, caused not by price changes but by fashion trends among young people. Declining tobacco sales have less to do with high prices than with health fears. High prices of housing did little to deter demand in 1987–8; cheaper credit and rising incomes were stronger influences.

However, some insight into the likely elasticity of demand for a product can be gained even without a full-scale statistical exercise. An intelligent appraisal of the nature of a product market can lead to some reasonably accurate conclusions about the product's price elasticity of demand. For example price elasticity of demand is likely to be low if the product:

1 Is not easily substitutable by something else, either a similar product from a competitor or by a different product altogether;
2 Involves only a small part of consumers' total expenditure;
3 Is used together with something else which has a low price elasticity of demand. The product might be complementary to the other, as with petrol and cars, or an input into the production of the other.

As an example of a product's demand being price inelastic take a box of matches. There are a few substitutes either in the form of matches produced by rival firms or as mechanical or electronic lighters. The more advanced substitutes now technically possible are unlikely to be commercially viable as they would have little appeal to people who simply want something to light something else with. The few pence needed to buy a box of matches represents a trifling expense for most users and few customers are likely to be deterred from buying if the price rises, say, from five to six pence even though this is a 20 per cent increase. If the buyer wants to use the matches in conjunction with another product with notoriously price inelastic demand – cigarettes – a price rise is unlikely to affect that person's overall consumption of tobacco, and thus of matches.

An example will help to illustrate some of these ideas. A firm wished to launch a novel business service. There were few if any competitors and the service would cost customers only a few pounds per week, negligible compared with their total spending. However, the service was novel to most of the target audience. They had not used it before and were unaware of its potential benefits. The problem was how to get a foothold in the market.

A price had been calculated and this promised a good return if the sales attained their expected levels. However, in a marketing drive the firm adopted a policy of deep price cuts of well over 50 per cent to stimulate demand.

An analysis of the product and its market, described in outline above, would rapidly reveal that we could forecast inelastic demand for the product and so it proved. The deep price cuts failed to boost demand significantly. Worse still, among the few customers who were attracted there was strong resistance to later attempts to restore prices to the original level where profits could be made. Although demand was inelastic, consumer resistance to a price rise of 100 per cent (needed to make good the earlier reduction of 50 per cent) was stronger than their response to the earlier cut.

On advice, when the product was re-launched, much more effort was put into other aspects of marketing, in particular to raising customer awareness of the product and the benefits it could bring them. The policy was much more successful. The product rapidly established a significant market. The basic price inelasticity of demand was confirmed by the ease with which subsequent customers accepted price rises after they had become familiar with the product.

Some Other Pricing Issues

Price Discrimination

We have already seen how a firm might look to make very different margins on different products if market conditions varied for its different products. It may also attempt to sell the **same** product at a different price to different customers, a practice called **price discrimination**.

This is attractive but rarely possible. It is attractive because it offers the opportunity to extract a high price from some customers without scaring away others who, while willing to pay a price more than sufficient to cover the costs of production, are less willing or able to pay a higher price.

It is rarely possible because, if a firm sells at a low price to one customer, an attempt to sell at a higher price to another could be frustrated by the first customer re-selling to the second at a price below that asked by the firm. As an example, consider the calls, often heard, for senior citizens to be sold coal at a discretionary discount price. The problem with this concession, well motivated though it might be, from the point of view of British Coal is that there would be nothing to stop senior citizens re-selling their concessionary coal to other people and thus effectively undercutting the producer.

For price discrimination to be **possible**, therefore, there must be some separation between the markets in which the different prices are to be charged. This separation would have to make it difficult, if not impossible, for customers to sell the product to one another.

For it to be **attractive** for the seller, demand conditions must be different in the various markets so that customers in each are prepared to pay a different price and respond in different ways to price changes. It will be **profitable** to the seller if the additional revenue gained from price discrimination is greater than any additional costs incurred as a result of departing from a policy of setting one common price to all buyers.

There are a number of different types of price discrimination and the following are common examples.

Haggling

Haggling is the term given to the attempt to achieve perfect price discrimination in which every buyer pays the price equal to his or her marginal utility. It is a process of individual bargaining in which the seller's bargaining skills are pitted against those of the buyer. The practice is familiar to anyone who has visited a small shop, market or bazaar almost anywhere outside Western Europe and North America. The potential rewards to the seller are illustrated in Fig. 6.5.

If one customer is prepared to pay £15, the second £14, the third £13 and so on, and if the seller is prepared to sell at any price down to £10, bargaining could achieve a maximum total revenue of £75 which is higher than could be gained from selling at the most favourable single price on this market demand curve. Haggling is not unknown in Britain. Think, for instance, of the house transfer and used car markets! Success, however, usually depends on the seller

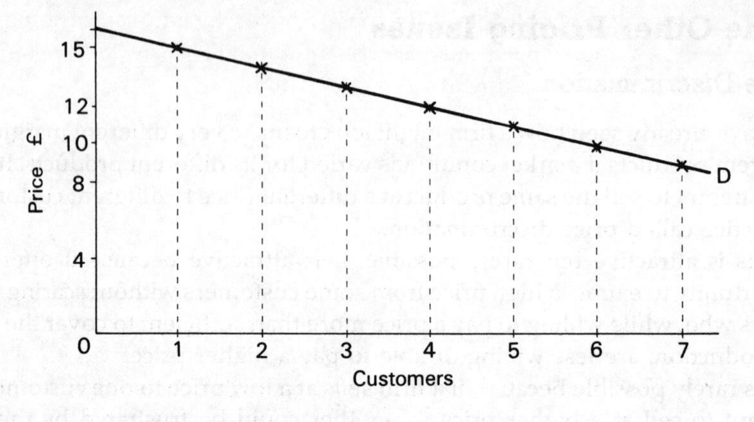

Fig. 6.5
If successful haggling achieves sales to each customer at a price equal to the value of the customer's marginal utility, total revenue is greater than can be achieved at any single price between £10 and £15.

having a financial stake in the bargaining process. It is not a suitable practice for large-scale retailing where paid assistants are employed.

Favoured pricing
Customers with more than average buying power are often able to ensure that they obtain **favoured pricing treatment**. The seller is prepared to accept a reduced profit from these rather than see them go to market rivals. Provided the practice is justified on the incremental grounds outlined earlier, the supplier will gain. The revenue implications of this practice are illustrated in Fig. 6.6. To qualify as genuine price discrimination the reduction allowed to such customers should be more than the cost saving resulting from any large-scale purchasing. This practice is often considered to be 'unfair' and

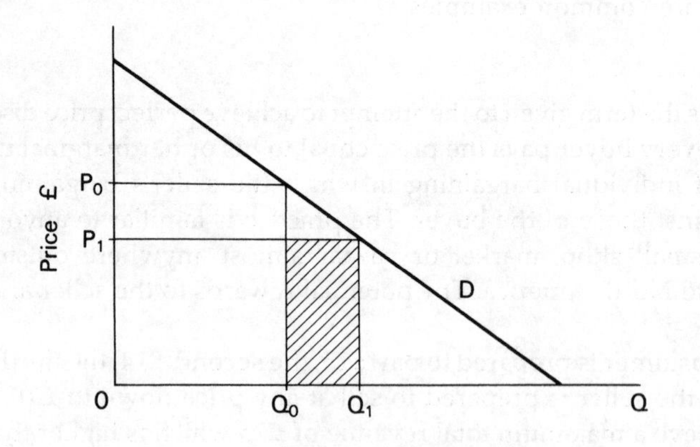

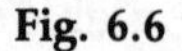
Fig. 6.6
The normal price is P_0 achieving total revenue equal to $P_0 \times Q_0$. Certain favoured customers are charged price P_1 to achieve additional revenue equal to the shaded area.

discouraged by competition laws. In the USA, for instance, the Robinson–Patman Act is aimed specifically at preventing it. However, this kind of legislation is notoriously difficult to enforce.

Different prices for different sections of the market

It may be possible to sell to different sections of the market at different prices. Provided the price elasticities of demand are different in the various market sections it is possible to raise total revenue by adopting profit maximising prices in each separate market. A theoretical model illustrating this idea is given in the Appendix to this chapter. There are a number of familiar examples which broadly follow this practice. For instance:

1 Multinational price discrimination can take place in different countries, especially where it is difficult for consumers to arrange personal imports from one country to another. It has been alleged that this has been the practice of car manufacturers when they charge lower prices in left-hand drive continental European countries than in right-hand drive the UK.

2 Pricing of services has a long history of 'charging what the market will bear'. By their nature services are not normally re-saleable from one customer to another – you cannot re-sell a haircut – so that it is possible to charge different prices to different customers according to believed ability to pay. There was often a social element to this practice. Before the formation of the UK National Health Service doctors frequently charged very little or nothing to poor or chronically ill patients – making good revenues from their more wealthy hypochondriacs. More recently, solicitors used to base house conveyancing fees on house values so that poorer people with low value property paid much less than the more affluent. Local bus companies used to allow passengers travelling before, say, 8 a.m. to buy cheap 'workmans' return' tickets. It was then assumed that the better paid 'white collar' workers started work later than the low paid manual workers.

Attempts to achieve rough social fairness through price discrimination are no longer fashionable. Transport companies have learned from economists that people who have to travel to work or to city business meetings present a market where demand is highly price inelastic so that these are charged significantly **higher** fares than those who travel for leisure and pleasure and who can choose between competing methods of transport and whose demand is thus more price elastic. Business executives, whose travel costs are likely to be paid by their employers, and indirectly by the buyers of their products, are also likely to be charged heavy fares for more comfortable business or first-class air travel whereas fares are reduced to very low levels for tourist class, package holidaymakers who have to pay their own travel costs.

Discrimination is also possible where re-sale of the product is difficult for technical or legal reasons. Re-selling coal was seen to present few problems but it is not technically or legally possible to re-sell mains gas or electricity.

3 Price discrimination may be used to try and reduce large variations in demand for products that cannot be stored and so allow producers to make greater use of spare production capacity. Certain public utilities suffer a severe peak loading problem. For example, there has to be sufficient electricity generating and distribution capacity to ensure that maximum demand is met on, say, the early evening of the coldest winter's day when there are peaks of both business and household use of electricity. For much of the rest of the time demand is well below possible production capacity. By charging reduced 'off-peak' prices the producer can stimulate and transfer some demand to the periods of surplus capacity as long as variable costs are covered and as long as charging the different prices does not add more to costs than to revenue. This is the logic behind 'Economy 7' electricity prices in the UK which reduce prices to around 50 per cent of 'normal' for electricity used between certain hours of the night, and the 'blue' travel days when British Rail reduces certain off-peak rail travel fares.

4 Price reductions for large-scale (bulk) buying are common. This practice cannot really be called price discrimination if the bulk purchase discounts are offered to any buyer wishing to take advantage of them and if the discount bears a reasonable relationship to the savings in storage, handling, transport, administration and other costs gained by the seller. The discount represents not only a recognition that there are cost savings from economies of scale to the seller but also an element of cost transfer to the buyer, e.g. goods are stored at the buyer's not the seller's expense. Only if the seller retains the freedom to choose whether or not to grant price reductions to different customers or groups of customers and/or offers discounts greater than can be justified on cost saving or transfer grounds would bulk buying discounts be viewed as price discrimination.

5 Price reductions are also sometimes given for long-term agreements. Some insurance companies, for example, may be prepared to charge reduced premiums if clients are prepared to sign an agreement to keep policies in force for, say, three years. Clearly there is a cost saving element in this as some marketing and administrative savings may be achieved. On the other hand these agreements are difficult to enforce in practice, cost savings are likely to be very small, and as they tend to be offered only to larger business policyholders they are really a form of price discrimination.

The above examples of price discrimination are not exhaustive and you may be or become familiar with others from your own experience.

Transfer Pricing

An interesting issue in pricing concerns the practice of charging internal prices within business groups for products or components which are transferred from one part of the group to another.

This practice may seem a little odd as it appears to involve the firm in charging itself but it does have a sound basis where the group is made up of a number of more or less autonomous units which trade with one another. Very often these units are designated as **responsibility centres** with their performance judged in terms of the profits they make or their success in operating within a

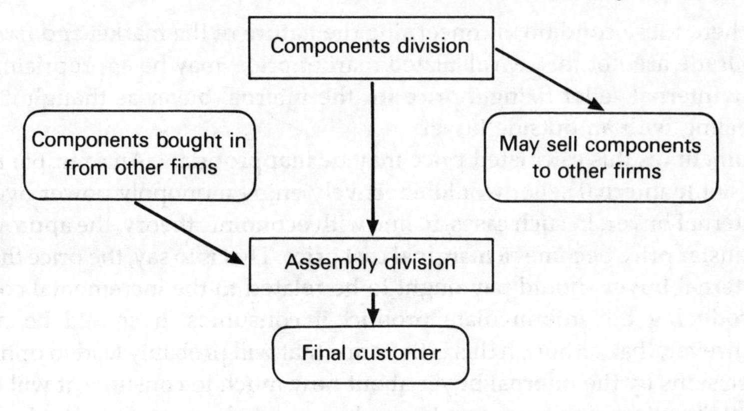

Fig. 6.7
The assembly division is regarded as a profit centre. Transfer prices are charged for components bought from divisions within the firm or groups.

budget. Suppose a firm is structured as in Fig. 6.7 and the assembly division, which uses components sourced from both inside the firm (from the components divisions) and from outside (from independent suppliers), is to be regarded as a **profit centre**.

To calculate the profit of the assembly division we need a figure for both its sales revenue and its costs. The latter will include the cost of the components transferred from the components division and for this purpose a **transfer price** needs to be put on these components.

If this transfer price is set artificially low a number of things will happen:

1 The profits of the assembly division will be artificially inflated as its costs are artificially low.
2 The assembly division will be induced to source only from the internal supplier even if there are more efficient external suppliers able to offer components at lower real prices.
3 If the components division is also to be regarded as a profit centre its profits will be artificially reduced.
4 The components division will probably regard the assembly division as a 'least favoured customer' as the price it pays is lower than that obtainable on the open market.

To avoid distortions of this kind a number of guidelines for the setting of transfer pieces can be suggested. These in outline are:

1 Where there is a competitive external market for the intermediate (transferred) product and both the internal customer and supplier have 'freedom to trade', i.e. the right to choose to source or sell outside the firm, then the appropriate transfer price is the going market price. There may, perhaps, be a small adjustment to allow for the fact that trade within the firm usually generates lower transaction costs than does external trade because there are lower marketing, purchasing and administration costs.

2 Where these conditions concerning the nature of the market and freedom to trade are not met, a 'calculated market price' may be appropriate, with the internal seller fixing a price for the internal buyer as though it were dealing with an outside buyer.
3 Sometimes this calculated price may be inappropriate. An example might be if the internal seller would effectively enjoy monopoly power over the internal buyer. In such cases, in line with economic theory, the appropriate transfer price becomes a **marginal cost price**. That is to say, the price that the internal buyer should pay ought to be related to the incremental costs of producing the intermediate product it consumes. It should be noted, however, that, although this is the price that will probably lead to optimum decisions by the internal buyer about how much to consume, it will mean that the internal seller can no longer be regarded as a profit centre because, with a transfer price based on marginal cost, it is likely to make reduced profits or even a loss.

Sometimes transfer prices are used for purposes other than to guide the pattern of internal trade in a firm or to help assess divisional performance. One of the most notorious uses – or abuses – of transfer prices arises in international trade. This was noted earlier in this chapter (see discussion on page 98). If the components division were located in a high tax area and the assembly division in a low tax area then a very low transfer price would mean that the components division would probably report a loss and the assembly division an inflated profit. This would reduce the tax liabilities of the firm as a whole. Transfer price changes are clearly ways available to adjust to differing taxation conditions.

This type of abuse can be checked by tax authorities but first they must be aware of it. This, for example, requires careful scrutiny of import prices on customs documentation, and then the authorities must normally be prepared to argue a legal case against the firm – which will usually have a plausible explanation of its pricing policy. In some parts of the world, including some states in the USA, systems of **unitary taxation** have been introduced to base a firm's tax liability on its world-wide earnings and not just those attributed to the territory concerned.

In defence, of course, firms may argue that they have to use transfer prices to correct the market distortions introduced by governments when they use taxes, interest rates and their power over currency exchange rates to pursue their own economic or political ends. This introduces a much wider argument that is beyond the scope of this book.

Loss Leading, Introductory Offers and Predatory Pricing

It is sometimes apparent that the price for a product may be set well below what would appear to be justified by any method of price setting, whether incremental or formula. The reasons for apparently 'give away' prices are usually to be found within the firm's total marketing and product strategy and not just in the pricing policy for a single product.

For example, **loss leading** is a practice whereby one of a number of products sold by a firm is offered at a heavily discounted price. This is a practice that, it is alleged, is often indulged in by multiple stores and supermarkets. A few 'lines', typically those for which there is a generally recognised going market price – coffee or bread, for instance – may be offered at a very low price in the hope of attracting to the store customers who are then likely to buy 'on impulse' other products, without checking their prices.

Sometimes a product may be offered at a very low price, or even free, for a limited period. This is appropriate where repeated sales are hoped for and where an attempt is being made to penetrate a market and overcome customer ignorance of the product or where there is an existing allegiance to an existing brand. Such introductory discount price offers might be appropriate for business services, periodicals or washing powders.

As we saw in Chapter 4, price cutting can be used to repel an attempt by another firm to enter a market. If one firm produces a range of products but faces the threat of competition on just one, it may use the profits earned on the range to subsidise heavy discounts on the threatened line. If the new competitor is also financially strong and has a range of supporting products it too may discount. The result may then be a **price war**. If the rival lacks financial and market power it may not be able to counter the **predatory pricing** tactics of the established firm.

Predatory pricing is usually regarded as an unfair business practice and is outlawed in most developed countries. Nevertheless it does appear to happen. After the collapse of Laker Airways there was a celebrated battle in which it was alleged that the major airlines had practised predatory pricing against Laker on the North Atlantic route.

Conclusion

We must not forget that pricing is part of the firm's total marketing mix and pricing strategies must be considered against the background of all the activities and objectives of the firm. Clearly, however, pricing involves issues that are rather more complex than the almost automatic responses to particular market structures that appear to be implied in some interpretations of economic theories. Economics, however, does have some very important lessons to teach the business manager. It has done much, for example, to spread awareness of the incremental approach, now widely understood in business firms which are much less likely than in the past to cling to formulae developed under vastly different market conditions. We must also recognise that modern electronic technology has made it possible for firms to acquire speedily a range of market and cost information that would have been beyond their reach two decades ago. Modern computer software includes some very powerful spreadsheet packages which permit firms to set up models and experiment on 'what if?' lines and so avoid some costly trial and error approaches. As always, however, it takes time for human understanding and imagination to catch up with the opportunities opened up by technology revolutions. What is certain is that these opportunities depend upon a sound understanding of market behaviour and this implies an ability to apply the basic concepts of economics to modern market conditions.

Discussion Questions

Discuss the pricing issues raised in each of the following:

1. A supplier of office and home copiers sells small machines at a low price. These use a replaceable cartridge capable of making about 3000 copies. The price of the replacement cartridge is around 7.5 per cent to 10 per cent of the price of a new machine. The same supplier also sells larger and more expensive copiers, usually with a service contract including the supply of chemicals needed for copying. The service contract is likely to have an annual price of around 2–3 per cent of the price of a new machine.
2. The price of a standard motor car sparking plug remained virtually unchanged between around 1938 and the early 1950s. Its price then actually fell for some years even though almost all other prices were rising. There are now more different types of sparking plugs but their price as a fraction of a new car price is less than it was in 1938.
3. First-class air fares can be as much as twice the price of tourist class air fares over the same route although both classes travel in the same aircraft and the difference in travelling conditions is unlikely to cost more than a fairly low proportion of the difference in fare.
4. Prices for tickets at some major international sporting events held in England, e.g. the finals of the FA Cup and tennis at Wimbledon, are usually set at levels which produce large numbers of 'ticket touts'.
5. Some camera films used by amateurs are often given away as part of a film developing marketing promotion. Others are sold with a 'free' developing and printing service.
6. Some leading insurance offices are able to produce national tables of house building costs enabling policyholders to calculate the cost of rebuilding their house if they make some simple area calculations. Nevertheless there are very great differences in the prices of similar sized houses situated only a few miles from each other and it is frequently difficult to have a clear idea of the selling price of a house without actually offering it for sale.
7. A group of holidaymakers staying at the same hotel at the same overseas holiday resort for the same number of weeks having arrived on the same aircraft, chat together and discover that they have all paid different prices for their holiday.

Suggestions for Further Reading

Davies, J. and Hughes, S., *Pricing in Practice*, Heinemann, 1975
Stokes, C. J., *Economics for Managers*, McGraw Hill, 1979

Appendix to Chapter 6

The Gains from Price Discrimination

Figure 6.8 shows a simplified model of two markets (A and B). In each the price elasticity of demand is different at the relevant price range. In market A demand is more price inelastic than in B and there are people prepared to pay a higher price than anyone in market B. Reflecting this, the demand curve in A is steeper and the curve starts at a higher price than the demand curve in B. At the right of the diagram the kinked curve represents the combined market of A plus B in which the demand curve is the arithmetic sum of A and B.

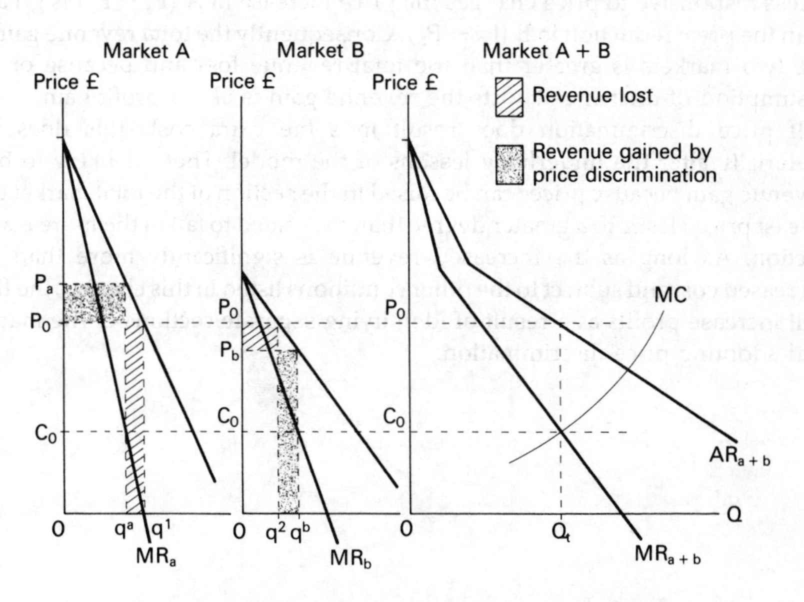

Fig. 6.8 Simplified model of two markets A and B
Without price discrimination the common market price is P_0 and the total quantity sold to the market is Q. Assuming costs remain unchanged, price discrimination does not change the total quantity sold but the price rise in market A is greater than the price fall in market B. The total revenue gain is greater than the total revenue loss. As costs are unchanged, profits rise. This model also assumes profit maximisation as an objective.

This model makes a further simplifying assumption that the costs do not change whether or not price discrimination is practised. This allows us to concentrate on revenues. Any change in revenue, given that there is no change in cost, will produce an equivalent change in profit. A further assumption of the model is that the firm is seeking to maximise profit.

In the combined market the profit maximising price, without discrimination, is P_0 at a total quantity level of Q_t, the level where marginal cost (C_0 on the MC curve) = marginal revenue (MR_{a+b}). This quantity would be apportioned between the two markets on the basis of q^1 sold in market A and q^2 in market B, where the upper horizontal line representing the common, non-discriminatory price cuts each of the market demand curves.

If the firm decides to charge discriminatory prices in each market it would aim to produce and sell that quantity in each where the separate market marginal revenues were equal to the unchanged marginal cost of C_0. This gives quantity q^a in market A and q^b in market B with separate prices of P_a (market A) and P_b (market B).

Notice that, in this model, the total quantity sold does not change. There is simply a redistribution of sales between the markets with a reduction in A ($q^1 - q^a$) and an equal increase in B ($q^b - q^2$). However, because demand in A is less responsive to price changes the price increase in A ($P_a - P_0$) is greater than the price reduction in B ($P_0 - P_b$). Consequently the total revenue gain in the two markets is greater than the total revenue loss and because of the assumption of unchanged costs the revenue gain is also a profit gain.

If price discrimination does result in some extra costs this does not materially alter the underlying lessons of the model. There is likely to be a revenue gain because prices can be raised in the section of the total market that is least price elastic to a greater degree than they need to fall in the more elastic section. As long as the increased revenue is significantly more than the increased cost and subject to the other conditions listed in this chapter, the firm will increase profits as a result of identifying separate sections of the market and adopting price discrimination.

7 The Investment Decision

In the last chapter we looked at the role of the pricing decision in the marketing of a product. In this chapter we look at a related set of decisions – what projects a firm should undertake, what investments it should undertake and how these should be financed.

The Investment Decision

Elements of the Investment Decision

All investment decisions involve a number of common elements, among the most important of which are:

1 The **objective** towards which the firm is working and thus against which we can measure the success or otherwise of an investment. Throughout this chapter we shall assume that the objective is the maximisation of profit, although if another objective were being pursued it would be possible to use the same techniques as long as a monetary value could be put on this objective.
2 There are a number of **alternative** courses of action. If only one course of action is possible then no decision has to be made.
3 There is a decision **technique** which can be applied in analysis.
4 There are decision **rules** which are to be followed once the calculations have been applied.

Whether this is a complete or even an adequate list is uncertain. Although most of this chapter is concerned with decision techniques and rules there is a great danger that over concentration on these will distort understanding of the full dimensions of the investment decision. Towards the end of the chapter we outline some of these other dimensions and some ways of taking them into account.

Discounting

Fundamental to virtually all the techniques of analysis examined in this chapter is the concept of **discounting**, that is putting a current value on revenues or costs that will be earned or incurred in the future.

A pound next year is not the same as a pound today. This would remain true even if there were no inflation – a condition that has persisted so long in the UK that almost everyone under the age of 60 now believes that money will automatically lose value with the passage of time. Even in the absence of inflation we would prefer to have a pound now rather than later, partly because there is always a degree of uncertainty over the future and partly because money can be 'put to work' even if we have no immediate use for it. A pound left to rest as a deposit in a bank or building society will earn some interest. We need, however, to be a little more precise than this. We need to know **how much** our preference is for money today rather than in the future.

Discounting is an attempt to measure this. If the **discount rate** is 10 per cent per year (per annum) then this means that £110 payable in one year's time has the same value as £100 payable now. This recognises that £100 left on deposit for a year to earn interest at the rate of 10 per cent per year will have £10 added to it at the end of the year. If the payment is not due for two years the difference between the present and future values is going to be greater. £100 left on deposit for two years at the same rate would earn £11 in the second year (£110 at 10 per cent) in addition to the £10 in the first year so that we would need to be assured of receiving £121 in two years' time to have an amount equivalent of £100 now. In three years' time the amount would be £133.10 and so on.

The general formula for finding the present value (V_0) of an amount payable at the end of n years (V_n) at a discount rate of d (where d is expressed as a decimal fraction, i.e. 10 per cent gives d = 0.1) is:

$$V_0 = V_n(1/1 + d)^n$$

Application of this formula to finding the present value of £100 payable in three years' time discounted at 10 per cent per year gives a value of £75.13.

There are commercially published tables of present values and there are also a number of easy-to-use computer programs for making suitable calculations.

Investment appraisal techniques which involve the calculation of the present value of a stream of future expenditures and earnings are known as **discounted cash flow (DCF) methods**. A general formula for finding the present value of a stream of future payments payable for n years, discounted at a per annum rate d, can be shown in the form:

$$V_0 = V_1(1/1 + d) + V_2(1/1 + d)^2 + V_3(1/1 + d)^3 + \ldots + V_n(1/1 + d)^n$$

Investment Appraisal Techniques

Payback Method

This is one of the simplest techniques and may be used with or without discounting. As its name suggests it involves calculating how rapidly a project will pay for itself. Consider the following example.

An investment involves an initial expenditure of £50 000. Thereafter it pays

Table 7.1 Investment example 1 showing project with a payback period of around eight years

Year	*Expenditure (£)*	*Earnings (£) (actual value)*	*Earnings (£) (discounted at 10%)*
0	50 000	10 000	9 091
1		10 000	8 264
3		10 000	7 513
4		10 000	6 830
5		10 000	6 209
6		10 000	5 645
7		10 000	5 132
8		10 000	4 664
9		10 000	4 241
10		10 000	3 855
11		0	0

a return of £10 000 per year for ten years. If these returns are not discounted the initial investment will obviously be recovered in five years so the payback period is five years. If the returns are discounted at 10 per cent there will be a stream of future earnings with a present value as shown in Table 7.1.

With a discount rate of 10 per cent it will be between seven and eight years before the initial investment is recovered so the payback period is about eight years.

The **decision rule** with the payback method involves comparing the calculated period with that for other projects or with some target payback period. For example, the project illustrated is to be preferred to one with a payback period of 10 years but not to one with a payback period of five years or less. In this way the payback method may be used in conjunction with some of the techniques described later. It may be used to **screen** all possible projects and only those with a sufficiently short payback period will then be considered for examination using the other, more expensive techniques.

The **advantages** of the payback method are considered to be:

1. Its simplicity. Especially if no discounting is applied it is very easy to understand and to use.
2. Its use to reduce **uncertainty**. All investment appraisal involves forecasts about the future and the further ahead, the greater is the uncertainty over the accuracy of forecasts. The use of the payback method:
   - **a** favours projects with shorter payback periods, thus reducing the uncertainties involved in forecasting;
   - **b** gives an indication of how rapidly a project will 'pay for itself' and thus how soon the firm will know with certainty whether the investment decision was profitable or not.

The **disadvantages** include:

1 The fact that it takes no account of the profile of the stream of earnings from the investment other than the point at which the total earnings equal the total expenditure. Look at the three earnings streams shown in Table 7.2.

Table 7.2 Investment example 2: earnings profiles

Year	*Project 1 (£)*	*Project 2 (£)*	*Project 3 (£)*
1	10 000	20 000	0
2	10 000	15 000	0
3	10 000	8 000	5 000
4	10 000	5 000	15 000
5	10 000	2 000	30 000
6	10 000	1 000	50 000
7	10 000	500	30 000
8	10 000	0	20 000
9	10 000	0	10 000
10	10 000	0	0
11	0	0	0

Project 1 has the same earnings profile as the investment outlined in Table 7.1. It does not really matter for our purposes here whether these represent discounted or undiscounted earnings as long as the payback method is to be applied to the earnings shown in Table 7.2. Project 2 pays higher returns in the early years but these rapidly drop away to zero by year 8. Project 3 pays very little in the early years but has very high earnings in later years.

If all three projects involve an initial outlay of £50 000, the payback period for them all is the same – five years. But if we apply the decision rule here we find we are indifferent between the three projects, despite the fact that project 3 offers much higher earnings than project 1 which, in its turn, has higher earnings than project 2. The method is completely insensitive to the pattern of earnings other than the payback period. There is valuable information here that is simply ignored in arriving at a decision.

2 Reducing uncertainty by accepting only short payback periods is not necessarily always the best way of handling uncertainty. After all, forecasts may not be over-optimistic. They may also err on the side of caution and pessimism. We shall return to this point later in the chapter.

Net Present Value Method

In contrast to payback the **net present value method** has been widely accepted as being the most 'correct' method.

To calculate the net present value (NPV) proceed as follows. Calculate the present value of all the costs and revenues associated with the project. Add together the revenues, subtract the costs and the result is the NPV. In

Table 7.1 the only cost is the immediate outlay of £50 000 which is thus the present value of costs. For the total earnings add together the figures in the right-hand column. This gives a total of £61 445 so the net present value is £(61 445 – 50 000) = £11 445.

Note that this is only true for a discount rate of 10 per cent. There will be different NPVs for different discount rates. A discount rate of 5 per cent will increase the discounted values of future earnings and thus the overall NPV. A higher discount rate will make these earnings less valuable and thus reduce the NPV. The NPV may well be negative, given a certain profile of costs or earnings or a particular discount rate.

The NPV may be represented by the following formula:

$$NPV = V_0 + V_1 + V_2 + V_3 + \ldots + V_n$$

where V_t is the total net present value of costs and earnings in any year (t). If there is a single discount rate (d) applied to all periods, this formula becomes:

$$NPV = V_0 + \sum_{t=1}^{n} \frac{V_t}{(1 + d)^t}$$

The **decision rule** with NPV is to accept projects with a positive NPV and reject those with a negative NPV. If a choice between projects has to be made then the project with the highest positive NPV is to be preferred.

The **advantages** of NPV include:

1 The inclusion of **all** costs and revenues whenever they fall. All are given the appropriate weight, following the discounting process.
2 The possibility of varying the discount rate if this is thought appropriate. For example, different discount rates could be applied in earlier and later periods. A higher discount rate, say, might be applied to later periods to allow for uncertainty. Strictly this is not a particularly 'scientific' way of handling uncertainty but may have intuitive appeal.

The **disadvantages** of NPV primarily centre on the rather abstract nature of the answer that it produces and this explains its unpopularity among many of the business people who are familiar with it. Look again at the answer that was produced for example 1 – £11 445. What **is** this £11 445! It is not money that is available now, nor is it any sort of measure of the 'real' money that will accrue to the firm in the life of the project. Many business people, even if they understand the concept of net present value and accept that it is theoretically correct for decision-making and resource allocation, prefer to work with something more concrete. The concept of payback, for example, is something that has real meaning, as does the 'yield', the third of the most popular investment appraisal techniques.

The Yield or Internal Rate of Return Method

Look again at example 1. An initial investment of £50 000 results in an annual return of £10 000 for ten years. Suppose that instead of stopping after ten years the return continued indefinitely at the same rate. It would then be clear that the initial investment was giving a **yield** or **return** of 20 per cent per year, indefinitely.

What, then, is the yield, or **internal rate of return** (IRR), of example 1 where the earnings stop after ten years? It cannot be as high as 20 per cent, as there are no earnings in year 11 or beyond. The answer lies in the formula for NPV, outlined earlier. This formula, applied to a perpetual stream of earnings of £10 000, at a discount rate of 20 per cent, produces a total present value of £50 000, i.e. the same amount as the initial investment outlay. So, at a discount rate of 20 per cent the NPV from this investment would be exactly zero. Thus the yield or internal rate of return from an investment is that discount rate (d) which will equate the NPV to zero:

$$V_0 + \sum_{t=1}^{n} V_t(1/1 + d)^t = 0$$

To solve the equation for d involves a lengthy iterative search procedure but this is now made very simple by programmable calculators or computers. It transpires that the yield of the project in example 1 is about 16 per cent, that of Project 2 about 2.5 per cent and that of Project 3 about 28 per cent.

The IRR of example 1 can be illustrated graphically as in Fig. 7.1. At a

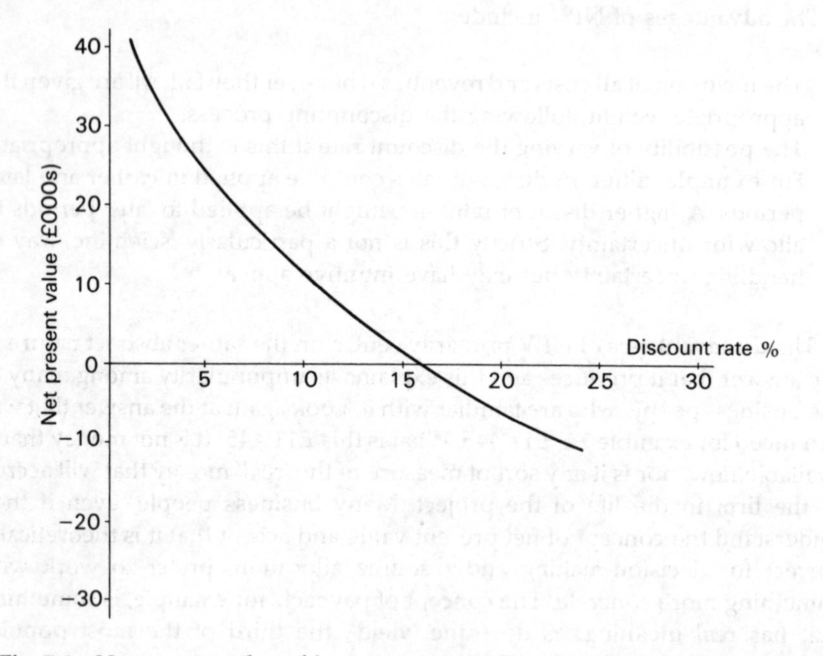

Fig. 7.1 Net present value of investment example one at various discount rates

discount rate of less than 16 per cent the project from example 1 would have a positive net present value (NPV). At a discount rate above 16 per cent it has a negative NPV.

The **decision rule** whether or not to accept a project then becomes: accept a project if its yield is greater than a certain **test discount rate**, which is normally the **marginal cost of capital** to the firm. So, in example 1, if the test discount rate is below 16 per cent the project is worthwhile. If it is above 16 per cent it should be rejected – notice that the NPV method gives the same result in this case. If a test discount rate of over 16 per cent is applied to this project it gives a negative NPV.

When it comes to a choice between projects the yield method cannot give such a straightforward answer. For example, faced with a choice between two projects both of which give a yield higher than the firm's test discount rate it might seem logical to accept the project with the highest yield. But suppose the other is a much larger project promising a much larger return in monetary terms?

This is a problem rather like being asked whether you would prefer a 25 per cent return from an investment of £40 or 20 per cent from one of £100. The first option would provide only £10, the second £20. The answer rests on what you could do with the other £60 (the difference between £40 and £100), if the first instead of the second option is chosen. The first is only worthwhile if the other £60 can be invested to return £10, i.e. about 17 per cent.

A similar problem arises when there are two alternative projects with one offering a higher total undiscounted return but with a high proportion of the receipts delayed until later in the project's life. It will be found that this project will have the higher NPV at low rates of discount but the alternative, with most of its receipts gained in the early stages of life, may have a higher IRR. Choice of the project with the higher IRR can only really be justified if the higher profits gained in the early years can be invested in some other project at a greater yield than they would have earned in the first alternative.

Clearly then, the use of the yield (IRR) to assess projects is inextricably tied up with the whole **capital budgeting** process of the firm. The firm cannot judge projects in isolation but must review all possibilities and select that **combination of projects** which promises to maximise the yield from the resources available for investment.

The **advantages** of the yield method rest chiefly on its intuitive appeal. Most people find it meaningful to think of the 'yield' from an investment and projects can be easily explained to boards of directors in these terms. Even when the pattern of returns is irregular, as in Project 3 in Table 7.2, the concept of a yield serves to give a mental idea of an average return from a project.

Incidentally, there is an intriguing arithmetical link between the yield and payback methods. If a project yields a constant return and if that return continues indefinitely then the undiscounted payback period is the reciprocal of the yield. Take the example we used earlier, an investment of £50 000 yielding perpetual returns of £10 000 per year. The payback period is clearly five years. The yield is 20 per cent; $\frac{1}{20} = 5$; 10 000 is $\frac{1}{5}$ of 50 000.

A moment's reflection shows that there is nothing surprising in this but it does help to explain further the popularity of the yield method among large numbers of those business managers who are familiar with DCF techniques. A payback period of, say, four years is on a quick rule of thumb, equivalent to a yield of 25 per cent. A yield of 10 per cent is likely to indicate a payback period of about ten years and so on.

It must, of course, be remembered that this handy rule of thumb is **only** true if the stream of earnings is constant and expected to continue indefinitely. There is no such easily recognisable relationship between payback period and yield where returns vary over the life of the project. The other two projects illustrated in Table 7.2 had the same payback period of five years but one yielded 28 per cent and the other 2.5 per cent.

We have already noted some of the **disadvantages** of the yield method. There are others which may make it give misleading results or, in some cases, be virtually impossible to use.

As a further example, suppose we have a project which is a slight modification of project 2 in Table 7.2. The earnings stream is the same but instead of having to lay out £50 000 at the outset, the firm needs to spend only £25 000. The remaining £25 000 can be borrowed and need not be repaid until the end of the project's life. There will be a cumulative interest charge of about 7 per cent to pay which will make the final repayment about £40 000. What now is the yield of the project?

Calculation shows that the yield is around 13 per cent but further calculations shows it is around 35 per cent! Which is correct?

Oddly they **both** are. Figure 7.2 illustrates this. At a discount rate of less than

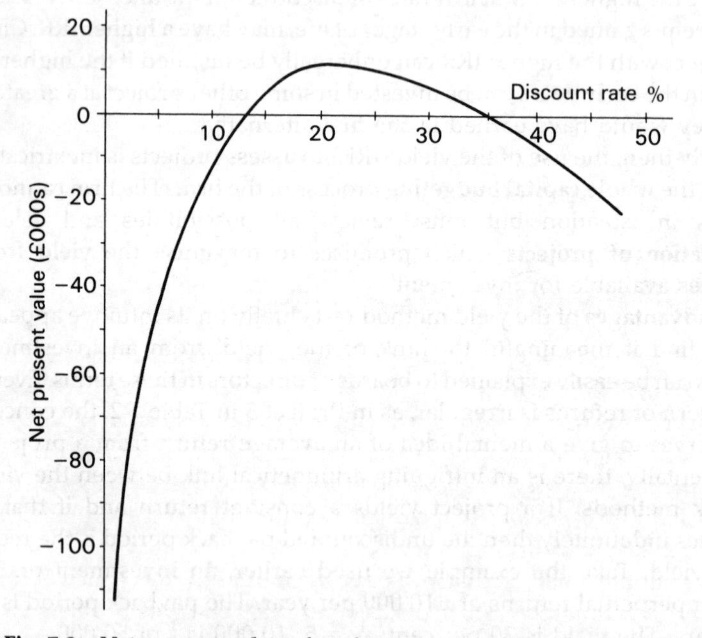

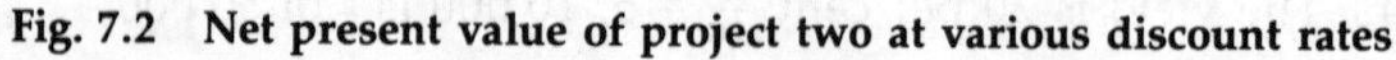

Fig. 7.2 Net present value of project two at various discount rates

13 per cent the project has a negative NPV; between 13 per cent and 35 per cent the NPV is positive; above 35% it is again negative.

This rather odd result – two yields – arises because, in this project, we have two periods of net cash outflow separated by several periods of cash inflow. The more such irregularities there are, the more turning points there will be in the curve which sketches out the NPV and, possibly though not necessarily, the more solutions there will be for the yield.

There is even the possibility that there will be no definite yield at all, in the sense of a discount rate which will set NPV = 0. For example, the rather bizarre but not impossible scenario of a project which yields net earnings of £15 000 in the first year, has net expenditures of £30 000 in the second and net earnings of £15 000 again in the third, has no such yield.

Although rules have been suggested to cover most of the difficulties that may arise with the yield method, it is difficult to make out a case for using them when the net present value alternative is available. Irregular cash flows present no more problems than regular ones for the NPV method. As it uses a single test discount rate or a single rate for each payment period, it is flexible enough to take into account anticipated future changes in the opportunity cost of capital (as explained in the next section of this chapter) and it always gives a single, unambiguous answer. The profit maximising answer provided by the NPV method is always reconcilable with answers provided by other methods where these are properly understood and applied. Often NPV will give a clear answer when others are ambiguous or fail to provide any answer.

Other Appraisal Methods

There are other techniques of investment appraisal. Details of these can be found in the more specialised business finance texts but for the purposes of this book it is more desirable to concentrate on the main principles and pitfalls of capital budgeting. If these are understood, further variations, most of which are applicable to particular groups of activities or which have little to offer that the main techniques do not provide, can be mastered if or when the need arises.

The Test Discount Rate and the Cost of Capital

Both the NPV and the yield, and the payback method when it is based on discounted cash flows, need to use a test discount rate or rates. In the NPV and, where used, the discounted payback methods, the test discount rate is used directly to discount the cash flows in the various time periods. In the yield method the calculated internal rate of return is compared with the test discount rate to screen projects for accept/reject decisions. How then do we select an appropriate test discount rate?

As an example, imagine that you have been offered the chance of investing £1000 with a guaranteed return of £100 per year. The only problem is, you do not have £1000 so, to take advantage of the offer you would need to borrow.

Clearly, if the borrowing will cost you more than £100 p.a. or 10 per cent of the necessary £1000 it is not worthwhile. If, on the other hand, you can borrow at well below 10 per cent, say at 5 per cent, the investment looks very attractive. The crucial factor in deciding whether or or not to go ahead, in other words, the test discount rate, is thus the amount that has to be paid to raise the necessary funds for investment, i.e. the **cost of capital**.

Note that the relevant cost of capital here is the cost of raising this particular capital. This is your **marginal cost of capital**. Once again we meet this fundamental concept of **marginal** analysis. It is irrelevant, for example, at least for the purpose of computing the cost of capital, if you have already borrowed £2000 at a rate of 6 per cent. Suppose you find that you could borrow £3000 at a rate of 8 per cent. It still would not help if you repaid the existing loan and used the extra £1000 for the new investment. £3000 at a rate of 8 per cent involves an annual cost of £240. This is £120 more than the existing interest payment of £120, making the effective cost £120 for the extra £1000, i.e. a marginal cost of capital of 12 per cent.

A firm must determine its cost of capital in a similar way. As we see in Chapter 8, a firm has many possible sources of finance. For simplicity these can be put into two divisions:

1 **internal** funds, the firm's own accumulated financial reserves;
2 **external** funds, finance raised from outside the firm whether from **borrowing** or from additions to share capital – a further injection of **equity** capital.

It may be tempting to look upon the internal funds as 'free', or to have a zero cost. This is not so. We can recall the economist's concept of **opportunity cost** and ask ourselves what **could** these funds be earning if we do not use them for a proposed project? Recall our earlier example of the personal investment opportunity of £100. This could, perhaps, have been financed by withdrawing £1000 from a bank or building society account where, presumably, it could have been earning interest of, say, 7 per cent. If this were the case then the cost of capital would be 7 per cent. The opportunity cost of capital is the potential earnings foregone when funds are used for a particular project.

If the funds are to be raised externally, then the cost of capital becomes the amount that must be paid to raise them. In the case of borrowings this is the rate of interest plus any dealing charges. If the additional funding is from a share issue the cost is a little less straightforward. We shall return to this later in the chapter but for the moment assume that the cost of this capital can be expressed as a stream of future payments which must be paid in much the same way as an interest rate. We can then construct a 'supply of capital curve' for a particular firm as illustrated in Fig. 7.3.

In Fig. 7.3 the amount of finance £0X is available from internal sources. The cost of capital for these funds is the interest that they earn if lent outside the firm. This is assumed to be constant. Amounts greater than 0X must be raised from sources external to the firm. There is a 'step' of discontinuity in the cost of capital curve at X because it usually costs more to borrow money than the

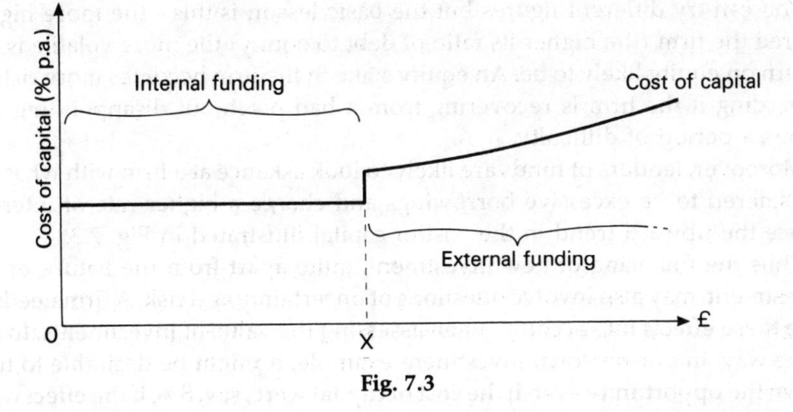

Fig. 7.3

amount that can be earned from lending it. An interesting question is raised when we consider the cost of capital curve to the right of X. Is this part of the curve horizontal or does it slope upwards as suggested by Fig. 7.3?

The curve is horizontal only if the firm can borrow any amount of capital, or raise any amount through shares, without having to pay proportionally more, i.e. a higher rate of interest. In reality it is likely that the higher the sum borrowed the more, eventually, has to be paid. Although there may be some economies of scale in borrowing large amounts of money to reduce the cost of larger borrowings a significant increase in the amount of external funding, either by borrowing or by new share issues, will alter the **capital structure** of the firm. The implications of using different sources of funds are explained more fully in the next chapter but one important example will illustrate the points to be considered.

If a firm raises a large amount of extra funds by borrowing, it will alter the ratio of **debt to equity** in the firm. This is known as the **gearing ratio** or **leverage**. A larger gearing ratio will have the effect of committing more and more of a firm's future earnings to servicing its commitments to interest payments. As an example, suppose a firm has capital employed of £1 million and earns a return on this amount of 10 per cent. The firm's earnings of £100 000 per annum are all available for distribution to shareholders or for retention in the firm.

Suppose it now undertakes a further investment of £1 million and finances this by borrowing at 10 per cent. If the new investment yields 10 per cent this will be exactly equal to the interest charges. The firm will be making £200 000 overall, half of which is committed to interest payments. If the new project yields 20 per cent, the firm's overall earnings will be £300 000, or 15 per cent on capital employed. But of this amount, £200 000 will be available for shareholders or retention thus providing a return of 20 per cent on equity. Notice how the increase in return on capital employed of 15 per cent has been 'geared up' (hence the term, 'gearing') to a 20 per cent return on equity.

Suppose, however, that the new investment yields only 5 per cent. The total earnings of the firm now become £150 000 – 7.5 per cent on capital employed. £100 000 must still be committed to interest charges, leaving only a return of 5 per cent on equity.

You can try different figures but the basic lesson is this – the more highly geared the firm (the higher its ratio of debt to equity) the more volatile is the return on equity likely to be. An equity stake in the firm becomes more risky – rewarding if the firm is recovering from a bad patch but disappointing if it enters a period of difficulty.

Moreover, lenders of funds are likely to look askance at a firm with what are considered to be excessive borrowings and charge a higher rate of interest, hence the upward trend in the cost of capital illustrated in Fig. 7.3.

Thus the financing of new investment, quite apart from the nature of the investment, may also involve questions of uncertainty and risk. A firm needs to take these effects into account when assessing the value of investments. In the same way, in our personal investment example, it might be desirable to turn down the opportunity even if the cost of capital were, say, 8%, if the effect were to exhaust all available credit. It might be thought better to turn down the possibility of earning an extra £20 per year, in order to retain the capacity to borrow and the ability to take advantage of any more profitable opportunities that might arise in the future.

As a final comment on Fig. 7.3 we must remember that this shows the cost of capital to the firm **at the present time**. It may well be different in the future. Interest rates can be expected to rise or fall and so increase or reduce the opportunity cost of capital. The firm's projected future cash flows may be such that more, or less, internal funds will be available for investment. One advantage of the net present value method of appraisal is that if the opportunity cost of capital can be confidently expected to vary over the life of an investment, this can easily be built into the calculations through the use of different discount rates for different payment periods. By comparison the yield method is relatively inflexible since the calculated internal rate of return is judged against a single test discount rate.

Mutually Exclusive and Dependent Investments

Mutually Exclusive Investments

So far we have concentrated on accept/reject decisions for individual projects, though we have indicated the choice criteria to be applied when choosing between projects. There are two basic reasons why the choice of one project may exclude another.

1. It is physically impossible to pursue both; for example, a single piece of land cannot be used for the construction of different buildings.
2. There is a **capital constraint** against undertaking both. For example, there may be a situation of **capital rationing**, that is only a fixed amount of money is available at whatever interest rate; or the raising of funds for one project increases the cost of capital so much that others are excluded.

In effect capital rationing is only a special case of the second type of problem – where the cost of capital for the excluded project becomes infinite – so we can handle them together. Here we shall concentrate on examining how the yield and NPV methods tackle this problem (as noted earlier the payback method can be seen as a crude approximation of the yield) and examine a simple example under conditions of absolute capital rationing.

Assume there are four possible projects, A, B, C and D. Each involves an initial outlay in Year 0 and yields constant earnings for five successive years:

	Outlay (Year 0) £000	*Earnings (Years 1–5) £000*	*Yield %*	*NPV (£000) discounted at 10% p.a.*
A	80	28	22	26.13
B	60	20	20	15.81
C	40	15	27	16.86
D	20	9	38	13.36

One way of approaching this would simply be to rank the projects in terms of yields and then work through these until the capital budget, which for this example we shall assume is £100 000, is exhausted. This would mean accepting projects C and D, which together would pre-empt £60 000, and rejecting A and B for which insufficient funds remain. This, however, would not be a correct decision. Even if we can assume that the unspent £40 000 could be invested at 10 per cent (the cost of capital), to produce another £4000 per year, the resulting yearly total earnings of £29 000 for five years and £4000 per year thereafter, would be less than could be achieved by different investment strategies. The **combined** yield of C plus D plus the investment income is, in fact, around 22 per cent and this is lower than the combined yield of projects B and C (nearly 23 per cent) and significantly lower than the combined yields of projects A and D of around 27 per cent even though, individually, these are not two projects with the highest yields. A and D represent the best combination of investments.

The yield method, therefore, requires us to look at all feasible combinations of projects, remembering to add the yield from any unspent part of the capital budget, and to choose the combination of investments which offers the highest return.

In the example used here, the calculations were reasonably straightforward. However, where projects have different time horizons, or where some may have rather irregular profiles of outlays and earnings, including, perhaps, closing costs, the calculations become rather more complex. In these cases it is difficult to make out a case against using NPV methods.

Essentially, use of NPV involves the same procedure of comparing the NPVs of different combinations. Many of the calculations are simplified. For example, the NPV of unspent funds is simply zero, by definition. In the example just given, the highest NPV is clearly obtained from a combination of projects A and D just as was calculated by the yield method – but with considerably less effort.

Mutually Dependent Investment Projects

A similar approach can be taken to mutually dependent projects. We should look for that combination of projects that gives the greatest yield or NPV. A point to note here is that, if a given project X depends on another Y being undertaken as well, it is best to calculate the yield or NPV of the combined project (X + Y), rather than that of X alone. Y can be considered separately if it could be undertaken independently of X.

Handling Risk and Uncertainty

Some Common Reactions and their Implications

Earlier in this chapter we saw how the rate of discount might be adjusted to allow for the degree of risk presented by a project or for uncertainty over the accuracy of the cash flow forecasts which had been made.

Critics of this approach point out that using a **risk augmented discount rate** is really confusing the elements of time and opportunity cost that **are** properly taken into account when choosing the discount rate, with the **uncertainty** surrounding the investment. After all, if the forecast is subject to genuinely random error, then it is as likely to represent an under- as an over-estimate of future earnings, in which case it is difficult to see why these should be subject to extra discounting.

Raising the discount rate, or the test discount rate used in conjunction with yield appraisal methods or reducing target payback periods, another common reaction to risk and uncertainty, all penalise most heavily those projects where earnings come relatively late in the life of the project, as well, of course, as ruling out projects that were marginally profitable at a lower rate. This is why it is commonly found that an increase in economic or political uncertainty results in a reduction in total business investment and in a reluctance to engage in long-term projects. Firms prefer to see their money back in the shortest possible time. This may be a natural reaction for the individual firm which is always vulnerable to sudden changes in both the market and the political environment but it can have long-term, damaging consequences for the national economy.

However rational these reactions may be in a climate of obvious economic risk, e.g. during a period of very high and rising price inflation, there is much less logic in their adoption in more 'normal' periods, particularly when inflation rates may be declining. Firms may well be turning their backs on long-term profit growth by taking too short-sighted an approach to investment.

Further Approaches to Risk and Uncertainty

A number of other approaches have been suggested to tackle the problems of risk and uncertainty. Here we have space to give just an indication of some of them.

One suggestion is to prepare a **pay-off matrix** to show the net present value of projects under various assumptions about the future. For example, suppose there are two projects under consideration, one of which can be seriously affected if future conditions are adverse and one which is likely to be less affected:

		Future conditions	
		Positive	*Negative*
NPV of	Project 1	120	40
(£000)	Project 2	70	60

Project 1 might be one where the predicted NPV is around 80, but there is a wide spread of possible NPVs according to how the forecasts are calculated. Project 2 has a predicted NPV of around 65 with a much narrower spread of possibilities.

A variety of decision rules have been suggested under these circumstances. For example, if the firm is looking for the highest likely return, whatever the circumstances, it can be expected to choose project 2 as this produces a pay off of 60. This is often known as the **maximin** strategy as it compares the minimum pay offs from various projects and then chooses the project that appears to guarantee the highest. This is a very pessimistic approach, always looking to the worst that could happen. In contrast a **maximax** approach compares the maximum from the different projects, then chooses the one with the highest possible pay off, a very optimistic approach.

The strategy likely to be adopted depends on the firm's attitude towards risk. This may be **risk-averse** with a tendency to try and reduce it, or it may be a **risk-taker**, prepared to take a gamble in the hope of a large gain. There is no 'correct' approach. The firm's decision-makers must formulate their own policy towards risk and then adopt an appropriate strategy.

It is possible to get over-concerned about the accuracy of forecasts and possible errors. Look at one more example. Project Q and project Z both involve initial outlays of £30 000 and their forecast returns, over a five year period, are as follows:

Project	*Year*					
	1	*2*	*3*	*4*	*5*	
Q	20	20	20	20	20	(£000)
Z	10	10	10	10	10	(£000)

There is a very high level of probability that the forecast for project Z will be achieved but that for project Q is subject to a possible 50 per cent error. Does this matter? A moment's reflection suggests that it may not. The **lowest** possible earnings from project Q is 50 per cent of £20 000, i.e. £10 000, the same as for project Z. On the other hand, earnings per annum could be as high as £30 000. Clearly, even on the most pessimistic assumptions, project Q offers as good return as Z and on any other assumptions its prospects are brighter.

The point here is that the choice of project Q is very insensitive to possible forecast errors. If errors are less than 50 per cent it is bound to pay more. There are several techniques of **sensitivity analysis**. These, really, involve seeing how much we would have to change our forecasts of cash flow before we would change our ranking of projects. Often such rankings are fairly robust so that inaccuracies in forecasting cash flows do not often change our decisions whether to accept or reject possible projects or to prefer one rather than another.

The Investment Decision – Some Final Comments

At the outset of this chapter we noted that there were common elements to all investment decisions. Among these was the need to choose between a number of possible courses of action.

All the criteria outlined in this chapter really fall into the same simple pattern:

1. **Evaluate options**
2. **Apply choice rule**
3. **Decision**

However, this really ignores certain key steps in the whole decision-making process. **Before** we can evaluate the options we must list them and this means generating possible courses of action that could be pursued. Even before we start trying to develop a range of strategies we have to **recognise** that investment decisions have to be made. A rather fuller framework can thus be shown:

1. **Recognition**
2. **Generate possible courses of action**
3. **Evaluate these**
4. **Apply choice rule**
5. **Decision**

This list is really common to all decisions, whether they concern investment, price or any other issue where choices have to be made and whether these are concerned with business or non-business matters. Sometimes the earlier stages are more important than the later. For example, if, while one is driving a car, the oil pressure warning signal lights up on the dashboard, it is wisest to go straight from recognition to decision, i.e. to stop the car, without first pondering the possibilities. The risk of the engine seizing up and the cost implica of this are high enough to make it worthwhile suffering some delay e use, a faulty switch perhaps, eventually turns out to be trivial. h business decisions, recognition that a choice has to be made f the available options and their financial consequences are as various choice rules indicated in this chapter. These are improve the quality of decision-making but they cannot of adequate research or for failure to seek and evaluate The investment decision can never be reduced purely to a mathematical process. Investment must always remain a matter of incurring expenditure now in anticipation that it will lead to increased returns in the future, but the future is never certain and can never be exposed simply by projecting the experience of the past. There is always the risk of the unexpected which, when it arrives, may be revealed as something that could and should have been expected. The oil price rises of the 1970s, the Iranian Revolution and the oil price falls of the early and mid 1980s were all events that profoundly altered the commercial environment within which world business operates but they were all largely unforeseen even by those major companies which had most to lose from them.

It is one of the dangers of the more advanced forms of investment appraisal that they can give a spurious appearance of accuracy to what is essentially little more than a sophisticated form of crystal ball gazing. The fact that an investment manager can present a computer printout with a prediction to three decimal places does not make it any more accurate than the information that was used to produce the calculation. On the other hand, it is one of the great benefits of the entire investment appraisal process if it is properly understood and carried out – whatever the mathematical techniques finally used – that it directs attention to the future events on whose outcome future earnings are most likely to depend. A careful investment appraisal may well **not** conclude by making a single prediction of future earnings from a given outlay but suggest that the outlay is likely to produce a return of £x **if** certain events take place or £y if they do not or if certain other events take place. The final choice and estimate of the likelihood of what is likely to happen in the future is left to the kind of business decision that does not rely only on mathematics and computers but on the broadest possible knowledge and experience and a realistic forecast of how **people** are likely to behave in the future. All investment, in the last resort, has an element of gambling and the ultimate decision must be subjective. It is the ability to recognise, enjoy and respond positively to this inevitable element of risk and uncertainty that separates the entrepreneurial business manager from the routine clerical administrator, however technically qualified, exalted in status and highly paid the latter may be.

Discussion Questions

1. Investment appraisal, market appraisal and pricing are all different aspects of the same decision-making process. Explain and justify this statement.
2. 'I always use internal rate of return. I do my sums and if the IRR is more than the present market rate of interest I go ahead with the project. If I am presented with more projects than I know the firm can cope with at once then I choose those with the highest IRRs because these will yield the most profit to the company.' Discuss this statement made by a senior business manager and point to dangers the manager may be running.
3. 'I never use DCF investment appraisal methods, possibly because I'm not sure I really understand them, but also because I find that both the bank and I are really interested in cash flow. So, I do a careful cash flow statement up to the time when I

estimate the project will have paid for itself and repaid the money I have borrowed. I find that if I can satisfy myself this way I have no trouble satisfying the bank and we go ahead with the project.' Discuss the merits and de-merits of this attitude to investment from the chairman and chief shareholder of an established family company.

4 Academics prefer investment decisions to be based on NPV calculations. The majority of those business managers who regularly employ DCF techniques appear to prefer IRR (yield) techniques. Explain the difference in these techniques and in the attitudes of the two groups. What are your views?

5 What is meant by the **opportunity cost of capital**? How can a business manager calculate this? Why is this calculation an important element in the investment appraisal process?

6 The following table sets out the estimated returns from two projects each requiring an immediate sum outlay of £100 000. The estimates are believed to have a similar degree of accuracy.

End of year	*A* *Return (£000)*	*B* *Return (£000)*
1	60	10
2	40	20
3	20	20
4	10	40
5	10	70

Use a computer package to help you answer and discuss the following questions:

a Which project is preferable on the basis of NPVs using discount rates of ***i*** 6 per cent and ***ii*** 12 per cent.

b At what discount rate, other things being equal, would a decision based on NPV be indifferent between these two projects?

c What are the yields (IRRs) of each project?

d Under what conditions might a decision based on IRR appear to differ from one based on NPV? How would you reconcile this difference?

Suggestions for Further Reading

You can make a more detailed study of investment appraisal in a number of business and managerial economics texts including

Pappas, J. L. and Hirschey, M., *Managerial Economics* Dryden Press (subsidiary of Holt Rinehart and Winston), 1987

Reekie, W. D. and Crook, J. N., *Managerial Economics*, Philip Allan, 1982

Stokes, C. J., *Economics for Managers*, McGraw-Hill, 1979

An educational investment appraisal program for BBC, Nimbus and Apple microcomputers is contained in the software package, *Introduction to Microeconomics*, prepared by Dave Blight and Tony Shafto (Tutor Software).

8

The Firm and Financial Markets

The Need for Finance Markets

In the previous chapter we saw that firms needed finance over a range of different time periods and for different purposes but the general factor underlying all demand for business finance was the recognition that if firms could make profitable use of money above the cost of obtaining it then they were likely to try to obtain finance in one form or another.

Firms, however, also needed to reduce the risks inherent in using money for which they were responsible to others. One danger is that the owner of the money may demand its return when it has been used in such a way that the firm cannot recover it sufficiently quickly to satisfy the owner's requirements. In the eighteenth and early nineteenth centuries, before organised financial markets had been adequately developed many reputable and profitable businesses were forced to cease trading simply because they were unable to meet demands to repay money without having to sell machinery or buildings without which the firm could not continue to operate. This risk has been reduced in modern business partly because financial institutions are usually well able to judge whether a business is financially sound and, if it is, can normally arrange for debt repayment through new borrowing, and partly because there is a greater general awareness that the terms under which finance is acquired should bear some relationship to the firm's ability to raise liquid cash. Consequently modern finance markets contain fairly clear sectors devoted to short-, medium- and long-term finance. The firm's need for finance in these time periods is summarised in Table 8.1.

Table 8.1 The firm and finance

Short term	*Medium term*	*Long term*
Bridge the time gap between expenditure and revenue	Acquire equipment	Finance internal expansion – purchase fixed assets
Meet current working expenditure	Acquire vehicles	Finance external expansion – takeovers, acquisitions
Finance exports	Cover production costs of longer term projects	

The Market for Short-term Finance

Sources of short-term finance are summarised in Table 8.2.

Table 8.2 Sources of short-term business finance

Internal	*External*
Retained revenue	Borrowings from banks and other financial institutions
Improved cash flow – minimise time gap between payments and receipts	Trade credit

The Very Short-term Money Market

Only the largest multinational companies, themselves financial institutions in their own right, are likely to have direct access to the wholesale money markets where money is lent for very short terms, often for 24 hours, overnight or 'on call' (repayable on demand). Most of the operators in this market are the wholesale banks, dealing in amounts of $1 million or more. They include the large high street banks, the foreign banks and the specialist dealers in very short-term money, the discount houses whose name originated in their business, still continued, of discounting, i.e. lending money on the security of, commercial bills of exchange. (These are explained in the next section of this chapter.) Nevertheless the existence of this market, dealing mainly in inter-bank loans, is important for business firms because it helps banks to lend to their business clients for periods longer than the repayment terms under which they themselves hold the money. For example, a bank can lend money for, say, a term of three months and use funds which it may have to repay on notice up to, say, seven days, because it knows that it can always balance its books by additional borrowing on the money market. It has a continuous turnover of borrowing and lending and if it comes under pressure to repay money it can refuse new requests for loans and quickly restore its funds.

Retail and Wholesale Banking

Although the modern banking system is classified as being retail or wholesale, this term applying to dealings in $1m or more, these terms refer more to functions than to institutions. Most of the major banks, whether they have clearing or merchant banking origins, operate in both sectors of the market, but the older merchant banks are likely to deal exclusively with large firms or with firms thought to have the potential to grow large quickly and with very wealthy individuals. The large British high street banks have their own merchant banking subsidiary operations and some can now fairly be described as financial composites represented in almost all of the financial sectors outlined in this chapter.

The term 'merchant bank' is still widely used but it now covers such a wide range of institutions that a clear definition is no longer possible. The original banks of this type were, as the name suggests, merchants whose national, and later international, reputation was such that their names were widely acceptable when used to guarantee the debts of others. Such guarantees were usually given in the form of acceptances on bills of exchange so that the firms became known as 'accepting houses'. This business is still transacted but now forms only a part of the activities of a recognised merchant bank. These include providing advice on and arranging investment and on raising finance, arranging stock issues, advising and administering takeovers and mergers – and also resisting them – and generally providing the financial know-how and back-up needed by a modern business organisation.

Retail and wholesale banking provides most of the short-term finance supplied to business organisations. Which sector of the market a firm uses depends mostly on its size, the countries in which it operates and its connections and standing with the financial community.

Forms of Short-term Finance

Forms of external short-term finance available from the finance markets are summarised in Table 8.3.

Table 8.3 Short-term finance from the finance market

Banks	*Specialist institutions (often bank owned)*
Overdrafts	Factoring and invoice discounting (mostly for export finance)
Loans	
Bill discounting (mostly for exports)	

The forms of finance likely to be used by the firm depend again on its size but also on the nature of its business activities. A supermarket chain or an importer of basic materials is likely to have little difficulty arranging overdrafts or short-term bank loans to finance the purchase of stock which is easily saleable and virtually as good as cash. A manufacturer of electrical generating equipment for governments in Africa and the Middle East would need to arrange rather more specialised finance to ensure that bank depositors' money was adequately protected. In fact, much of the demand for short-term finance results from international trade and as this is a highly specialised banking activity which has built up over a long period it is examined in the next section.

One form of finance which is not obtained directly from a bank is that provided by **trade credit**. The trader taking time to settle a debt is, in effect, trading on the creditor's money and the creditor may have to obtain a bank loan or overdraft in order to keep production going while debts remain outstanding.

This is one of the most controversial forms of finance. While some degree of credit is an essential element in almost all business transactions it is the deliberate delays to debt settlement that cause the most problems. It is widely recognised that taking extensive trade credit can be costly because suppliers are likely to set prices quoted to known bad payers high enough to cover the anticipated credit cost. Buyers with this reputation are in a relatively weak position when bargaining over price because some suppliers can be unwilling to supply at any price.

However, this is not always the case. When small firms sell to large firms the bargaining power usually remains with the large buyer who may deliberately discriminate against the small supplier in the knowledge that the supplier has few alternative markets but other actual or potential competitors.

In some cases, including many institutions in the public sector, long periods of trade credit may be more the result of poor administration than of deliberate policy. These institutions are likely to be subjected to high prices imposed because of their reputation.

From time to time appeals are made to reduce credit periods imposed on payments to small firms and practices do vary considerably in both the public and the private sectors.

It should also be recognised that firms can often reduce their need to obtain money from external sources by paying more attention to their internal cash flow. By careful attention to ordering and payment times they can often reduce the time gaps between the accounts they have to pay and the amounts they receive. It is wasteful to borrow money to acquire stocks which wait in storerooms until they are needed.

Finance for International Trade

This is a specialised sector and only some of the most important features are outlined in this section. The 'big four' high street banks and the older accepting houses play a key part in this international market.

Commercial Bills of Exchange

Although the growth of intra-Community European trade and intra-firm trade within the large multinational companies is ensuring that an increasing amount of trade finance is being handled within and between banks in much the same way as domestic payment and credit arrangements, the **bill of exchange** remains an important part of international trading finance.

A bill of exchange is essentially a commitment to pay a definite sum of money in a specified currency at a specific place on a definite date. Although the bill is a form of payment for goods or services the obligation to pay is quite separate from the trading contract. Payment cannot be refused, for example, on the grounds that the goods were faulty or not as ordered. Bills are drafted by the supplier of goods who thus establishes the payment terms on which the business is to be transacted. The draft is then sent to the buyer who **accepts** the commitment to pay by signing across the face of the bill. In practice the supplier is likely to specify that payment should be by a **bank bill** or **London bank bill**. This means that the acceptance must be in the form of the signature of a recognised London accepting house which thus effectively guarantees payment under the terms of the bill. The bank makes its own arrangements to ensure that its risk is minimised. The most desirable bills are those accepted by an accepting house recognised as eligible by the Bank of England – the most prestigious being members of the London Accepting Houses Committee. These are first-class securities eligible for discounting in the London discount market at the best available discount rates and re-discounting at the Bank of England.

The banks, by accepting and discounting bills, make it possible for suppliers to sell goods on credit knowing that they have the best possible guarantee that payment obligations will be met. The holder of an accepted bill can obtain immediate payment from a bank by discounting the bill, that is by using it as a security for payment of the face value less the bank's rate of discount. The rate depends on the class of risk and the length of time before the bill is due to be paid. Bills are usually drawn for periods of 30, 60 or 90 days after acceptance though some can be payable **on sight**. Term bills, allowing time before payment becomes due, allow the buyer a period of credit.

Much trade is conducted on the basis of 'documentary credits'. Under these arrangements import buyers provide a supply of accepted bills to a bank in the exporter's country and the bank is authorised to release bills to the exporter or credit the exporter's bank when specified documents are presented showing that goods have been duly loaded on ships or aircraft as required by the terms of the credit.

Factoring and Invoice Discounting

A factor is one who is empowered to act for another on certain specified matters and subject to agreed conditions. In finance markets the term is used to refer to an institution which takes over the approved, invoiced debts of a trader, usually an exporter, and assumes the trader's powers of collecting the debts and the risks of non-payment. The factor purchases the debts for a sum which is, of course, less than the face value and so, in effect, provides finance for the exporter who looks upon the factor's charge as the cost of obtaining the finance and of being released from the costs and risks of collecting the money due. Factoring is **not** a low cost method of obtaining finance.

Where the exporter does not wish customers to know that a factor is involved and has the resources to administer the accounts collecting, factoring can be concealed by the device of appointing the trader as the factor's agent for the actual work of collecting the accounts due.

Most factors are departments or subsidiaries of a major bank, and in addition to having the backing of the bank's financial resources are also able to use the bank's extensive connections to check the creditworthiness of the trader's customers and the exporter's own trading reputation.

When full factoring services are not required traders can often arrange to have the invoices of approved export customers discounted. When finance is raised by invoice discounting the risk of non-payment remains with the exporter who must refund any money loaned against an invoice for which payment is not received. In this system the invoices are not sold as in factoring but used as securities for loans which are normally repaid as the payment is received from the buyer. Failing this payment the exporter remains responsible for clearing the debt to the finance house.

Forfaiting

The financing of capital goods projects can cause problems because of the length of time involved in production. The buyer does not want to pay until the goods are delivered but the exporter has to meet production costs and to borrow money to cover the production and payment period adds substantially to the total costs. If the buyer is prepared to co-operate the banks can ease the burden to the advantage of all. Under a forfaiting arrangement the buyer supplies a series of bills of exchange dated at various stages of the production process. Each bill must carry the **aval** (guarantee) of an approved international bank. Receipt of these bank guaranteed bills enables the exporter to obtain bank credit on the lowest possible terms and may assist the exporter to quote keen prices to the buyer. In effect, therefore, the cost of credit is shared between buyer and exporter and the banks are able to ensure that the credit they extend is backed by satisfactory payment guarantees.

Medium-term Finance

Forms of medium-term finance available from the finance market are summarised in Table 8.4.

Table 8.4 Medium-term finance from the finance market

Banks	*Specialist institutions (mostly bank owned)*
Loans	Hire-purchase
Forfaiting (mostly for export finance)	Leasing

There are no universally accepted definitions of the length of time needed to classify borrowing as short-, medium- and long-term. However, for borrowing extending more than a year up to around five years would, in most cases, be regarded as medium-term. In modern markets the importance of this time distinction has been reduced by the involvement of the large banks in all three sectors.

The banks, both high street and merchant, tend to dominate the medium-term market through their ownership or financial association with specialist hire-purchase and leasing institutions. They may also provide financial support for the financing arrangements sometimes made available by the suppliers of goods such as motor vehicles.

The main use by business firms of borrowing over terms of several years is to finance the acquisition of equipment and vehicles. The precise terms under which equipment may be acquired often depends on the current tax laws and on the nature of the equipment and its use. The firm's main objectives are usually to acquire the use of equipment with the smallest immediate outlay possible so that most of the cost can be met from the increased earnings made possible by its use. A coach company, for example, hopes to meet most of the financial cost of a new coach from the fares paid by the passengers carried by the coach. Similarly another firm may hope to pay the costs of a computer system from the savings in administration costs that it hopes the new system will make possible. At the same time the firm also wishes to retain some flexibility in its use of the equipment. For example, if a better coach or computer system becomes available during the period of the financing the firm wishes to be able to make a change without incurring heavy financial penalties.

These objectives can often be met by hire-purchase, leasing or hiring with or without an option to purchase the equipment at the end of an agreed term. In a period of rapid change, purchase of equipment can leave the purchaser with assets that are obsolete and with little re-sale value even though they have many years of useful and reliable life in them. However, failure to replace with more modern equipment can undermine the firm's ability to compete with other suppliers which have more effective assets.

Under most instalment credit schemes the financial institution becomes the legal owner of the assets which are the subject of the agreement and these are then hired or leased to the user, often with an option to purchase exercised when the final instalment is paid. An exception is the credit sale agreement where legal ownership passes to the borrower when the agreement is signed. Company borrowers and hirers do not have the special protection provided by the Consumer Credit Act of 1973, it being assumed that they are capable of obtaining the proper professional advice before entering into credit arrangements.

Where equipment is hired or leased with no option to purchase, strictly there is no credit involved. The hire charge is for the use of the goods and not for any financial loan. On the other hand, the option of hiring may be chosen as the more flexible option to borrowing for purchase so the effect on company finances is much the same.

Markets for Long-term Finance and Permanent Capital: The Capital Market

The Basic Sources of Capital

Forms of long-term business finance are summarised in Table 8.5.

Table 8.5 Sources of long-term and permanent company capital

Internal	*External*
Retained revenue, including capitalised profits (scrip share issues)	Share (rights) issues: ordinary, preference, convertibles
	Freehold mortgages
	Sale and lease-back
	Long-term borrowing
	Debentures and loan stock (secured and unsecured)

It is not difficult to understand the business need for long-term finance. This was implicit in the discussion of investment appraisal/capital budgeting in Chapter 7. If the firm decides that the cost of such finance can be justified in terms of profitable investment opportunities, its next problem is to raise the finance in the most advantageous manner available to it. In practice the two issues are rarely separated in this clear-cut way. It is more common for the firm to have to ration its investment projects according to the finance that its investment advisers believe it to be prudent and practical to raise.

It is common to suggest that the firm has three main sources of capital: revenue retentions, borrowings and equity. In addition it can capitalise some of its assets. We can better understand the choices made by firms if we examine the particular features of each of these basic sources.

Retentions of Revenue

This is often referred to as **ploughing back profit** and is the single most common source of business capital. On average firms retain around 50% of their gross profit for use within the business. The attraction of retentions to business managers is that they do not have to account directly to any outside financial authority for their use of these funds. If their profit record is considered to be satisfactory the use of retentions may escape detailed scrutiny almost completely. If, however, their profits come under criticism the market's fund managers and financial specialists representing institutional shareholders are likely to look at past investment decisions very carefully. Companies seeking public capital for the first time or seeking to enter a more prestigious sector of the capital market are also likely to find their past investment record examined in some detail.

Retentions are not, of course, costless to the firm. There is always an opportunity cost measured in terms of the next best alternative use of the finance. All opportunity costs are notoriously difficult to measure because of lack of agreement on what the next best alternative actually is, and whether the risks of the compared options are strictly equal. At the very least the cost of any retention must be the interest that could be earned by depositing the money with a finance market institution.

The legal owners of earned profits are the ordinary shareholders and all profits are available for distribution to the ordinary (also known as equity) shareholders as dividends. Retained revenue is thus money held back from shareholders on the grounds that its profitable investment in the business will increase future profits. To a large extent this must be true. If a firm does not ensure that it is operating with the most efficient available technology, if it neglects research and development and if it does not develop its product and market range, it is unlikely to maintain, much less increase, future profits.

However, ignoring any special consequences of taxation or market speculation, the true market value of any company share must be based on the dividends that the shareholder anticipates earning in the future. For simplicity we can say that the market value of a share is the present value of the discounted stream of future dividends, expressed formally as:

$$M = \sum_{t=0}^{\infty} \frac{(1 - r_t)\, P_t}{(1 + d)^t}$$

where

d = discount rate chosen
P_t = expected profit in period t
r_t = the expected retention ratio (proportion of profit retained by the company).

An increase in retentions not matched by an equivalent increase in profit available for distribution will reduce the anticipated value of future dividends and will reduce the value of M. We saw earlier that this process provided the grounds for Marris' theory that the managerial desire for business growth was likely to be constrained by the fear of takeover when the ratio of a share's market to asset value fell to a level where takeover became attractive to a market raider. Even before such a stage is reached managers are likely to find that their company's shares are becoming unattractive to investment advisers and their ability to raise capital through the market is curtailed. No company can afford to ignore market opinion and in practice managers, especially senior managers, are usually keenly aware of their shares' market standing. Thus the capacity to increase retentions depends on capacity to increase profits. This puts pressure on managers to invest profitably. Failure to do so jeopardises their company's and their own futures.

Borrowings

Borrowing is also attractive to business managers whenever there is inflation. If they are able to borrow at a fixed rate of interest, even though this may appear high at the time of borrowing, the real cost of the interest charge is likely to fall in the future. Companies that borrowed over a twenty-year term or more during the 1960s at interest rates of around 7 or 8 per cent actually paid negative interest to their debt holders when market rates of interest rose to more than double that figure in the 1970s.

There are a number of ways in which companies can borrow money:

1 They can arrange long-term loans from banks and financial institutions if any are willing to lend on these terms.
2 They can arrange mortgages on any property they possess as freeholders or long lease holders. A mortgage is a loan on the security of property under terms which allow the borrower to retain the use of the property almost as an owner as long as the terms of the mortgage are met. In fact, financial institutions prefer to buy freeholds or long leases and lease them back to the seller for fixed periods, say five or seven years, with an option to renew leases on re-negotiated terms. This can still be attractive to firms during inflationary periods because the full impact of inflation can be delayed and its uncertainty reduced. Financial institutions may be willing to arrange such **sale and lease-back** contracts because they receive the benefit of capital gains as property values rise.
3 Companies may be able to issue debentures or loan stock. The two terms are really interchangeable. There is, however, an important distinction between stock which is **secured** and that which is **unsecured**. Secured stock gives the stockholders agreed rights to specific property in the event of the company failing to meet interest repayments or being unable to repay the debt when it becomes due for repayment. Unsecured stockholders would have to sue for the proceeds of assets along with other debtors and are thus less well protected in the event of company failure.

   Private companies can issue debentures and loan stocks but cannot advertise them for sale to the public. They can, of course, be issued to banks, other financial institutions and to private individuals.

   Loan stocks are usually issued on terms which require companies to repay within certain dates, the company having the choice of the most favourable time within these dates. As long as the company is making satisfactory profits and subject to market sentiment regarding fixed interest stocks the company is likely to be able to repay one stock by issuing another if it so wishes.

Borrowing also has its limitations. These arise partly from market sentiment towards fixed interest stocks and partly from the firm's ability to meet its legal obligations to pay interest.

The market's attitude towards fixed interest stocks depends on market anticipation of the future course of inflation. The bad experience of lenders during the 1970s and early 1980s turned sentiment against fixed interest lending. Institutions insisted on having an equity interest and consequently an interest in any growth of profits as a condition of providing financial help to growing firms. Falling inflation and the stock market crash of 1987 brought a revival for the fixed interest market but this was again threatened by rising inflation in 1988. There is always some demand from investors for stocks which provide a fixed rate of return. Pension funds, for example, usually need to have a proportion of any investments in these, but if people expect inflation and interest rates to rise in the future they will expect high current rates of return and will usually only be interested in lending money for fairly short periods. Firms wishing to borrow money during periods when the market is unfavourable for the issue of debentures and loan stock may have to borrow for short periods from banks at interest rates which are adjustable whenever the banks change their base rates.

No company can borrow unlimited amounts of money. All will be subject to a **safe gearing ratio**. Gearing (or leverage) as explained in Chapter 7 is the term given to the ratio of a company's debt to its ordinary shares. The actual ratio depends on the current market rate of interest and on the activities of the company. The lower the rate of interest the more a company can borrow. In the short term an increase in interest rates can actually increase the amount borrowed as banks add the higher interest charge to existing loans or overdrafts. This, of course, reduces profits and most companies will seek to reduce borrowings from retained revenue as soon as possible. Companies which trade in stocks which are readily saleable and which thus have a high proportion of liquid or near liquid assets are able to borrow more safely than those whose physical assets are highly specialised with no ready market value in the event of a forced sale. A supermarket group can borrow on the security of stocks with little difficulty. If faced with increased debt charges it can simply delay some orders, keep lower stock levels or take a few weeks' extra trade credit until borrowings are reduced. A haulage contractor, however, would normally keep a lower gearing ratio because it could not sell vehicles to meet debt charges without seriously reducing its earnings capacity. Companies with high gearing are very vulnerable to any downturn in economic activity or any failure in the markets in which they operate.

Companies always have to remember that debt interest is a legal charge whatever the state of profits. Failure to pay interest to a secured debenture stock holder could quickly lead to a forced sale of essential assets and the downfall of the company.

Ordinary Shares

Known also as **equity** and as **common stock** in the USA, ordinary shares provide the permanent capital for a normal business company. Under the Companies Act 1985 companies can repurchase shares subject to certain conditions but shareholders cannot demand repayment so that effectively they must continue to be regarded as finance held permanently by the company. The only practical way the shareholder can turn shares back into cash is to sell them to someone else. The more active the market in the shares of a company the closer that company's shares come to being liquid assets to the shareholder. Share markets are examined later in this chapter.

The number of shares that a company is permitted to issue is established by its memorandum of association, but this can be altered by a special resolution of the shareholders. Under the current rules of the International Stock Exchange of the United Kingdom additional ordinary shares for companies whose shares are traded on the exchange must be offered to the existing shareholders. This frequently takes place under what is known as a **rights issue**. Each existing shareholder is given the right to buy a stated number of new shares at a stated price. This is usually a price below the current share market value. Shareholders not wishing to exercise any or all of their rights to buy new shares can sell them. It is felt that this benefit should be given to the shareholders as compensation for the **dilution** of their shares through having to divide profits among the increased number of shares. There is no guarantee that the company will be able to increase its profits proportionally to the increase in shares. Share prices often do fall for a time in response to a rights issue, recognising the possible threat to the company's ability to maintain the current rate of dividend. Another method of increasing share capital is to offer shareholders additional shares instead of cash for part of the dividend payment. Income tax is payable on the issue as though it were a cash payment. This effectively allows companies to increase their retentions with the express permission of shareholders willing to reinvest part of their share of profit in the company.

As already noted the share price depends ultimately on future dividend expectations. As dividends rise with the growth of a company and its profits so too rises the market value of the share. British stock markets dislike shares that have too high a value on the grounds that this reduces selling flexibility. When, therefore, a share price rises to what is currently thought to be a high level additional shares are usually issued to shareholders without payment and without any proportional increase in profits. This is known as a **scrip issue** and in itself does not change the total value of each shareholder's holding.

Share price movements generally depend on market expectations of the future trends in the economy and of interest rates and inflation. Market movements are measured by a number of indices the best known of which for the UK market are: *The Financial Times* Stock Exchange 100 Index (based on the 100 largest UK companies) and *The Financial Times* Industrial Ordinary Index (based on 30 leading industrial companies).

Companies try to arrange new share issues in periods when share prices are high relative to the general level of dividend yields. They thus obtain a relatively large amount of finance in relation to their commitment to distribute profit. Consequently there tend to be a large number of new issues at times when share prices are high and rather fewer when prices are thought to be low. In either event it is evident that a company's ability to increase its total equity depends on its ability to continue to increase profits. If profit expectations fall so does the share price and it becomes difficult and expensive to issue new shares.

Preference Shares and Convertibles

Preference shares were developed to try to give certain groups of shareholders greater security and to ensure that they had preference in the payment of dividends from profits. However, the principle of dividend preference implies that this can only apply to a fixed amount of dividend and the dividend on preference shares is usually expressed as a percentage of the nominal value of the share whose capital or market value depends, of course, on the relationship between the yield on the share and the current market rate of interest, modified by the market's view of the degree of certainty that the company can continue to afford to pay dividends. Unlike debenture or loan stock interest the company has no legal obligation to pay preference dividends if there are no or insufficient profits to distribute. Companies do find themselves unable to pay preference dividends. Most preference dividends are cumulative, i.e. arrears of unpaid dividend must be paid before the ordinary shareholders can receive any distribution from profit. This can become a very big burden for a company trying to recover from some bad years and the preference shareholders can come under pressure to accept some lesser settlement. If, however, they refuse – and again this does happen – then the company has to meet its dividend obligations as best it can.

For the company, particularly during a period of inflation, the preference share has the attraction of a fixed charge on profits without the debt burden imposed by loan stock. For investors a definite return can also be attractive and the return is usually slightly higher than for an equivalent debenture. However, there is the risk that the real value of the dividend will fall if the inflation rate rises and the preference shareholder receives no benefit from any growth and increased profitability of the company. To try and overcome this to some extent the participating preference share was developed but the right to participate in profits above the set dividend is strictly limited and does not really meet the objections to a fixed dividend share.

A more satisfactory way to try to get the best of both worlds of fixed yield and share of growing profits has been developed with the convertible loan stock. This is a loan stock repayable between stated dates and paying a fixed rate of interest. At the same time it gives lenders the right to convert their stock to ordinary shares at a stated conversion rate between specified future dates. If the company prospers and its ordinary share price rises the option to convert at a fixed rate can be profitable. If not, the stock is still a fixed interest loan security. Naturally the market value of this kind of stock depends on current market interest rates, the ordinary share dividend and future dividend expectations, and the length of time before the conversion option becomes operative and the time before the loan is due to be repaid. These stocks can be attractive during periods of market uncertainty when no one is sure how inflation and the economy are likely to develop. Such a period occurred in 1988 when memories of the crash of 1987 were still strong, when the economy was growing but inflation was also rising and there were balance of payments problems combined with a government whose economic strategy seemed to be limited to interest rate adjustments.

Choice of Securities

The overriding interest of the company wishing to raise finance is to obtain the money it needs on the most advantageous terms, i.e. at the lowest possible cost and with the least possible risk currently and in the future. As already indicated, in a period of rising inflation it will try to obtain money on fixed dividend or fixed interest terms. However, by the 1980s investors had learned the lessons of high inflation in the 1970s and were demanding either very high interest rates or a right to share in future growth and profits. In a period of economic growth and rising profits investors may be eager to share in this expansion through ordinary shares whose current yields then fall and present opportunities for companies to make rights issues on terms that effectively provide low cost finance.

Clearly, choosing both the type of instrument and the best time for raising money through the capital market demands specialist advice and a thorough knowledge of the finance market. Multinationals also need to know which of the growing number of international finance markets is the most suitable for their needs. Advising on new issues is the function of the issuing house which, today, is most likely to be a division of a major merchant or high street banking group. Over the years an established company is likely to build up a capital structure containing different kinds of securities each being the result of a particular set of past conditions.

Specialist advice is equally important for the individual investor who must adapt his or her savings portfolio to individual requirements and the demands of prudence and reasonable security. Investment institutions are likely to seek to build up a balanced portfolio with a mixture of securities so that the conflicting demands of profit and security can be met to a reasonable degree whatever the market conditions. The institution must also be ready to adapt its portfolio as conditions change.

A fuller description of some of the more important institutions which have developed to channel private savings into business and public sector capital investment is given in the next section.

Institutions of the Capital Market

The Role of Banks

The old strict segregation between short- and long-term sectors of the finance market has been breaking down for some years and some of the main demarcation lines disappeared in the revolutionary changes known as the 'Big

Bang' in 1986. One feature of the revolution was that outside bodies were permitted to own members of the Stock Exchange and thus gain direct entry to the capital market. This opened the door to entry by the large banks, including international banks not necessarily British owned. The effect was to aid the growth of large financial banking composites which could give a comprehensive financial service to their business clients, including the major multinational companies, and give this service on a genuinely world-wide basis by operating in all the main world financial centres.

This development also recognised that firms themselves have to have access to all sectors of the market and do not wish to have to deal with a series of different institutions. A company cannot delay commencement of a major investment project while it waits in a queue for the right time to make a new share issue. More often it will depend on bank finance and rely on the bank to advise when part of this debt can be **funded** by issuing loan stock or ordinary shares. Inevitably the major international banks are likely to take an increasing part in the full range of financial services needed by the modern business company. An example showing one major bank group's UK operations is shown in Table 8.6.

The Stock Exchange

The British Stock Exchange has become the International Stock Exchange of the United Kingdom and the Republic of Ireland Ltd but it is still generally known as the Stock Exchange. Since the 'Big Bang', computerisation and the end of the jobber system, trading on the floor of the Exchange has virtually ceased. Dealing now takes place within the offices of brokers and market makers and is based on computer screen quotations. The market makers have replaced jobbers as dealers in shares and may also operate as brokers. All bargains are recorded on the computer dealing system so that price movements can be very accurately seen.

The International Stock Exchange encompasses three distinct markets and embraces two areas of activity. The three markets are:

1 **The main Stock Exchange** Here trading takes place for all securities listed in the Official List. It is the security that is listed so that a company may have, say, its ordinary shares listed but not its preference or debenture stock. Shares of the largest and most actively traded companies are known as alpha stocks and these are indicated in the major daily press lists of share prices.
2 **The Unlisted Securities Market** This market, known usually as the USM, was introduced following criticism that the exchange had become restricted only to large companies. It introduced less stringent and costly entry procedures more appropriate to smaller and less actively traded companies. It was accepted that the degree of risk associated with shares in this market would be higher than with those traded on the main exchange. The market has been successful but the costs of entry have risen so that it can be accused of no longer fulfilling its original purpose.

Table 8.6 The financial services and group structure of the National Westminster Bank PLC in the UK

	National Westminster Bank PLC Over 3100 Branch offices throughout the United Kingdom	
SUBSIDIARY COMPANIES **Coutts & Co** Banking and Investment Services Chairman D B Money-Coutts Managing Director A J Robarts Head Office 440 Strand, London WC2R 0QS	**National Westminster Home Loans Limited** Home Mortgage Finance Chairman M A Lydon Managing Director H A Gillis Head Office PO Box 156 38 Colmore Circus, Queensway, Birmingham B4 6AL	**Ulster Bank (Isle of Man) Limited** Deposits Chairman A J Sayle Managing Director D J McCawley Head Office 46 Athol Street, Douglas, Isle of Man
Coutts Finance Company Short and Medium Term Deposits Chairman D B Money-Coutts Managing Director (acting) G T Spencer Head Office 27 Bush Lane, Cannon Street, London EC4R 0AA	**National Westminster Insurance Services Limited** Insurance Brokers Chairman P A Girle Managing Director B A Carte Head Office PO Box No 106, 37 Broad Street, Bristol BS99 7NQ Registered Office 41 Lothbury, London EC2P 2BP	**Ulster Bank Dublin Trust Company** Trustee and Income Tax Services Investment Management Chairman F J O'Reilly Managing Director P Caulfield Head Office PO Box 145, 33 College Green, Dublin 2
Isle of Man Bank Limited Banking Services Chairman J C Dean General Manager J C Allen Head Office PO Box 13, 2 Athol Street, Douglas, Isle of Man	**NatWest Export Finance Limited** Financial Services Chairman T R Finlow Director J E McIntosh Head Office National Westminster Tower 25 Old Broad Street, London EC2N 1HQ	**Ulster Bank Trust Company** Trustee Services, Home Loans Chairman R D Kells Managing Director J T Hart Head Office PO Box 233 35–9 Waring Street, Belfast BT1 2ER
Lombard North Central PLC Banking Services, Credit Finance, Leasing and Contract Hire Chairman Sir Hugh Cubitt CBE JP DL Chief Executive B C Crittenden Head Office & Registered Office Lombard House, 3 Princess Way, Redhill, Surrey RH1 1NP	**NatWest Stockbrokers Limited** Retail Brokers and Investment Managers Chairman M A Lydon Managing Director N F Stapley Head Office & Registered Office Garrard House, 31 Gresham Street, London EC2V 7DX	**Ulster Bank Insurance Services Limited** Insurance Brokers Independent Life Assurance and Pension Advisors Chairman D Went Manager G P Davidson Head Office Ulster Bank House, Shaftesbury Square, Belfast BT2 7DL
	Ulster Bank Limited Banking Services Chairman F J O'Reilly Chief Executive D Went Head Office 47 Donegall Place, Belfast BT1 5AU	

Table 8.6—*contd.*

		PRINCIPAL ASSOCIATED COMPANIES
Lombard NatWest Commercial Services Limited Factoring Services, Invoice Discounting Chairman P A Girle Managing Director M A Maberly Head Office & Registered Office Smith House, PO Box 50 Elmwood Avenue, Feltham, Middlesex TW13 7QD	**Ulster Investment Bank Limited** Merchant Banking Chairman M Rafferty Chief Executive B W McConnell Head Office 2 Hume Street, Dublin 2	**The Agricultural Mortgage Corporation PLC (26%)** Agricultural Mortgage Finance
Lombard Tricity Finance Limited Instalment Credit and Credit Card Facilities Chairman B C Crittenden Managing Director J M Morgan Head Office & Registered Office Lombard House, Baird Road, Enfield, Middlesex EN1 1TP	**Lombard & Ulster Limited** Medium Term Finance, Hire Purchase, Leasing and Deposits Chairman H S E Catherwood Chief Executive C F S Gibney Head Office Canada House, 22 North Street, Belfast BT1 1JX	**International Commodities Clearing House Holdings (22.2%)** Clearing Services for Futures Markets **3i Group plc (23.5%)** Permanent and Long Term Investment Finance
National Westminster Growth Options Limited Venture Capital for Small Businesses Chairman G A Robinson Director R C King Head Office 41 Lothbury, London EC2P 2BP	**Lombard & Ulster Banking Limited** Medium Term Finance, Hire Purchase, Leasing and Deposits Chairman M Rafferty Chief Executive R Robinson Head Office Lombard & Ulster House, 54–7 Lower Mount Street, Dublin 2	**The Joint Credit Card Co Ltd (30%)** Credit Card Operations **Yorkshire Bank PLC (40%)** Banking Services

Extract from the Group Report and Accounts, 1988.

3 **The Third Market** Partly to meet criticisms that the USM had become too costly for small companies and partly to bring most of the growing 'over-the-counter' trading developing in brokers' offices outside the exchange within the regulation of the Stock Exchange a Third Market has now been introduced. This is now established as an active market with daily share price quotations in the leading journals. There is still an over-the-counter market conducted by some brokers operating outside the Exchange and this is recognised to be the riskiest sector of the business capital market. The shares traded in this 'fringe' market are not always approved by the London International Stock Exchange.

The two activities of the Exchanges are:

1 **Channelling new money into business and the public sector** Strictly this is the new issue market but in practice it is difficult to separate it from other

market operations. The main distinction between a new issue and other dealing is that the new issue is made by a bank or broker/issuing house on behalf of the company or other authority actually issuing the shares. Payments for the shares or other securities are passed to the company or authority and become part of that organisation's capital. However, no one will buy the new securities unless they know that they can be sold on a recognised market so that an essential feature of all new issues made through the Stock Exchange is that permission to deal on one of the three exchanges is given.

With the exception of the privatisation stocks issued by the government as part of its denationalisation programme, it is rare for first entry to the market to be made through the main exchange. A first entry is usually made through one of the smaller markets. Even then the Stock Exchange will expect the organisation to have been trading successfully as a private company for some years before 'going public' and raising new money by one of the procedures allowed by the Stock Exchange. As a company grows and prospers it may wish to raise more money and enter a higher level of market so that it is possible for a company's shares to start on the Third Market and proceed to listed status via the USM. Some may even start on the over-the-counter market.

2 **Trading in issued securities** Most of the daily activity of the Exchange is concerned with trading in issued shares whereby ownership changes and money passes from the new to the old owner but no new money goes to the company or public authority. Without an active securities market some other method would have to be found for allowing people to recover cash. Few people would be willing to make their savings available to business companies or the government if that money could not be recovered at all or for a period of many years. If companies were legally obliged to re-purchase shares on demand by shareholders they would always have to raise more money than they needed in order to keep liquid cash available constantly. The device of the Stock Exchange enables the proceeds of share or debenture sales to be used entirely for purchase of assets and to become permanent or long-term capital for the company. To the investor, however, securities traded on the Exchange are almost liquid assets because they can almost always be sold for cash, accepting, of course, the risk that the value of a share may fall drastically if the company fails to make profits and is unable to pay a dividend to shareholders.

Some Other Institutions in the Capital Market

Much political capital has been made of the large number of individual shareholders that have entered the Stock Exchange as individual investors as a result of the large privatisation issues of the later 1980s. In fact relatively few of these 'investors' hold more than the small number of shares originally allocated at the time of privatisation and the amounts involved tend to be small compared with the major channels for personal savings which still remain the building societies and other institutions.

Apart from the privatisation issues there has been a steady decline in the proportion of individual direct investment on the Stock Exchange since the early 1960s. Direct investment in Stock Exchange securities is dominated, in Britain, by the financial institutions. On the other hand, these institutions are using the savings of millions of individuals very few of whom are aware that they are providing the funds for stock market dealing.

A high proportion of these funds have come from contributions to pension schemes made by workers and employers. Since an employer's pension contribution is seen as a cost of employing labour it is also a payment that would otherwise have been available for adding to the worker's wage. In effect, therefore, workers are contributing a significant amount of the money flowing through the Stock Exchange. This money is controlled by the investment managers of pension funds and life assurance offices. The possible consequences of this dominance by professional fund managers for business firms was discussed in Chapter 2. At this stage we need to consider possible effects on capital market behaviour.

Some have argued that the greater involvement of professional investment managers steadies the market. Speculation is controlled and takes place in response to genuine information rather than rumour and 'crowd reactions' and the managers are able to exert pressures on companies whose performance is considered inadequate by the market.

Others point to the fact that the fund managers do tend to move as a crowd. They adopt similar investment and analytical techniques and procedures and these can produce huge and sudden swings in share prices. So-called 'insider trading' becomes a much more serious matter. Sensitive market information gained by one or two individuals may have little effect on market prices (though their conduct may offend against current moral or ethical standards). However, when such information is passed to investment institutions the very large sums which then become involved do have a significant impact on the market. Quite apart from this aspect it is also clear that the professional fund managers do regularly have access to information that is mostly denied to individual investors. When a fund is a very large shareholder and when it can influence the company's prospects of raising new capital, its managers have to be treated with respect and are likely to be given information not generally available. Even when they do not have privileged sources of information the institutions are able to employ professional analysts capable of making forecasts much more accurately than the distorted and biased information available to individual investors would allow. The services of the most skilled brokers and their market analysts are normally only available to the larger trading clients. Individual investors with active investment portfolios less than £100 000 are unlikely to receive anything like the quality of information regularly fed to the financial institutions. In practice a high proportion of those with investment funds of this size will hand over active management of their portfolios to the investment departments of banks or other institutions.

Individual investors with smaller sums to invest are frequently advised not to enter the market directly but to buy unit trusts or the shares of investment trusts. There are even unit trusts which specialise in government securities (known as **gilts**) which can easily be bought and sold through banks or through the government's own bonds and stock office at Lytham St Annes with forms and information available at Post Offices. An investment trust is a company whose business is investment and whose shares are traded like other shares with their value depending on the investment success of the company's managers.

Unit trusts are widely known as a means of entrusting savings to Stock Exchange forces without incurring the risks of buying the shares of individual companies. The unit trust managers form a fund which is used to purchase securities of a type and purpose specified by the managers. The total fund is then divided into units which can be bought by individual investors who may also sell their units back to the managers. Unit trust holders, therefore, do not have to deal with agents but part of their savings are used to pay the expenses of fund management. The trustees of the fund are usually major banks. Their duty is to ensure that managers obey both general law and the rules of the fund.

For most individuals a unit trust is the most practical way of investing in foreign securities and foreign markets. Most specialise in securities of one kind or another and a glance at the financial pages of any of the 'serious' daily journals gives an indication of the number and range of today's trusts. Although most trust activity is in issued shares their funds are also available to the new issue side of the capital market so that they are usually considered to be an important channel whereby individual savings are made available for business and public sector investment.

Finance for Private Companies

Throughout most of this chapter it has been assumed that the companies under discussion were free to appeal to the public for funds, usually through recognised Stock Exchange channels. These channels are, of course, available only to public companies or companies proposing to 'go public'.

Large numbers of companies, some of them large organisations, are not public and they also need finance for development. In Britain a private company is able to issue the full range of shares and loan stocks described in this chapter and there is no longer any restriction on the number of its share and debenture holders. What it cannot do is advertise its securities for sale to the public. Many private companies are subsidiaries or associates of British public companies and are thus dependent on them for finance. Another group of the larger private companies are subsidiaries of foreign companies and, through them, have access to the international capital markets. Our main concern in this section is with the genuinely independent private companies, most of which are owned and managed by the members of one or two families.

The retention of personal control is generally highly prized by the owner-managed company so that an opportunity for expansion can often pose a real dilemma. If a company is profitable and capable of expansion it is rarely difficult to obtain finance while retaining private company status. However, the finance may not be available in the form preferred by the owners. These may seek to borrow, believing that they can meet the costs of borrowing from their anticipated increases in net revenues. Their bankers or other financial advisers may claim that the company is already borrowed up to its safe gearing limit or be unwilling to provide additional loans under prevailing conditions where future inflation is feared. Consequently additional finance may be available only in the form of ordinary shares with all or the majority being purchased by the financing institution. In many cases this means that legal control of the company passes to the institution and the owners may see this as too high a price to pay for expansion both because they see the lion's share of the fruits of their work and enterprise passing to others and because they fear that the institution will sell the enterprise to a large company should it be in their interests to do so.

Redeemable ordinary shares were introduced in the early 1980s as a possible remedy for this dilemma. The shares or sufficient of the shares could be bought in by the company to restore control to the family management when profits permitted. Nevertheless control was still lost during the intervening period and further expansion could be checked by the need to re-purchase shares to restore independence.

Nor is going public an effective remedy. While it might seem that the family's block of shares might prove a more powerful force than a shareholding diffused through large numbers of shareholders, this might not be the case. The shares of a small public company are more likely to be bought by specialist financial institutions which could easily co-operate to force through changes not desired by the family management. The effect may be little different from expansion as a private company.

There is no simple solution to this problem and it could be argued that a solution is not really desirable. When expansion of a family controlled company expands substantially it may reach a size where fundamental changes in management style and structure become essential for continued stability and success. Financial institutions which provide the funds for this expansion may feel that they need to have control to force through changes made necessary by the changed character of the enterprise. Highly successful managers of small enterprises do not always make successful leaders of large corporations. The qualities that bring success at one stage of development can be disastrous at another. Professional financiers are more likely to recognise this than the owner-managers themselves.

Discussion Questions

1 The Stock Exchange is only a market for 'second-hand' stocks. Why then is a healthy stock exchange thought to be essential for the provision of capital to industry?

2 Look carefully at the stock market pages of one of the 'serious' journals such as *The Financial Times* or *The Times* and note the yields of the shares listed. What is the yield of an ordinary share? Why do yields differ **a** between different classes of share and **b** between different companies of the same class? As an investor what considerations would influence your choice as to shares with high or low yields?

3 Discuss the considerations likely to influence:

a a public company in its decision whether to raise additional finance by borrowing or by equity;

b an investor in the choice between purchasing fixed yield stocks or ordinary shares.

4 Why do exporters have special needs to borrow finance? Examine and discuss the services provided for exporters by the large high street banks.

Suggestions for Further Reading

Some of the most useful reading in relation to business finance lies a little outside the mainstream of 'academic' literature.

To learn more of contemporary banking practices and services obtain and study the widest possible range of booklets issued by the banks. Also of particular value are the bank booklets describing their services for exporters and for the financing of exports and imports.

To absorb an awareness of the modern capital markets there is no real substitute for regular reading of the money sections of one or more of the 'serious' daily and weekly journals.

From time to time the accountancy bodies and the leading firms of accountants and business consultants issue their own booklets concerning sources of business finance. Be alert for these and enquire about them from any suitable local sources.

The Consumers' Association, publishers of *Which?* also publishes a very useful guide to private investment, and other practical guides are advertised periodically.

9 The Firm and the Public

Profit and Efficiency

The Assumptions of Market Economics

The basic assumptions of classical market economics, dating from the observations of Adam Smith in the eighteenth century, are that people, whether buyers or suppliers, act from self-interest. Buyers seek to obtain the highest possible level of satisfaction from the money they spend on goods and services while suppliers try to obtain the highest possible level of profit from the supply of these goods and services. If the market is functioning effectively, these intentions interact in the marketplace in such a way that available economic resources are used to achieve the greatest good for the community as a whole. This is largely because suppliers are only able to achieve profits by providing those goods and services that people are prepared to buy. This is what is meant when it is said that a market economy is based on a system of consumer sovereignty.

As we might expect this justification of the free market system is deceptively simple and we need to examine more closely the qualification 'if the market is functioning effectively'. We need to be rather more precise in identifying those conditions most likely to achieve the highest possible degree of consumer welfare. Economists have long been conscious of the need to develop an analytical framework to take welfare into account and to show how it may be achieved. They have usually identified the condition of best possible (optimum) welfare and, therefore, of the use or the allocation of economic resources as that pattern of production where it is impossible to make any alteration aimed at making one person or group better off without making some others worse off. As long as it remains possible to increase the welfare of some without reducing the welfare of others then the ideal, optimum position has not been reached.

Welfare, Marginal Cost and Price

If we think in terms of a market for any particular product then the demand curve for that good can be seen as the aggregation of every individual's personal demand curve for that product. Each point on the curve represents the valuation placed on that product by a particular individual or group of people having similar values. If the price is above that point it is higher than the value they place on it and they do not buy. As it falls, however, the price comes to equal their valuation and they enter the market. At each point on the curve there are marginal consumers just prepared to buy because price equals their valuation of the product, i.e. the value of its utility to them. Looked at in this way the demand curve becomes a marginal social valuation curve.

From the supplier's viewpoint each unit of the product produced has an additional (marginal) cost which is based on the cost of the additional resources required for that extra unit of production. This cost reflects what this producer has had to pay in competition with other producers wishing to use these resources to produce other products. The marginal cost curve may thus be seen as a kind of resource opportunity cost curve. As these opportunity costs also reflect society's valuation of the resources in their various possible uses we can see the marginal cost curve as the **marginal social cost curve**.

Figure 9.1 illustrates these assumptions and shows how the best output level for this product is the level where its marginal social cost just equals its marginal social valuation. At any other level the cost is either greater than marginal value and the resources would contribute to greater total consumer satisfaction if used elsewhere, or less than marginal value and society's total utility would be raised by the diversion of more resources to the production of this product.

This leads to the deduction, familiar to economists, that optimum consumer welfare could be achieved if resources were allocated to the various competing

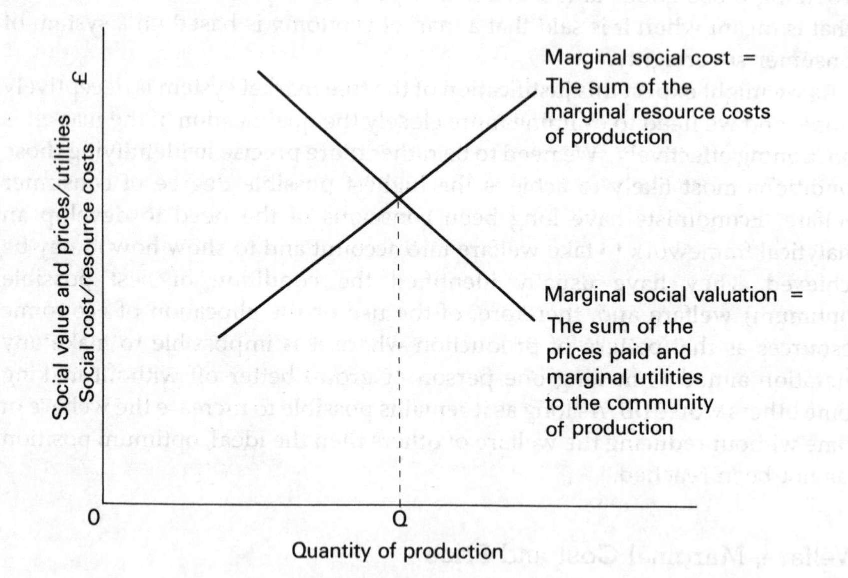

Fig. 9.1 Maximising community welfare
The best output level is at 0Q where marginal social cost = marginal social valuation.

forms of production in such a way that marginal cost equalled price in all markets. This view of the use of resources is also known as **allocative efficiency**, i.e. the most efficient allocation of scarce economic resources.

Market Conditions for Achieving Allocative Efficiency

If it is assumed that the firm is seeking to maximise profits then this would require it to aim at achieving that level of production where marginal cost is equal to marginal revenue. It can only combine profit maximisation with the consumer welfare optimising condition of marginal cost equalling price if price and marginal revenue are identical. This can only be achieved if the individual firm is able to sell as much as it can produce at a given price. Under this condition the additional revenue received from an extra unit of sales is the unit price. If the firm had to reduce price in order to increase sales then the marginal revenue would be less than price as explained in the Appendix to Chapter 3.

There are a number of possible ways in which marginal revenue can be equal to price over a significant range of output. One is when the firm's supply is small in relation to the total supply to the market so that changes in the firm's supply have no significant impact on market supply and, therefore, do not affect the market price. This can occur under the market structure known as **perfect competition**, discussed later in this chapter (see also Chapter 3), or when the market price is determined by one or more dominant firms in the market and other, smaller firms have to accept this price.

Another possibility is that the product price is determined by some regulating force outside the market. This may be a national government, a body with price fixing powers confirmed by the government under authority of the legislature, or an international body supported by the national government. In the European Community many farm prices are established within the framework of the Common Agricultural Policy.

The position where price is equal to marginal revenue so that the firm can maximise profits and contribute to consumer welfare is shown in Fig. 9.2.

If the assumption of a profit maximising objective is abandoned more possibilities arise. If there is no attempt to equate marginal revenue and marginal cost then it becomes possible for the firm to come closer to the welfare maximising condition consciously or unconsciously. For example a firm wishing to maximise revenue subject to making a level of profit considered by shareholders and financial institutions to be satisfactory, is likely to produce more than one seeking to maximise profits. The result is illustrated in Fig. 9.3.

In this diagram profit maximisation would require an output level of 0Q and price 0P. Revenue maximisation unconstrained by the need to achieve a particular profit level would require an output level of $0Q_1$ and price of $0P_1$. If there is a profit constraint production and price are likely to be between these two levels, i.e. closer than profit maximisation to the welfare optimising points of $0Q_2$ and $0P_2$. Some economists point out that the firm might produce at a level higher than $0Q_2$, as indicated in Fig. 9.4, to produce a consumer surplus.

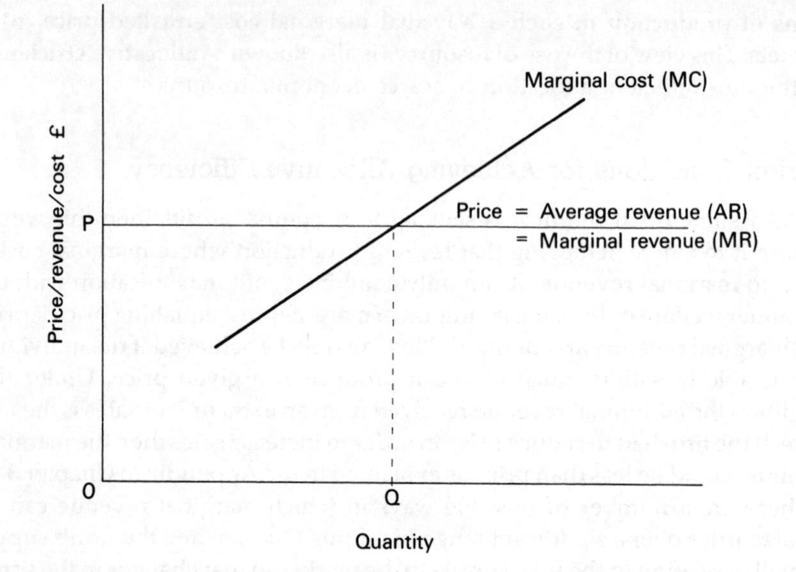

Fig. 9.2 The condition for price = marginal cost
When a firm has to accept a ruling price and cannot change this price on its own the profit maximising condition of MR = MC is also the welfare maximising condition of price = MC. (See also Chapter 3 and appendix.)

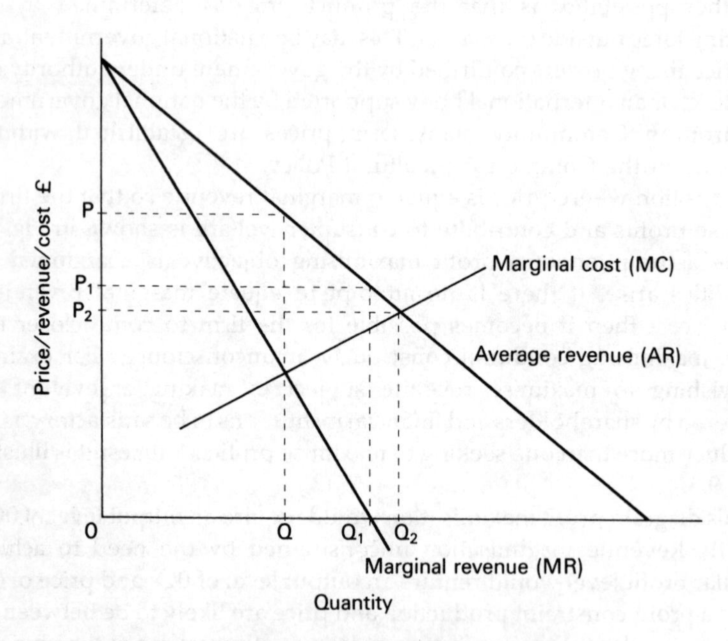

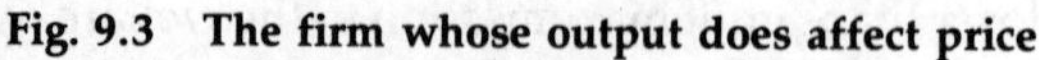

Fig. 9.3 The firm whose output does affect price
Profit maximisation is achieved at 0Q and 0P. Revenue maximisation is achieved at $0Q_1$ and $0P_1$. Welfare maximisation is achieved at $0Q_2$ and $0P_2$.

This is theoretically possible but less likely than the position illustrated in Fig. 9.3.

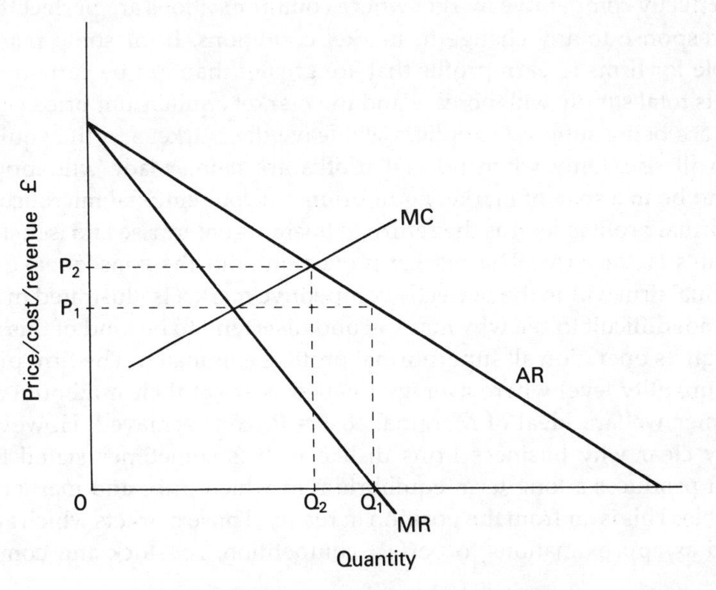

Fig. 9.4 The firm and welfare maximisation

It is possible for a firm wishing to maximise revenue to produce at a quantity level higher ($0Q_1$) and a price lower ($0P_1$) than those required for welfare maximisation ($0Q_2$ and $0P_2$). This would produce a consumer surplus.

The Firm's Conduct and Performance under Perfect Competition

The Conditions for Perfect Competition

In the previous section we noted that the market structure known as perfect competition could produce conditions favourable for a profit maximising firm also to fulfil the welfare optimising requirement of Price = Marginal cost.

As explained in Chapter 3 perfect competition is an ideal of **pure** economic market structure under which the market forces of supply and demand are thought to interact completely free from any imperfection internal or external to the market. It is useful in showing what would happen if the imperfections found in real life did not exist. This helps us to achieve a better understanding of the distorting effects of the various conditions found in markets which fail to achieve the **pure** economic state. The term **perfect** thus relates only to a state of perfect economic interaction. It contains no social, ethical or moral implication. Indeed, under certain conditions, e.g. a food supply collapse, the consequences can be socially and morally most **undesirable**.

The conditions for achieving perfect competition were outlined in Chapter 3. You should make sure that you are fully aware of these before moving to the next section.

The Consequences of Perfect Competition

In a perfectly competitive market where communications are perfect there is a swift response to any change in market conditions. If for some reason it is possible for firms to earn profits that are greater than can be earned in other markets total supply will increase and the market equilibrium price will fall. If losses are being suffered suppliers will leave the market and the equilibrium price will rise. Only when normal profits are being made will supply and demand be in a state of market equilibrium. In conventional microeconomics this normal profit is seen as the return to business enterprise and is included in the firm's factor costs. The market movement and the consequence for the individual firm within the perfectly competitive market is illustrated in Fig. 9.5.

It is not difficult to see why many economists tend to be fond of this market. Through its operation all supernormal profit is eliminated. The firm produces at the quantity level where average total costs are at their minimum and the consumer welfare ideal of Marginal cost = Price is achieved. However, it is equally clear why business firms dislike it. It is sometimes stated that the market produces a long-term equilibrium in which price and market supply are stable. This is far from the position in reality. Those markets which are often quoted as approximations to perfect competition, i.e. stock and commodity

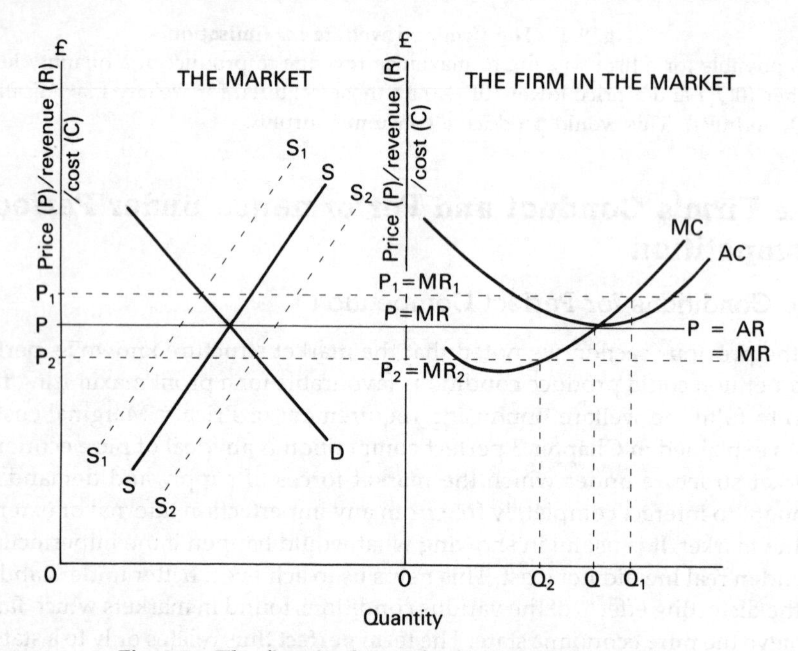

Fig. 9.5 The firm in the perfectly competitive market

If supply is at S_1S_1, price is at $0P_1$ and the firm produces quantity $0Q_1$, it makes profits above the normal ($0P_1$-AC at Q_1 where $0P_1 = MR_1 = MC$).
If supply is at S_2S_2, price is at $0P_2$ and the firm produces quantity $0Q_2$, it suffers losses (AC-$0P_2$ at $0Q_2$ where $0P_2 = MR_2 = MC$).
Only when supply is at SS is the firm in equilibrium where $P = AR = MR = MC = AC$ at quantity $0Q$. Here profits and consumer welfare are maximised.

exchanges, are notable for their extreme price instability. This is because the market equilibrium is only partial. It shows how supply responds to demand and has nothing to say about market demand. Any shift in demand is followed by a swift supply and price reaction. Price instability is not favoured by business firms. It creates uncertainty and administrative costs and makes forward planning difficult.

More serious for the community and for the achievement of optimum welfare is the removal of profit above what is rather vaguely described as **normal**. The full analysis of what is termed the **Pareto optimum**, from which is derived the ideal of marginal cost-price equality, shows that perfect competition is likely to lead to the best possible productive use of economic resources as well as the best allocation of resources to meet community wants. However, this is a static condition assuming a given level of technology. The analysis says nothing about the dynamic processes which produce changes in technology and the development of new resources. It is this process of technological and resource development that has produced the high and rising living standards associated with modern, industrial market economies. Perfect competition provides no incentive for technology development because perfect communications ensure that no individual firm is able to achieve a monopoly of knowledge and so secure the additional profit that this monopoly is able to secure.

It is possible to argue that it is the struggle to break away from or avoid perfectly competitive market conditions that provides the incentive for firms to seek technical knowledge (a term including commercial as well as production skills) beyond that possessed by their rival suppliers, and to use this knowledge to secure profits above normal. Possession of this knowledge and the ability to use it to achieve supernormal profit does not necessarily increase market supply because new firms will not wish to enter the market unless they also have superior technology.

In fact, for this and other reasons, it has to be admitted that economic analysis alone is incapable of indicating whether perfect or imperfect economic markets are more likely to raise the total level of consumer welfare. It also has to be recognised that most markets in the advanced, industrial economies are far removed from perfect competition. The tendency for firms to grow in size and to seek dominating positions in their markets has produced conditions under which oligopoly, where supply is in the hands of a few large firms, is now a common market structure, and a great deal of attention is now paid to the nature of competition in oligopolies and the conduct and performance of oligopolistic organisations.

Resistance to Competition in Oligopolistic Markets

Collusive Tendencies

All the main approaches to the analysis of oligopolistic markets indicate a tendency towards collusion. This is not surprising. Common sense suggests that where only a few firms operate in a market, continued competition, price or non-price, will only harm all suppliers. The logical conclusion of an unending price war would be to pay customers to empty the shelves – hardly the purpose of a business operation! If advertising were to escalate without check all revenue would be passed to advertising agencies and all profit would disappear. Following competition to its extreme absurdity reminds us that it is almost always likely to be subject to some checks if business is to operate under conditions of reasonable stability.

It has long been recognised that the prices of many products sold in oligopolistic markets tend to remain steady in spite of fluctuating raw material costs. One explanation for this has been based on the **kinked demand curve** model. This is illustrated in Fig. 9.6.

This model is based on the assumption that suppliers arrive at a given product price, 0P. If the individual firm tries to increase this price the rival suppliers of competing products – assumed to be close substitutes – do not follow the price rise. However, if the supplier tries to reduce the price they make similar reductions so that each firm's market share is unchanged. Thus the individual supplier's demand curve is more elastic above the current price than it is at lower price levels. The kink in the demand/average revenue curve produces a discontinuity in the marginal revenue curve (see Appendix 9A) and this allows marginal cost to move between 0R and $0R_1$ without any change in the profit maximising quantity and price.

This model has been criticised on the grounds that:

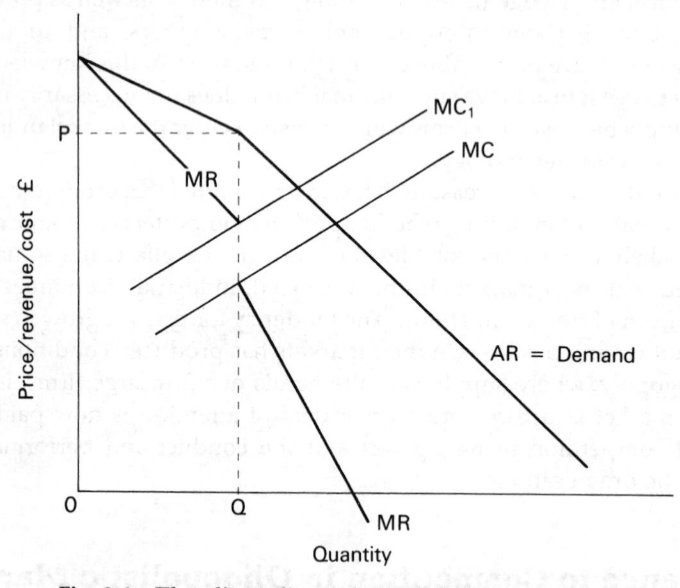

Fig. 9.6 The oligopolist and the kinked demand curve
At the established price 0P there is a kink in the demand/average revenue curve if it is assumed that competitors will match price reductions but not price increases. This produces a discontinuity in the MR curve and marginal costs can move between MC and MC_1 without affecting the profit maximising price and quantity (0P and 0Q).

1 It does not explain how the 'sticky price' (0P in Fig. 9.6) is arrived at.
2 It breaks down in periods of price inflation when behaviour is reversed, i.e. firms quickly support an individual price rise but ignore a price reduction in the belief that it cannot be maintained for very long.
3 It only applies to special conditions where a limited number of large firms are selling roughly homogeneous products.
4 It ignores non-price competition which influences costs.

The behavioural approach towards examining oligopolistic behaviour recognises the importance of **uncertainty avoidance** and the consequent search for a **negotiated environment** within which managerial decisions can be taken with more predictable consequences. This, of course, suggests that there will be strong managerial pressures for co-operation and at least tacit collusion whatever anti-trust or monopoly laws are in force. The spread of information-sharing agreements following the banning of openly collusive restrictive trade practices in the UK shows how strong these pressures are. However, the behavioural approach is widely criticised on the grounds that it is essentially descriptive rather than analytical. It shows that firms will seek to avoid uncertainty but does not add much to our understanding of how they do this or with what economic consequences.

Another approach to the problem is based on **game theory**. This can be studied at many levels but a very simple example is sufficient to illustrate how it may help to explain the options available to oligopolists.

Suppose there are two firms selling two close substitute, competing products, say Wizz and Splurge. Suppose also that the makers of Wizz believe that their probable profits and those of their competitors resulting from sales of the products at two possible prices are represented by the following matrix:

		Splurge	
	Price	£2	£2.50
Wizz	£2	100	130
	£2.50	90	120

This suggests that if both Splurge and Wizz are priced at £2 the profits on Wizz will be 100. If, however, the price of Wizz is raised to £2.50 and Splurge stays at £2 then profits on Wizz will fall to 90.

For their part the makers of Splurge believe that their profit possibilities are as set out in the following matrix:

		Splurge	
	Price	£2	£2.50
Wizz	£2	100	90
	£2.50	130	115

Thus, if Splurge is priced at £2 and Wizz is also at £2 the makers of Splurge believe that their profits will be 100, but if Wizz were priced at £2.50 then the profits on Splurge would rise to 130.

If the firms operate independently their safest course of action is to each charge £2. To charge £2.50 risks a response by the rival of £2 and reduced profits. On the other hand, if they collude and each agrees with the other to charge £2.50, then each is able to increase profits. At the same time an even bigger profit can be made if one firm is able to cheat successfully and secretly charge £2 while the rival keeps to the agreement and charges £2.50. This over-simplified and rather unrealistic example illustrates the important fact that collusion offers oligopolists higher profits than are likely to be gained by operating completely independently. At the same time there is always the temptation to cheat.

Collusion can take many forms. In its extreme form, firms can form a **cartel** to make agreements on such matters as price, advertising and distributors' commission rates, and, in some cases, agreements may be reached to divide the market either geographically or by product range. Most of the older industrial countries now have laws and agencies to discourage open collusion. These have to be alert to attempts at evasion through secret arrangements such as those to share information. Tacit collusion may take place without any meetings or agreements of any kind. Firms may simply keep away from certain products, agencies or areas known to be strong supporters of their rivals in the expectation that the rivals will respect their own known interests. All participants in the market may simply be anxious to avoid a damaging competitive conflict. Unwritten codes of market conduct can develop and be preserved for some years. One form of conduct that can arise is that of following an acknowledged **price leader** who may also set the market norm for such major costs as wages through trade union negotiations. Again there need to be no formal agreement as all established firms believe it to be in their interests to follow market custom and practice.

Barriers against New Competitors

If established firms have developed their own methods of survival and profit security in what is potentially a competitive market they are likely to resist attempts by newcomers to enter the market and introduce uncertainty and insecurity. If the market is not protected by substantial **natural barriers** such as very high capital costs in relation to maximum market size or dependence on rare skills, firms are likely to erect artificial barriers.

Price can be used as a barrier to discourage new entry and the idea of limit pricing as an entry barrier is frequently linked with the **Sylos Postulate** (from the original analysis by the Italian economist Sylos-Labini). This suggests that firms considering entry to a market expect established firms to continue their former production. Consequently the effective price that they have to consider is not the pre-entry price but the one resulting from the combination of pre-entry supply plus the additional supply from the new entrant. This postulate can be examined against a variety of situations but one example would be where there are scale economies and a minimum efficient scale of operations. This is illustrated in Fig. 9.7.

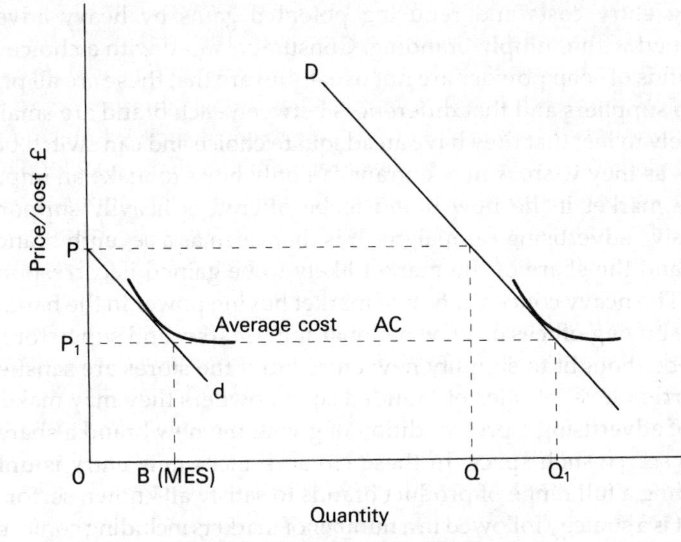

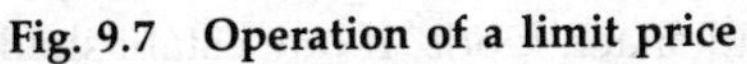
Fig. 9.7 Operation of a limit price

Market demand is DD, market price 0P and quantity supplied 0Q. A potential new entrant, given an MES of 0B, would raise market supply to $0Q_1$ and reduce market price to $0P_1$ where profits are not possible. The entry barrier limit price is thus 0P.

Here the pre-entry market supply is 0Q which, given market demand DD, produces a market price of 0P. AC represents the long-term average cost curve of a supplying firm and its shape suggests that the minimum efficient scale of output is 0B. If this quantity of output is added to the pre-entry supply then total market supply rises to $0Q_1$ and the market price falls to $0P_1$ which is not high enough to provide profits for the new entrant. 0P is thus a limit price deterring entry. If the established firms raise price above this level and reduce their total supply below 0Q they are risking the danger of a successful new entry and disturbance to the established market.

There is, of course, always the danger that a new entrant may be a large firm operating in an associated market or in the same product market in another country. It may also have developed new production or commercial technology that enables it to operate profitably below the limit price. If this is suspected the established firms may be prepared to start a price war against the entrant forcing prices down to levels where no profits are possible and heavy losses are inevitable. The established suppliers may have sufficient reserves or financial support or be able to call on subsidies from other profitable markets to force the new competitor to withdraw. They may then be able to recoup losses by suitable price o: quality adjustments. It may not actually be necessary to enter such a conflict. Awareness that the established firms are prepared and have the resources to take this action may be sufficient to deter entry – especially if one or more of the firms have been known to have followed this option in the past.

Studies of oligopolistic market behaviour suggest that there are other entry discouraging practices. These include:

1 Raising entry costs and reducing potential gains by heavy advertising combined with multiple branding. Consumers faced with a choice of, say, six brands of soap powder are not usually aware that these are all provided by two suppliers and that differences between each brand are small. They are likely to feel that they have an adequate choice and can switch between brands as they wish. A new entrant can only hope to make an impression on the market if the new brand to be offered is heavily supported by expensive advertising campaigns. It is then seen as a seventh brand, not a third, and the share of the market likely to be gained is correspondingly small. The heavy concentration of market buying power in the hands of the central buying offices of a few national supermarket and superstore chains might be thought to simplify new entry but if the stores are satisfied with the current level of sales of branded soap powders they may make a high level of advertising a pre-condition of giving the new brand a share of the store's scarce shelf space. In these circumstances new entry is unlikely.
2 Providing a full range of product brands to satisfy all known sectors of the market is a strategy followed in a number of markets including confectionery, alcoholic drinks and snack foods. If one established firm identifies a new sector and provides a new, slightly different brand other suppliers will quickly follow with a close substitute. This both enables them to share in the new demand that has been identified and it also prevents a new entrant from taking the opportunity to come into the market through this opening.
3 Established firms can signal their commitment to the market and thus warn potential entrants that attempted entry would be expensive and damaging. Awareness that price wars have been used in the past has already been noted. Firms may also retain spare capacity to warn competitors that this would be used to force down the price if this were considered necessary. In some markets established firms have had to make a major commitment by purchasing expensive and highly market specific equipment. Finance has thus been **sunk** in this capital spending and cannot be recovered by switching to another market. For such firms trading at any price above variable cost would be preferable to withdrawal and potential competitors are well aware of this.

In all these entry deterring practices it is assumed that established firms have the advantage of knowing the conditions of market demand and are able to move towards satisfying any shift or identified gap in the market before a new competitor can react. It is also assumed that the established firms are able to influence the attitudes of the senior managers of potential competitors.

Further Aspects of Oligopolistic Competition

By now it should be evident that because a market is oligopolistic and appears to be free of actual competition this does not mean that participants are totally freed from the fear and discipline of competition. The awareness that other firms could, if they so wished, enter the market can be a healthy constraint on the conduct of the established firms. These may adopt entry deterring strategies but they must also ensure that they keep their customers satisfied and be ready to close any perceived market gaps in order not to encourage new competition. It is also probable that the fear of potential competition acts as a constraint to preserve quality standards, keep prices well within market expectations and avoid profit levels that attract the attention of expansion-minded firms in other markets.

Contestable Markets

The threat of new entry increases with the ease of entry, and the lower the costs of entry and exit the less will be the effective market power that established firms are able to exercise.

A perfectly contestable market is one where there are no barriers at all to entry. A new entrant incurs no entry costs that cannot be recovered on exit. Specialist pig farmers, for example, complain that other farmers can enter or leave pig production whenever they wish. Such farmers already have land and buildings and only have to buy stock when they enter the market. Stock is easily sold and not replaced when they decide to leave.

Under such conditions the established firms have to behave as though they were in a perfectly competitive market. This is true even if there are only two existing suppliers to the market. The threat of entry is so powerful that only normal profits can be earned and price is likely to satisfy the **Pareto** condition of price/marginal cost equality. Such a market is not likely to be one where advanced technology is important. It is more likely to be found in service markets with a low technological requirement and a relatively low requirement of capital investment and very few economies of scale.

The higher the level of technology and the greater the commitment in capital investment the less contestable the market and the greater the market power of the established firms.

The Countervailing Power of Buyers

The prevalence of oligopolistic markets thoughout industry makes it likely that an oligopolistic supplier of an intermediate product is selling a large proportion of output of any one product to another large firm. A metal can manufacturer, for example, might find that a major customer is a pet food manufacturer operating in another oligopoly who, in turn, is selling a high proportion of output to superstores in a sector of retailing which is itself becoming highly concentrated.

Loss of the major buyer would seriously disrupt the supplier's business, probably bringing production below the minimum efficient scale of operations and, in effect, forcing closure. Even if this were not the immediate consequence the supplier must be aware that the buyer has the option, and the resources, to enter the market as a supplier if this appeared to be advantageous. The capital investment and technology for metal can production are well within the means of a major pet food manufacturer. The existing supplier must, therefore, ensure that no incentive is given for such an option to be exercised. Once again we see potential competition, this time from a customer with the ability to become a rival producer, as a powerful constraint limiting market power over prices, profits and quality standards.

Competition from Other Products

The real extent of competition in a market depends very much on how the market is defined. To continue the example of the metal cans: the can manufacturer may dominate supply of this particular product but the same function can be carried out by other kinds of containers, e.g. those made of plastic or glass. Even if metal is the only safe material for some substances at the present state of technology the metal can manufacturer must beware of providing incentives to plastic container manufacturers to undertake the research that could lead to a safe substitute for metal.

Another common example to illustrate the need for careful definition of the market is that of the railways. British Rail may be a monopoly supplier of passenger rail travel but in the market for passenger travel it is in a highly competitive market together with long distance coaches and private cars. Subject to other influences such as protection or underpinning by governments, the behaviour of firms is more likely to reflect the competitive condition in the wider market. It is readily conceivable that a high degree of market power, making possible technical research, high capital investment and scale economies in the limited market, may be a condition for long-term survival.

Rivalry within Oligopolistic Markets

It is clear that firms with substantial market power may nevertheless face competition and potential competition strong enough to modify their behaviour in ways that benefit consumers and make for a more efficient use of scarce resources. It is also likely that many are subject to considerable competitive pressure within their product markets even though there is negligible price competition. This pressure is the result of what is sometimes called **non-price competition** and which is also referred to by modern economists as **oligopolistic rivalry**.

One of the most outstanding features of rivalry in consumer markets is the continual battle to achieve and maintain brand leadership, i.e. to have the largest market share in a set of competing brands. Some consumer product suppliers spend very large sums in maintaining their position and have been successful for long periods. It is difficult to think of baked beans, for instance, without also thinking of Heinz. There are many advantages which producers consider to justify their expenditure and efforts. Identification with a product in the public mind must account for a large proportion of impulse purchases in stores. Many consumers may not even by aware that there are competing products made by other manufacturers. To be the acknowledged brand leader ensures that the brand is given favoured shelf positions in supermarkets and a generous allocation of shelf space. It also ensures favourable receptions from central buying offices in the large store chains and it becomes easier to launch new products and brands because stores will give 'new runners from a successful stable' a fair trial.

Producers, of course, are well aware that most products follow what marketing people term a **product life cycle**, which suggests that successful products go through various stages from their market launch through growth, saturation, stable demand and finally decline. The difficulty with this concept, which was discussed in Chapter 5, is that there is no way of forecasting with certainty the timescale of the cycle. In some cases the eventual and inevitable decline can be delayed for a very long period. However, we have already noted the importance given by business managers and capital markets to business growth so that before products reach the stage of market saturation and stable demand producers will be looking for new products and brands and market openings that look capable of exploitation. Rivalry, therefore, includes a constant search for new product development and companies are always seeking to be the first to open up a new market and launch a successful new brand. To be first in the field gives a good prospect of becoming brand leader.

Most of the oligopolistic effort to defend market positions and open up new markets requires substantial advertising and product promotion. In the UK the largest share of advertising is carried out by manufacturers direct to consumers. Retail stores are obliged to stock heavily advertised brands to meet consumer expectations. In practice they may make substantial advertising and promotional support a pre-condition of allocating shelf space. In other countries it is the retail groups which advertise and promote their own brands. Manufacturers must, therefore, concentrate their efforts on selling to the retail groups. There has been an increase in retail **own brands** in the UK but the established manufacturer brands tend to dominate most product markets. Nevertheless a large and growing marketing effort is directed towards the distribution networks. Perhaps the best known examples of this kind of marketing rivalry occur among travel agents where agency employees are given attractive inducements to direct buyers of packaged holidays to certain of the large tour operators. Less well known but somewhat similar examples of oligopolistic rivalry in an international market are the inducements offered to business secretaries to direct their business travel bookings to particular airlines.

Although most of the rivalry concerns various aspects of marketing of what are often very similar products, oligopolists in modern markets cannot entirely neglect production technology. The ability to produce an article at a lower cost than rivals clearly gives advantages to producers. Much of the effort in this direction is concerned with developing large-scale production processes that enable firms to achieve consistent quality standards at low cost. The snack food industry, which developed from origins in potato crisps, was revolutionised when unreliable batch production was changed to a highly mechanised form of continuous production. Changes in packaging materials also extended shelf life and brought the crisp packets on to supermarket shelves. Further packet snack foods became possible on the basis of materials that could be mass produced to almost any shape or design. Production technology, design and marketing are all part of the same process of product development and sale and the firm that neglects one of these elements is unlikely to achieve long-term success with the others. The fact that oligopoly has become the dominant market structure in most advanced market economies does not necessarily mean that business competition has declined.

Competition, Efficiency and the State

Competition and Efficiency

Although it seems evident that the degree of competitive rivalry in modern business markets is greater than some economists have been prepared to admit in the past, it is less clear how this affects economic efficiency. We must remember that the term **efficiency** is used in two senses:

1 **Absolute** (also termed **technical**) **efficiency**, i.e. the effective use of scarce resources in the production of goods and services. Given that human wants are without limit but that the resources available to satisfy those wants are scarce then the community requires its business organisations to use the resources entrusted to them as effectively as possible. Efficiency along these lines has been described as X efficiency. This relates to the ability of some firms to produce more with fewer resources than others. Observers have noted the very great differences in the production achieved from a given quantity of labour and capital. The main cause of efficiency differences is often given as differences in competitive pressures, competition being regarded as a powerful spur to increased efficiency. There are, however, problems in measuring and making comparisons of X efficiency and different measures tend to give different results. There are also, of course, important differences between products, quality standards and the conditions under which workers are employed.
2 **Allocative efficiency**, i.e. the use of scarce economic resources to produce that combination of goods and services that the community most requires.

Earlier in this chapter we pointed out that, in the past, economists have argued in favour of perfect competition as the market structure most likely to bring about the **Pareto** welfare optimum to achieve both kinds of efficiency. At the same time, however, some doubt was cast concerning the ability of perfectly competitive markets to achieve dynamic improvements in technology so that levels of technology could be raised. Similar doubts apply to the more recent concept of perfectly contestable markets as these seem likely to achieve the same behaviour patterns in relation to prices, profits, investment, and research and development as perfect competition.

A further school of modern economic thought, chiefly associated with a group of economists often known as the **Austrian school** (because it includes a number of influential Austrian economists), has argued that the rivalry between large organisations is evidence of business firms' attempts to meet consumer wishes and is likely to lead to the kind of technological and product development that is needed to achieve constantly rising living standards.

Another famous modern economist, the American Professor Milton Friedman, has followed a somewhat similar line of argument to suggest that completely unregulated markets are the structures most likely to maximise consumer welfare. This, he suggests, is largely because failure to satisfy consumer wants and aspirations leads, in the long run, to business collapse, while long-term profit can only be achieved through consumer satisfaction and support.

Some of the dangers of leaving quality and safety standards entirely to market discipline are examined in Chapter 10. At this stage our concern is more with the market's ability to provide for all consumer wants and aspirations. We need, therefore, to examine how far oligopolistic markets are capable of achieving both absolute and allocative efficiency.

It is often argued that the desire to gain the benefits of monopoly profits stimulates technical research because these profits go to the firms which can take the lead in the technical race. Research and development are seen to be important activities of the large firm. Expenditure on research and development is an investment cost which is met from profit in the hope that it will generate increased profit. If it is successful the public gain from the improved productivity of scarce resources while the firm and its shareholders gain the benefit of increased profits.

Against this argument it is pointed out that much of the research activity of large firms with established market power is concerned with relatively superficial aspects of product modification aimed at making what is essentially an unchanged product more attractive to target groups of consumers. To take the private motor car as an example, the fundamental design of the internal combustion engine has changed very little for most of the twentieth century. Most of the changes have been concerned with making what is essentially the same product more reliable and attractive – assuming that speed is one of the features that make it attractive to consumers.

Really fundamental changes in products tend to come with the threat of extinction from alternative technology. Economists sometimes refer to the **sailing ship effect**, pointing out that more progress was made in the technology of sailing ships in the last half century when sail faced competition from steam than in the previous five centuries when it had no serious rivals in ocean transport.

It is also notable that war is a major incentive to technical innovation and development. Much of the economic growth of Europe in the 1960s and 1970s may well be accounted for by converting to peace-time use the major developments in materials technology, electronics and in air and land transport that were made during the Second World War. Even some quite simple products owe their development to war. The hand-held chain saw was developed in Germany to meet a military need for rapid tree felling.

If there is some doubt concerning the ability of oligopolistic markets to generate fundamental technical advance there is even greater uncertainty over the market system as a whole to meet the demand for an increasing range of public goods on which so much of a modern community's welfare depends. British history of the eighteenth and nineteenth centuries suggests that major advances in the national infrastructure of communications and the public health and public order services of sewers, piped water, street lighting and the police force only began to attain standards that we would now regard as the minimum needed for healthy and civilised living when the state started to play a serious role. It usually did so through legislation supported by inspection and enforcement services, and by entering the market as a major producer in its own right. Although, as we see in Chapter 12, there is considerable controversy over the extent of the state's involvement in production, few would deny that it does have an important role in making good the allocative deficiencies of unregulated markets, especially in the production of public goods where self-interest is not a sufficiently powerful force in generating effective supply.

At the same time we must be careful in our identification of market inadequacies. We need to separate those gaps which history suggests are rarely, if ever, closed by normal, profit inspired, business enterprise from those where the market failure has itself largely been brought about by state intervention and controls. Examples of the former would probably include a public sewerage system, and an instance of the latter would include the various housing shortages that have appeared in the UK during this century. It is difficult to blame private housing markets for failing to provide adequate housing when supply has been discouraged and hampered first by rent controls (dating from the First World War) and, since 1948, by rigid controls over land use designed to protect the environment so that it can be enjoyed by those who are already adequately housed or who benefit from the scarcity which controls help to create.

Failure to analyse correctly the cause of market failure can lead to 'solutions' that aggravate the problems. If failure is due to the market's fundamental inability to provide supply considered necessary by current social expectations then more state intervention is likely to be desirable. If, however, the failure is due to outdated state controls and political policies seeking to reconcile irreconcilable conflicts, such as the desire to improve the quantity and quality of housing while also increasing leisure space on a finite stock of land, then the remedy may be more likely to lie with less state control and allowing the community to express its priorities for houses and green fields through the marketplace.

One further criticism of unregulated markets as the means of allocating scarce resources to production is based on the belief that misallocation arises because of the inequalities of wealth in the community. The wealthy have more votes in the marketplace than the poor. In an unregulated housing market the wealthy would build houses on green field sites while the poor might be herded into inner city slums. To each according to need, rather than ability to pay, is a socially and morally attractive slogan. Unfortunately there is no guarantee that decisions taken by a bureaucracy controlled by the political machinery of the state provide a morally more pleasing result. Given the fundamental economic truth that human wants exceed what can be produced with available resources at any particular time, someone has to decide that A's need is greater than B's. Observation of countries where resources are allocated in this way indicates that, in practice, decisions are still based on self-interest and the exercise of money and power.

There are no easy answers to difficult choices. Economic analysis alone cannot provide a formula to guarantee technical and allocative efficiency. The perfect market structure is as difficult to attain as Utopia itself. The search for the ideal economic market structure is probably as hopeless as the ancient quests for the Holy Grail or the Philosopher's Stone. An imperfect world has to accept economic imperfections but it can try to set up structures and institutions to limit the harm that these imperfections can cause. The next chapter considers some of the ways modern communities have sought to do this.

Discussion Questions

1. 'There is no such thing as absolute monopoly. Every economic organisation has to compete for its share of available income.' How far is this true? Take into account services, including legal services and public sector bodies, as well as manufacturing companies.
2. 'Neither perfect nor competitive and an impossible position for a producer to be in.' Discuss this view of perfect competition.
3. With reference to at least one consumer product market, discuss the ways in which producers defend themselves against actual and potential market rivals.
4. 'All producers compete in international markets even if they never export a single item of their own.' Explain and discuss the implications of this statement.
5. Politicians refer to the **iron law of oligarchy** meaning that all political systems tend to move towards a situation where power is concentrated in the hands of a relatively few people. Is there a similar economic **iron law of oligopoly?** If so does this mean that there is little genuine business competition?

Suggestions for Further Reading

Most microeconomics and industrial economics texts discuss competition, barriers to entry and limit pricing, but there is a growing body of literature concerned with taking a new look at competition and challenging the 'traditional' analysis in which all markets are judged against an ideal of perfect competition. The term **rivalry** is often used to move away from 'competition' which has become overloaded with older economic associations.

Clarke, R., *Industrial Economics*, Blackwell, 1985 presents a balanced account of the contemporary academic position on competition in general.

Classic texts on market structure include:

Scherer, F. M., *Industrial Market Structure and Economic Performance*, Rand Mcnally, 1980
Schumpeter, J. A., *Capitalism, Socialism and Democracy*, George Allen and Unwin, 1987

Other writers who have influenced thinking in this general area include:

Leibenstein, H., 'Allocative efficiency vs "X-efficiency"', *American Economic Review*, **56**
Reekie, W. D., *Industry, Prices and Markets*, Philip Allen, 1979
Reekie, W. D., *Markets, Entrepreneurs and Liberty. An Austrian View of Capitalism*, Wheatsheaf Books, 1984

The emerging theory of contestable markets is presented in:

Baumol, W. J., 'Contestable markets: an uprising in the theory of industry structure', *American Economic Review*, **72**

Appendix to Chapter 9

To understand why a kink in the average revenue curve will produce a discontinuity in the marginal revenue curve it is helpful to examine Table 9.1

Table 9.1

Price per unit (£)	*Quantity (units per time period)*	*Total revenue (£)*	*Marginal revenue (change in TR) (pence)*
1.40	0	0	
			130
1.30	10	13.00	
			110
1.20	20	24.00	
			90
1.10	30	33.00	
			70
1.00	40	40.00	(60 or 20)
			0
0.80	50	40.00	
			−40
0.60	60	36.00	
			−80
0.40	70	28.00	
			−120
0.20	80	16.00	
			−160
0	90	0	

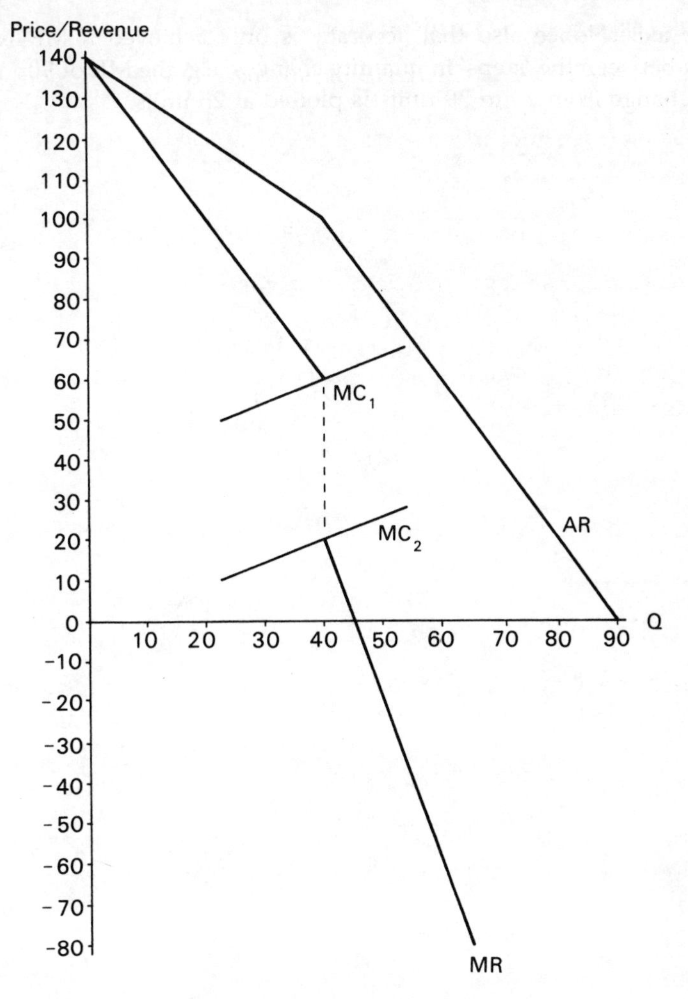

Fig. 9.8 The kinked demand curve

and Fig. 9.8. In this set of figures the kink occurs at the price of £1.00 and quantity level 40 units. At prices above £1 demand falls at the rate of 10 units for each 10p rise in price. At prices below £1 the fall is 5 units for each 10p price rise.

This produces two possible marginal revenues at the 40 unit quantity level. The higher (60p) comes from the continuation downwards of the upper part of the marginal revenue curve. The lower (20p) from the upward continuation of the lower marginal revenue curve.

Notice that each section of the marginal revenue curve obeys the rule that the MR curve **bisects** the horizontal distance between the AR curve and the revenue axis. If you take a ruler and extend the lower parts of the AR and MR curves you will find that they both meet at the same point above the vertical, revenue axis. Notice also that accuracy is only achieved if MR is plotted midway between the 'steps' in quantity changes, e.g. the MR of 90p resulting from a change from 20 to 30 units is plotted at 25 units.

10

Competition, Consumer Protection and Public Policy

The Case for Government Intervention in Economic Markets

Competition and the Consumer

It must be stressed that this chapter is essentially concerned with economic issues. It does not attempt to become involved in the socio-political argument that people in the mass are not the best judges of what is best for them and that judgements are better made through a political system. Supporters of this view would argue that the basic economic decisions of 'what, how and for whom?' are most effectively reached in the best interests of the community by those most fitted to identify them. This debate has continued without clear resolution at least since Socrates and doubtless long before him. Nor, in this chapter, would we wish to challenge or subject to close analysis the more common view that communities need to be protected against minorities whose behaviour is held to threaten the community as a whole, including the minorities themselves. Consequently we shall not be examining in detail laws relating to such issues as drugs, alcohol, tobacco smoking or the wearing of vehicle seat-belts. This is not to suggest that these are not important aspects of consumer protection or that they are not of legitimate concern to economics. They all do, in fact, have important economic as well as social and ethical implications but our main concern in this chapter is not so much with the goods and services being traded as with the market conditions under which trade takes place and the effect these may have on individual and community welfare.

In Chapter 9 we examined the relationship between market structure and competition and we identified some of the problems of identifying competitive pressures. We saw that there was no certainty that any one market structure was guaranteed to offer the maximum benefits to consumers. Nevertheless there is more general agreement that competition is of benefit to consumers. When firms either compete amongst each other for business or if they operate with the knowledge that others are ready to take over their customers if they do not keep them fully satisfied then customers obtain a number of real benefits. These include:

1 **Reasonable prices** Price cutting is the most obvious and direct way to 'steal a customer' and established suppliers are aware of the need to avoid giving this opportunity to competitors or potential competitors. The suspicion that suppliers are making excess profits from a product is also likely to tempt rivals so that established firms will try to avoid arousing that suspicion. Price stability may, therefore, indicate that suppliers are being careful to charge competitive prices rather than the more readily assumed absence of price competition.
2 **Product choice** Competition allows consumers to choose both product and supplier. Awareness that others have the potentiality to enter the market as suppliers ensures that established firms make an effort to meet the product requirements of customers.
3 **Customer service** As products have become more complex and technically advanced and as services have taken a more important place in consumer budgets trust in the supplier's ability to meet warranty obligations, to replace or repair defective products and to make an effort to make good deficient services has become a major element in consumer welfare. Many defects in electronic equipment only become evident during use. Often the only satisfactory remedy is speedy replacement. The tourist who finds that holiday accommodation is not as described by the travel agent needs immediate, sympathetic and efficient attention on the spot. Competition and rivalry are the surest ways to ensure a satisfactory quality of customer service. Many of today's motorists are able to recall the way vehicle warranty conditions and services improved when European and American manufacturers started to face significant Japanese competition in their home markets.

If competition and the fear of competition make it difficult for firms to achieve excess profits and ensure that they keep prices low and quality of product and service high we can expect that business managers will seek to limit these constraints on their ability to make profits and achieve a secure, problem-free environment. We have already noted that oligopolies have a tendency towards collusion. There is a similar tendency in markets containing a large number of small firms as suppliers for these to combine together in associations. These frequently claim an objective of 'fair trading' or the avoidance of 'unfair competition'. From the consumers' point of view such objectives look more like setting limits on competition to preserve profits and ensure the survival of the less efficient suppliers. In the UK many of these associations ceased their anti-competitive practices after the passing of the Restrictive Trade Practices Act of 1956. Others, such as the Building Societies Association and the Fire Offices Committee (an insurance association) survived but were weakened when continued mergers changed market structures.

It is possible, therefore, to base a case for state intervention in product and service markets when, left to themselves, these appear to tolerate barriers to effective competition powerful enough to deny to consumers the benefits that they could have expected from more competitive supply conditions.

Competition and the Economy

The pressure of competition can also improve the efficiency with which scarce resources are used. If firms are forced to keep prices low the desire to make profits will ensure that they produce at lowest possible cost and this will usually mean that resources are used as effectively as possible. It could also provide an incentive for firms to pass costs to external sources. For example, firms could try to dispose of waste in rivers or dumps without adequate safeguards so that the community as a whole pays the cost in lost amenities or dangers to health. They may also be tempted to operate with inadequate safety precautions and so pass some costs to injured employees or workers who suffer sickness and loss of life expectation. Competitive pressures may also force employers to pay low wages and give inadequate training so that, in fact, labour is not used efficiently. We should remember that most of the occupations which have a history of **sweated labour**, i.e. employing labour under poor working conditions for long hours at low pay, are precisely the ones which feature in competitive markets where there are large numbers of small firms operating with each other.

It was this kind of competitive market structure in the nineteenth century which led Marx and Engels to develop their theories of worker exploitation and alienation leading to inevitable revolution. To avoid the distortions and abuses that can arise from totally unregulated competition the state tends to become involved in establishing public and worker safety legislation and in setting up the machinery to enforce it. It may also establish machinery to ensure that pay and working conditions do not fall below socially acceptable standards. It is for these reasons that the UK has had effective Factory Acts for well over a century and had wages councils for much of the twentieth century.

It is also frequently claimed that competition provides incentives for technical research leading to improved use of resources and the development of new and improved products. Desk-top computing, which has revolutionised so many aspects of business life, is a product of competition, and the struggles of firms to survive and develop in fiercely competitive markets has helped to bring about the extraordinary progress of the microcomputer during the 1980s.

Nevertheless there is always the danger that lack of profit limits the research capabilities of firms. This danger, however, can be exaggerated. The modern banking system in countries such as the UK is very flexible and there is always venture capital available for profitable opportunities. An entrepreneur able to prove ability to develop a profitable product should be able to obtain the finance needed for development at the price of sacrificing some independence to financial managers and some of the profits to the financial backers.

On the whole, therefore, genuine competition is likely to be beneficial to the community as a whole subject to some safeguards to ensure socially acceptable practices. This is not, of course, the same as suggesting that the market structure known as perfect competition is the ideal structure to achieve maximum consumer welfare. The doubts surrounding perfect competition expressed in Chapter 9 should not be overlooked.

Anti-competitive Practices

Most anti-competitive practices are associated with oligopolies but, as noted earlier in this chapter, small firms may also form restrictive associations to protect themselves from the pressures of competition. Such associations usually sought to ensure that prices were fixed at a level that allowed the survival of all members and that there was no undercutting of those prices. Attempts were also made to ensure that member firms were provided with a degree of local monopoly, e.g. that there was not more than one grocer or one greengrocer in a particular locality. It was also common in the past to ensure that shops did not cross the boundaries of their own specialist trade. In the early 1960s, for example, in the UK it was still unusual to find grocers selling meat, fresh fruit or vegetables while butchers sold meat only and often specialised in one kind of meat such as pork, beef or lamb. These local monopolies broke down with the spread of supermarkets cutting across the old trade specialisms and with the legal end of resale price maintenance when it was no longer possible for large suppliers to discipline over-competitive shops by withholding supplies of popular branded goods.

It is worth recalling the restrictive tendencies of small firms to show that the desire to achieve a defence against competitive pressure is not confined to large oligopolists and monopolists. However, much of the economic concern over anti-competitive practices has centred on the activities of large firms which have achieved a significant degree of market power. The methods which have been used at various times to gain and maintain this power are now widely recognised and can be summarised quite simply.

Cartels

In its extreme form a **cartel** is a formal association of firms which agree to observe clear rules relating to such issues as product prices, wages, payments to agents and distributors, advertising and restrictions against 'poaching' each other's customers. In some cases there can be an agreement to share markets according to some agreed pattern. The basis of market sharing may be geographical so that each member gains an effective monopoly in a defined area, by product so that each has a monopoly in the supply of agreed categories of product, or by turns or quotas. Where, for example, it is customary to invite competitive tenders before awarding contracts for, say, building or removal work, a ring of suppliers may so fix their tender prices that work is shared equally among members of the ring. Each may take turns in submitting the lowest tender. Although cartels and the practices associated with them have been effectively illegal in the UK since the Restrictive Trade Practices Act of 1956 later cases have come to light and it would be optimistic to suppose that some are not being continued in a number of business sectors.

Price fixing and price wars

Freedom to vary price is an essential element of a competitive market. If prices are fixed consumers will tend to buy from established suppliers whose reputation is known. There is no incentive to risk buying from new or unproved suppliers. Established oligopolists have been known to take extreme measures to preserve price fixing arrangements. An effective method is to apply generous price reductions on any products or in any areas where a new supplier – or a rebel against an 'agreement' – is seeking to compete. When constantly faced by low prices the would-be competitor is unable to supply at a profit and is eventually forced out of the market. The established firms are then able to restore prices and profit margins and recoup any losses suffered.

Blocking essential supplies
A powerful firm can use its power as a supplier of popular goods to withhold supplies to distributors which it believes are trading in ways that threaten the stability of the market or which are supporting rival suppliers. If it is also an important buyer of basic materials it may be able to persuade the suppliers of these to withhold supplies from rivals.

Gaining financial control over competitors or their suppliers
Given the legal constraints against the more blatant forms of anti-competitive practice now common in the advanced industrial nations and public hostility to these practices the modern large firm is more likely to use its financial power to limit competition. It may simply buy out a competing firm. Observers of business mergers suggest that the elimination of competition is a significant motive of a high proportion of horizontal mergers, i.e. mergers between firms producing similar products at the same stage of production. Proposed mergers between two firms which already have a large share of a product market are likely to attract the attention of bodies, such as the British Monopolies and Mergers Commission, which have a responsibility towards resisting attacks on competition. On the other hand they are less likely to notice when an established large firm swallows a new, small company. The managers of the large company would have little difficulty in finding reasons why the takeover was necessary. They would be unlikely to suggest that their real motives were to suppress or take control of a technological or marketing development which seemed likely to change an existing price and market structure.

It is not always necessary to take over a competitor firm completely to control its actions. Purchase of a significant proportion of its voting shares would, in most cases, ensure representation on the main board of directors and access to information and to the people who make strategic decisions. At one time the apparently competing tobacco companies were linked in this way so that actual competition in the market was fairly carefully regulated. This practice has also been made more difficult in countries such as the UK where there are rules providing for the disclosure of the identities of people or organisations owning a certain proportion of the ordinary shares in a public company.

It is clear that there are pressures for firms to limit competition and many devices whereby they can seek to do so. The general course of government measures to try and preserve or restore competition has been to stop the measures that do come to light. Firms then seek other ways to achieve their purpose. This inevitably raises questions regarding the value of legal measures designed to influence or modify business behaviour. Some will argue that laws are ineffective and that markets should be left to the regulation of normal market pressures. Others will suggest that business should be subject to very strict and detailed laws, while there will be some who believe that the only remedy is for a complete change in the structure of the economic system with state control replacing private profit as the driving force of economic activity.

We return to these issues towards the end of this chapter but it is now desirable to examine the way in which UK competition policies have developed in recent years.

The Development of UK Competition Policy

Policies on Restrictive Trade Practices

Before the Second World War there was really no official UK policy towards competition and business behaviour. The legal courts had shown a marked disinclination to apply the law of conspiracy to business activities even when there was clear evidence that firms had acted together to remove competitors or had forced other firms to conform to anti-competitive rules set by established market leaders. If anything there was a general public suspicion against **cut-throat competition** which was thought to force employers to pay low wages and which created unstable conditions in labour markets. In a period of long-term high unemployment when business cycles were thought to be the cause of a great deal of human suffering and political instability these attitudes are not surprising. It was hoped that large firms might offer more stable employment and some protection against the uncertainties associated with periodic economic booms and depressions.

Experience of economic management during wartime when the government itself became the main buyer of industrial production and when civil servants had to administer purchasing procedures gave ministers and the civil service an insight into the extent of collusive practices in the industry of that time. Naturally these were denied and it was difficult to obtain detailed facts. The first need, therefore, was to establish a means of acquiring accurate and unbiased information. Accordingly the Monopolies and Restrictive Practices (Inquiry and Control) Act of 1948 set up a Monopolies and Restrictive Practices Commission with power of investigation and a responsibility to make reports on its findings.

The reports of the Commission started to show that anti-competitive restrictive trade practices were indeed widespread and damaging to consumer interests. In response to these reports – and in the opinion of some observers to stop the Commission from discovering too much – the issues of monopoly and of restrictive trade practices were, perhaps artificially, separated by the Restrictive Trade Practices Act of 1956. This Act set up a Restrictive Practices

Court to register collective agreements made by firms within industries, to examine selected agreements and to decide if these were 'against the public interest'.

The Act introduced a presumption that restrictive trade agreements were against the public interest but associations of firms could argue on the basis of certain **gateways** that their agreements were, on balance, in the public interest. The gateways were based on such issues as employment, exports and public safety. It was left somewhat uncertain as to how the public interest should be determined and how, say, an increase in local unemployment should be balanced against freedom for firms to enter into price competition.

While the 1956 Act set up a high court to investigate and make judgements on collective trade agreements it actually strengthened the powers of companies to set the prices at which their products could be distributed to consumers. This apparent anomoly was corrected in the 1964 Resale Prices Act, later consolidated into the Resale Prices Act 1976. These extended the 1956 ideas of balance of public interest and defence gateways into the areas of resale price maintenance by individual firms. It soon became clear that for most consumer products the court would be reluctant to accept that any price fixing arrangement could be to the public advantage and most of the main agreements, e.g. on tobacco, chocolate and confectionery, were abandoned.

The Fair Trading Act of 1973 abolished the separate office of Registrar of Restrictive Practices, its functions being absorbed into those of the Director General of Fair Trading who thus became responsible for registration, investigation and bringing relevant cases to the court. Although there is a legal duty for firms to register restrictive and price-fixing practices with the Court and, if they wish the practices to continue, seek exemption from the Director General of Fair Trading, there were, in 1988, no penalties for failure to do so. The Office of Fair Trading had no special investigative force and had to rely on normal sources of information, or disclosure by aggrieved firms or individuals, to discover concealed practices. In 1988 a White Paper suggested that there should be serious penalties for continuing to operate an unregistered restrictive practice.

Monopolies and Mergers

In 1956, stripped of its responsibility for investigating restrictive trade practices, the Commission set up in 1948 became simply the Monopolies Commission. In 1965, however, the Monopolies and Mergers Act gave it powers to investigate mergers on the grounds that by the time a monopoly had been created it was too late for the government to take effective action. It might be more effective to try and prevent new monopolies from being created by exercising some control over the merger process. In 1973, the Fair Trading Act strengthened and clarified the investigatory powers of the Commission which was re-named the Monopolies and Mergers Commission (MMC).

The 1973 Act defined a monopoly situation as one where a firm or group of firms acting together controlled at least 25 per cent of the supply of a given category of product. Earlier definitions had been broadly similar but based on control of one-third of supply. The Act also brought the Commission under the wing of the Director General of Fair Trading whose Office thus became the main body concerned with monopolies, mergers and anti-competitive practices. Much of the work of the Commission since 1973 has been related to mergers and takeovers. Under this Act it has powers to investigate proposed mergers and takeovers likely to create or strengthen a monopoly situation as just defined or concerned with the acquisition of assets of a value over £5 million (raised to £15 million in 1980). There were also special provisions relating to mergers of newspaper companies. Merger references to the MMC are made by the Secretary of State but recommendations can be made by the Director General of Fair Trading.

In 1988 the Director General had no special powers to acquire information on proposed mergers and had to rely on normal sources of information unless the participants chose to consult privately. Unlike the position over restrictive trade practices there was no assumption that monopolies or mergers were or were not in the public interest. Each case was to be judged in the light of its effect or likely effect on competition, there being a more general assumption that competition was desirable, though no attempt was made to define it. If anything, merger policy can be seen as 'permissive', in that unless a strong case (usually on competitive grounds) can be made out against it, a merger will be permitted to go ahead. This is in direct contrast with the position over restrictive trade practices, which will be struck down unless a strong case can be made out in their favour. The view of the UK government, in the 1980s, was quite clearly that, in the main, issues of whether or not mergers went ahead should be left to market forces, unless clear competition issues were raised.

In 1980 the Competition Act brought public sector activities within the scope of MMC investigations and gave the Secretary of State powers to order **quick references** (reports within six months) for mergers and activities suspected of being anti-competitive. By the 1980s, therefore, the Secretary of State had very wide discretionary powers to order investigations and to hold up mergers, and the decision whether or not to make such an order itself constituted considerable powers to intervene in the operation of the capital market.

Competition Policy and the European Community

The national policy of any member of the European Community on matters of such economic significance as competition, monopolies and mergers has to be reconciled with and to some extent complement the general policy of the Community.

Community attitudes to competition arise from Articles 85 and 86 of the Treaty of Rome. Article 85 forbids the majority of restrictive agreements affecting trade between member countries and Article 86 forbids the abuse of market dominance. To some extent the Community provisions are rather wider than those of the UK legislation. Article 85 applies to exclusive dealing agreements between producers and distributors and between the licensors and licensees of patents. These agreements are largely ignored by the UK rules but they have a significant impact on international competition because they tend to partition markets, preventing a supplier in one country from competing with suppliers in another and at the same time protecting that supplier from challenge within his own exclusive area. The Community has also been concerned with discriminatory pricing policies in different countries resulting from different market structures in the various member states.

Enforcement of Community competition rules is the responsibility of the European Commission which has wide powers of investigation. It is not certain how effective action on a European scale has been. Member governments have not always been anxious to encourage competition within their national markets from stronger firms in other countries. Political pressures within states has often tended to be anti-competitive in the interests of preserving established national industries and employment and there has been a suspicion that cases have been brought to the notice of the Commission more in the interests of hindering entry to a national market by a powerful foreign competitor than in fostering consumer interests and encouraging competition. It should not be forgotten that the Community's Common Agricultural Policy is one of the most powerful barriers to competition seen in modern international trade and a forceful reminder of the weakness of consumer interests in the face of long established, well organised and politically influential producer groups.

Relaxation of intra-national trade barriers within the Community due to take effect in 1992 might be expected to encourage competition throughout all member nations. However, the history of most unregulated markets suggests that firms with established market power will seek to limit the real extent of competition through the various oligopolistic practices that have already been noted. There is little evidence, so far, that the institutions of the Community are prepared to set up effective measures to combat the kinds of restrictive trade practices that may be anticipated.

Effectiveness of UK Competition Policies

Attitudes to UK competition policies vary considerably among both economists and business managers. Academic critics tend to stand at opposite ends of a debate as to whether the measures are ineffective because they do not go far enough or ineffective because attempts to control business conduct are misguided anyway. Both groups agree that they are not very effective.

The Case for Stiffer Controls

It has been argued that there is now sufficient evidence to show the collusive and anti-competitive tendencies of virtually all business firms which operate in highly concentrated markets so that the government should take a firm stand against the existence of monopolies and highly concentrated oligopolies.

A policy on these lines would imply that the government should:

1 Seek to break up those large firms which appear to have a controlling influence on specific markets.
2 Introduce statutes that forbid mergers of large firms in the same or related markets, subject, perhaps, to exceptions considered to be necessary in the public interest. However, the onus would be upon companies wishing to merge to show that the benefits to the public from the proposed merger outweighed the loss of competition which it would involve. Placing the onus on proof of the firms would thus follow existing provisions over restrictive trade practices.

Supporters of this kind of policy argue that it would introduce a greater degree of certainty over the government's attitutudes and that business firms would know where they stood. Many mergers would be discouraged as firms would only go to the trouble, publicity and expense of seeking to prove that their union was in the public interest if they had a strong case and if their past record was such that they could afford to have it subjected to the spotlight of publicity.

Critics argue that in the USA where there is an apparently strong, statutory anti-trust (i.e. anti-monopoly) policy the position is little better than in the UK. Firms have developed techniques of complying with the letter of the law while breaking its spirit. The main group to gain from the legislation is the lawyers whose fees have to become part of production costs. There are very great practical difficulties in breaking up existing business groups, and in trying to establish legally watertight definitions of business concentration too much emphasis tends to be given to horizontal monopolies and oligopolies where firms at the same level of production are operating in the same product market. Not enough attention is given to vertical monopoly, i.e. where firms at one production stage are able to control important inputs to the production process, or major distribution outlets for the finished product. This is more difficult to define and is also liable to change as technology changes.

The Case for Fewer or No Controls

The opposing point of view is usually based on one or both of two arguments:

1 Government legislation and controls are ineffective in that they simply create legalistic attitudes and lead firms to enter into complex and expensive procedures to appear to comply with the law.
2 Controls are unnecessary because the best guardian of community interest is the freest possible marketplace. If firms abuse market power to make abnormal profits or to produce inefficiently this will be observed by other firms who will gain entry to the market whatever the established suppliers do to try and prevent them. If customers are not satisfied with the products and service supplied they will seek new sources so both are best guaranteed by consumer freedom to buy what and where they choose. It can also be argued that in modern communities monopoly power is almost

an impossibility in the private sector. No one is forced to buy anything so that all suppliers are competing for a share in each consumer's disposable income. The individual might have only, say, three possible sources of supply for a new family car. However, the individual can choose whether to buy the car, take the family on a foreign holiday, buy new furniture, have the family house redecorated or buy a larger house. The suppliers of all these products are in competition with each other even though they do not operate in the same product market. Given the reality of this kind of competition the fact that there is a restricted choice of cars is not worth the expense and trouble of legal market controls.

Any form of control which has its origins in Parliamentary statutes runs the risk of becoming out of date. UK policies, as they existed in early 1989, were based on implied assumptions that mergers involved the takeover of a smaller firm by a larger organisation. In practice modern, sophisticated capital markets can make it possible for the smaller firm, if it has sufficient financial support from other institutions, to take over a larger firm. If the takeover raider is successful it must then sell parts of the acquired group to repay its financial backers. Critics of this practice point to the possible loss of jobs involved when assets are **stripped** in this way. Supporters of free market economics suggest that the victim must have been operating inefficiently for the takeover to be possible. Awareness that this kind of takeover can be mounted keeps even the largest company alert to the dangers of not operating all its assets to the maximum level of efficiency and profitability. The takeover raider is simply fulfilling the historic, economic function of looking for under-use of scarce economic resources and putting them to more effective use when suitable opportunities are located.

Another modern situation is that where two, or sometimes more, companies are seeking to take over another. Sometimes only one of the raiders is exposed to the threat of reference to the Monopolies and Mergers Commission under existing practices. An intervention by the Secretary of State for Industry to refer one of the bids to the Monopolies and Mergers Commission, leaving the other bidder free to pursue the takeover, then looks as though the government is taking sides in what should be a purely commercial battle.

Nevertheless the argument that controls do not always work very smoothly does not necessarily prove that controls are never necessary. We have to remind ourselves of the evidence produced by the Monopolies Commission in the 1950s, that unregulated markets could lead to monopolies achieved by some rather ruthless practices, to be suspicious of suggestions that, left entirely to themselves, firms will choose competition and efficiency in preference to collusion, market sharing and price fixing.

Business Attitudes to Controls

The main business complaint over UK monopolies and merger policy is that it has been very uncertain. The possibility of a proposed merger being referred to the Monopolies and Mergers Commission is very small. Only a proportion of all mergers eligible for reference under the Fair Trading Act 1973 are even considered seriously by the Office of Fair Trading. A small proportion of these are put to the Secretary of State as possibly justifying a reference. The Secretary of State takes no formal action over the majority of these and in most cases is not required to justify the decision publicly. In the event only a tiny fraction of **eligible** mergers are referred and in many of these the MMC recommends that the merger is permitted, subject, perhaps to some safeguards such as disposal of companies that would otherwise give the successful takeover group a very high degree of market control.

Nevertheless there is always the possibility that a reference will be made but as the risk is low companies whose merger plans are blocked feel that they have been unjustly picked on. Unlike other areas of the law it is not possible to consult an independent lawyer who, after consideration of precedents, can advise with some confidence what the legal position actually is. The Commission has been accused of some inconsistency in its reports and is not required to follow the precedent of earlier decisions.

Companies may approach the Office of Fair Trading informally to find out probable reactions to merger proposals but the Office cannot guarantee the political reactions of the Secretary of State who, in any event, may be put under intense political pressure sufficient to force a change of mind. While it may seem to be taking a sensible precaution to sound out possible official reactions to proposed actions – and indeed proposals on these lines have been made in a 1988 White Paper – it has to be remembered that civil servants and politicians do not have the same sense of urgency as business managers operating in the capital market. It has also become apparent that they cannot always ensure secrecy. News of a merger proposal can make a sudden and significant difference to the share price of the target company as well as alerting the proposed victim and providing time for defensive action. Business managers have also pointed to the very great cost of Commission investigations and the length of time the Commission takes to reach its conclusion.

In general, therefore, business managers would prefer to have no controls over their efforts to improve their share of product markets, but if there have to be some controls they would prefer these to be clear and precise so that the views of both the Secretary of State and the Monopolies and Mergers Commission can be accurately predicted.

Proposals for the Reform of UK Policies on Mergers and Monopolies

By 1989 there was a widespread belief that policies formulated at the beginning of the 1970s were not adequate for the conditions of the 1990s. Nevertheless there was less agreement over the form that changes should take. The government had made it clear that new legislation was needed in order to encourage increased competition throughout many sectors of UK business.

Firm, detailed proposals for changes were still awaited in March 1989 but ministers had indicated that they proposed to retain the broad principles underlying UK policies, i.e. that there was a desire to encourage genuine competition in the interests of business efficiency and protection for consumers, and that the approach was to remain essentially 'pragmatic', i.e. each case was to be judged on its merits against its implications for competition. The main reforms anticipated were:

1. The Commission was to be encouraged to carry out its work more swiftly.
2. Arrangements would be made for companies considering merger to pre-notify their intentions to the Office of Fair Trading (or whatever body might take its place). The OFT could then consult the Secretary of State and negotiate legally binding undertakings or actions (such as the sale of individual companies) that might help to avoid a reference and reduce the costs faced by the companies concerned. It was proposed that companies would have to pay a charge towards the cost of vetting proposed mergers.
3. The law relating to restrictive trade practices would be stiffened. The Office of Fair Trading (or its successor) would be given powers to investigate suspected hidden practices and be able to impose substantial financial penalties on companies found to be operating concealed anti-competitive agreements.
4. Any necessary changes would be made to harmonise UK law and procedures with European Community requirements and practices.

It is clear that these proposed changes would be unlikely to meet the critics of UK competition policy which would continue to chart a cautious passage between those who believed that unfettered markets offered the best chance of preserving consumer sovereignty over business behaviour and those who were deeply suspicious of business practices and who wanted these made subject to precise and detailed government regulations.

Protecting Consumers

The Need for Consumer Protection Law

Extreme supporters of free markets argue that there is no need for governments to pass laws to protect consumers because competitive markets ensure that business firms operate to satisfy consumers and failure to do so leads inevitably to business failure. This may be true in the long term but actual practices of some firms can certainly cause suffering and loss to individuals, some of whom may not survive to witness 'the long term'. It is not much consolation to the person dying from food poisoning to know that the guilty food producer will eventually go out of business. That person would prefer the producer to be forced to comply with legal controls to prevent the production and sale of contaminated food.

In fact there is a very long history of measures designed to protect the consumer. UK legislation concerning quality standards of gold and silver dates back to the thirteenth century and silver has been quality tested and **hall-**

marked since the year 1300. Most ancient civilisations have records of official attempts to ensure quality and safety standards for food, weights, measures and house building. It has apparently always been necessary to protect people against those prepared to make profits regardless of the consequences to their fellow beings.

The modern consumer movement in the UK has its main origins in the creation of the Weights and Measures inspectorate in the last century, and in the codification of the common law as it had developed through court decisions in the first Sale of Goods Act 1893.

The main arguments supporting the establishment of a body of consumer law are:

1 A body of law has to emerge in any case because disputes inevitably lead to legal cases so that in time a collection of case law is built up. When this becomes large enough it is desirable to give it greater certainty and clarity through legal statutes. This was the background to the first Sale of Goods Act.
2 Under modern conditions it is necessary to restore a balance between the powers of consumers and producers. When most producers were small firms operating in very competitive markets and most buyers of durable goods were from the wealthier sections of society the principle of **let the buyer beware** was not unreasonable. Today, when production is dominated by very large companies with vast financial resources and access to the best legal brains the individual consumer is not usually able to fight a legal battle on equal terms and needs the protection of Parliament.
3 It is no longer possible to inspect goods and be certain that they are satisfactory and safe. Electronic goods can only be tested fully in normal use while prepacked goods can only be examined by destroying their protective packing. In these circumstances there is a special onus on the supplier to ensure that goods are sold in safe, working condition and this onus has to be created by the legislature.
4 The chain of supply can be very long and cross several countries and continents. To trace a guilty producer can be a long, complex and expensive process with little guarantee of financial compensation at the end. Parliament may be able to fix immediate responsibility for defects on the retail supplier and leave it to business organisations to share this responsibility without further cost or delay to the consumer.
5 Reputable traders are in just as much need of protection from the unscrupulous as consumers and they generally support moves to drive rogues away from product markets.

Principles of UK Consumer Law

Consumer law has both a criminal and a civil side. The purpose of criminal law is to forbid certain actions which are considered to be dangerous in the hope that injuries and losses to people in the community can be avoided. Thus people who allow customers to enter dangerous premises may be committing a criminal offence, as are those who manufacture children's nightware out of highly inflammable materials or allow food to be prepared under unhygienic conditions and sell it to the public. People accused of criminal acts can be prosecuted and be liable to punishment on behalf of the community as a whole but this, in itself, does not provide a remedy to people who have suffered as a result of the act.

People who suffer injury or loss as a result of the actions of others may have the right to seek a civil remedy which usually takes the form of financial compensation. In some cases trading standards officers may be able to prosecute an offending trader and obtain financial compensation for people who have suffered loss but, for the most part, the onus and cost of a civil action falls on the injured individual.

Partly as a result of the cost and difficulty in obtaining help through the civil courts the UK government has sought to encourage **self-regulation** whereby industrial or service sectors set up their own bodies to 'police' the actions of producers and suppliers, and provide a less costly and less formal system of settling disputes between buyers and retail markets. Most sectors of business activity now have their own self-regulatory body handling complaints made by members of the public and this system has been the basis for the regulation of the financial services under the Financial Services Act of 1986.

Another aspect of official interest in consumer protection is the establishment of agencies to provide a channel of communication between government and business, to keep a watch on business practices and to advise government on necessary legislation in the light of practices both in the UK and in other countries. Under the Fair Trading Act of 1973 the body set up to carry out these functions was the Office of Fair Trading which was also responsible for the Monopolies and Mergers Commission and the work of the Restrictive Practices Court. The OFT was still the main agency for overseeing and administering government policies on consumer protection and business competition at the beginning of 1989.

Some Economic Implications of Consumer Protection

As with any other measure the main purpose of which is probably social and ethical, i.e. arising from a desire to protect innocent individuals from harmful business practices, there are costs in terms of the resources they employ and opportunity costs in terms of benefits that might otherwise have been gained by the alternative use of these resources.

No law is effective unless resources are devoted to its enforcement. Where resources are provided through the public sector, e.g. the trading standards officers, costs have to be borne by taxation. Consumers are also taxpayers if only because most goods are subject to value added tax. Where there is self-regulation the immediate cost falls on producers, but this becomes a production cost which has to be met from revenues received from sales to consumers. Ultimately, therefore, all the costs of consumer protection are paid by consumers either through taxes or through the price paid for products.

Opportunity costs, though real, are notoriously difficult to define and measure because no one knows how the resources would otherwise have been employed. Clearly if business were to become subject to a mass of detailed regulations then an army of public sector employees would be necessary to interpret and enforce these regulations and these people would not be available for employment in the actual production of goods and other services. We might also expect that these conditions would lead business firms to employ skilled lawyers to find ways of evading the more restrictive regulations and of challenging official decisions. All this activity would be at the expense of producing other desired goods and services.

The Benefits of Consumer Protection

The main benefits of consumer protection lie in the reduction of costs and losses which would have been suffered by people as a result of harmful business practices. In 1989 it became apparent that failure to enforce adequate safety and health standards in chicken and egg production had resulted in some avoidable illnesses and deaths. Adequate consumer protection can eliminate, or much reduce, the costs of bad practices suffered by unfortunate individuals.

Consumer protection can also reduce costs to the community. If safety standards reduce death and injury then the community is relieved of the medical costs of repairing broken bodies and the welfare costs of mending shattered families and lives. Any measures to reduce the daily toll of road casualties would have obvious social benefits but would also provide economic benefits in reducing the need for police, legal and accident services.

The Balance of Costs and Benefits

It is difficult to produce a generally agreed balance sheet of costs and benefits because no one really knows what accidents and injuries have been prevented by consumer protection measures. It is possible, say, to measure trends in road accidents and to argue that any reduction is due to measures such as the compulsory wearing of seat-belts. On the other hand trends may also owe something to increased public awareness of the dangers of road travel, to improved vehicle design or to a reduction in the numbers of young people between the ages of 17 and 25!

It is probably reasonable to reject the claims made by extreme free-market economists that the market is always the best preserver of community interests because ultimately the consumer is always sovereign. There are many UK consumers who would testify that competitive markets did not protect them from injury or losses in areas as diverse as chicken and egg production, the supply of fitted kitchens, hearing aids, slimming foods, telephone chat lines, holiday time-shares and investment advice.

On the other hand there must clearly be limits to the resources which a community can be expected to provide to protect all its individuals from the consequences of their gullibility, ignorance, carelessness and sometimes plain greed. Economists can assist in the identification and measurement of costs and benefits but in the last resort decisions over the extent of consumer protection to provide and the main ways in which it should be provided are essentially political and must depend very much on the social and political conditions and attitudes of the time.

Discussion Questions

1 Choose one report of the Monopolies and Mergers Commission issued during the past five years. Identify the issues under investigation, the position as seen by the MMC and the Commission's recommendations. Were these recommendations accepted and put into effect by the Secretary of State? From your observation have business practices changed as a result of the MMC report?

2 Discuss the view that competitive markets are the most effective guarantees for consumer protection.

3 Outline and discuss the case for replacing UK law and institutions concerned with competition policy by European Community law and institutions.

4 'Self-regulation usually ensures that producer interests are preserved at the expense of those of the consumer. The only effective regulation of business practices is that carried out by bodies established by Parliament.' Discuss this view of the regulation of business practices.

5 Almost all restrictive trade practices are defended on the grounds that they are necessary to preserve standards of quality and to protect the public. Retail pharmacists, opticians, medical practitioners and barristers are among those who have pleaded this defence. Examine and discuss its validity as applied to at least one of these groups or to any other group of which you have up-to-date knowledge.

Suggestions for Further Reading

Two government Green (discussion) Papers provide an excellent foundation for much of the content of this chapter. They are:

Review of Monopolies and Mergers Policy, Cmnd 7198, HMSO 1978
Review of Restrictive Trade Practices Policy, Cmnd 7512, HMSO 1979

Monopolies, mergers and restrictive trades practices policies are discussed in:

Clarke, R., *Industrial Economics*, Blackwell, 1985

At the time of writing full details were still awaited of proposed legislation on the whole area of competition policy and you should examine the main elements in this legislation when available. The 1988 White Paper referred to in this chapter is *DTI – The Department for Enterprise*, CM 278.

The costs and benefits of consumer protection and public safety are examined in:

Old, J. L., 'Economics and Disasters', *Economics* **XXIII**, part 2, no. 98, Summer 1987.

11 Business Location and the Community

Influences on Locational Choice

One of the most important decisions a firm has to make at some stage of its development is where to locate its activities. The initial decision for a completely new firm is, of course, made when the firm starts life and for very small firms there may not be a great deal of choice. The owners will probably choose the first available and affordable location that is reasonably close to where they live. For larger firms or for firms which have become established and which are seeking to extend their business the question of choice is more open and those in control may be able to select from a number of viable options.

The question of choice between scarce economic resources – in this case land – is clearly of interest to economists who will wish to discover both what influences firms in the choices they make and what the effects of these choices are on the wider economic community. Even where firms are not able to exercise any significant degree of choice, economists are still interested and will wish to discover why certain activities are associated with certain areas and why firms in some areas survive and prosper when apparently similar firms, engaged in similar activities in other areas, fail to survive. It is not only economists who are concerned with these matters. Geographers too are concerned with these spatial aspects of economic activity and business location is a major part of studies in economic geography.

Business Location and Business Costs

Clearly cost must always be an important influence on choice of where to conduct business operations. If it is assumed that the sole objective of the firm is to maximise profits then cost is the dominant, if not the only, influence. Much of the work carried out by economists before around 1950 on this question appears to make the assumption that, where firms could exercise choice, they would do so on the basis of finding the least cost location, taking into account all purchasing, production, distribution and transport costs. Costs were also held to be mainly responsible for explaining why certain activities were more likely to be carried on in some areas rather than in others.

If we take this view then locational choice becomes little more than a fairly complex mathematical problem involving such issues as the relative costs of transporting materials and components to the place of manufacture and those of transporting and distributing the finished product to the market centres, the unit cost of labour resulting from net labour costs and labour productivity, land costs and local or regional costs. Theoretical models which only take some of these influences into consideration are defective and of little use in explaining or predicting the choices made by business organisations.

Another cost influence that has to be taken into account is the relationship between transport costs (for simplicity this term is used to include all transport and distribution costs) and the economies likely to be gained from large-scale production in a single plant. At this point you should make sure that you fully understand the term **minimum efficient size (or scale) of production (MES)** as outlined in Chapter 4. If the MES is low relative to the size of the market then we would expect transport costs to outweigh production economies at a relatively short distance from the point of production so that we would then expect to find the industry containing many plants throughout the product's market area. Whether these plants are controlled by many firms or by a much smaller number of firms raises other aspects of company growth not directly related to the locational issue. If, however, the MES is large relative to market size and if we expect the firm to be seeking to minimise costs in pursuit of profit maximisation then the whole market might be served by a very few, perhaps even one plant situated at the point of lowest final unit cost.

This relationship between unit transport and production costs will also affect the way in which suppliers respond to competition. If transport costs are relatively high then each supplier enjoys an important cost, and hence potential price, advantage within a certain area around each firm's point of production. Without a significant change in the technology of production and/or transport there may be many suppliers in the national or international market but the real degree of competition between them may be very little. In fact competition may take the form more of growing or aggressive firms seeking to take over suppliers in other areas – the pattern that has emerged in the brewing industry, for instance. If, on the other hand, production economies are relatively high we may find relatively few firms located close together at the point of lowest final unit cost but these either engaging in competitive rivalry, or tacitly or formally colluding to avoid the profit destroying consequences of continual market rivalry, or, perhaps something between these two extremes, a kind of market competition played according to tacitly understood rules, whereby there is rivalry over some issues such as new product development and advertising but there is no price competition and no aggressive attacks to secure each other's known major customers.

A further criticism of the locational theories that have sometimes appeared in economics studies is that they may be unduly concerned with present costs and present supply and market conditions and they appear to assume that these are not subject to change in the future. It must be remembered that locational choice is a form of business investment of the kind considered in Chapter 7. It was then stressed that investment involved looking into an uncertain future. Locational investment is no exception. A decision to move or

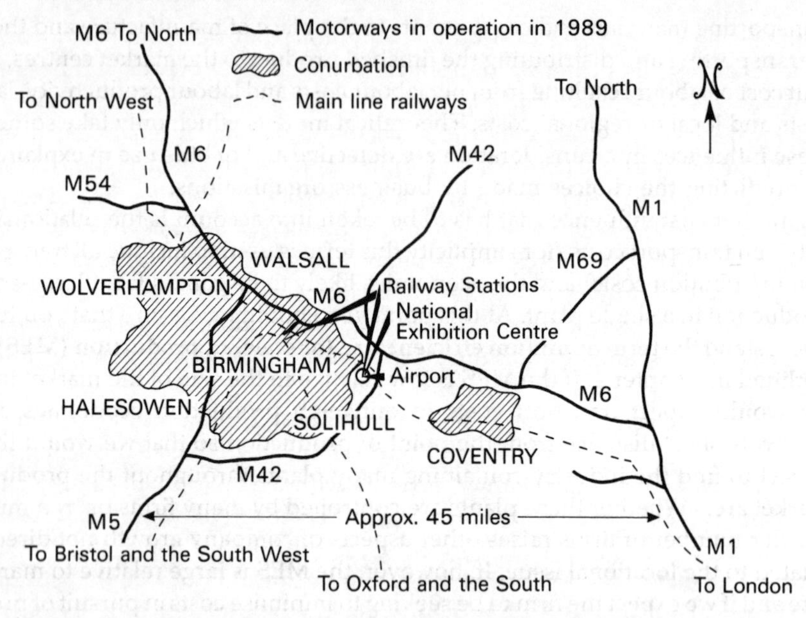

Fig. 11.1 Motorways, airport and railways of the West Midlands conurbation
The National Exhibition Centre is slightly to the east of the Birmingham International Airport. Birmingham International railway station is by the side of the airport and links Birmingham to the North and London.

to concentrate production at one locality rather than another commits the firm for a number of years in the future. Locations cannot be switched as readily as advertising budgets. Locational choices must take into account probable developments in future production and transport costs and in market conditions. Where possible they must minimise the risks of uncertainty. One way to do this is to allow for a degree of flexibility so that transport and distribution arrangements can be changed if conditions change. These help to explain the locational attractions of areas in the UK that are close to motorway access points, especially if these are also close to rail and air access points. Firms in these locations can quickly adapt to changing sources of supply, markets and transport conditions without themselves having to move. Figure 11.1 shows part of the English West Midlands region. Notice how the centre of the motorway network, a major railway station and an international airport are all close together. The attractions to business of this region are clear. You may be familiar with other areas with similar transport links.

Markets and Location

It has been argued that firms find it attractive to be located close to their major markets for reasons other than reducing transport costs. Close proximity to the market keeps decision-makers in close, personal touch with market trends and with customers. The ease of personal communication can stimulate ideas for product development and warn suppliers of the need for product modification. This can be particularly important for services, especially the financial and technical services which must be constantly adapting to changing market needs. Telephones and fax are no substitute for personal contact when it comes to stimulating ideas and responding to atmosphere. The benefits of being at the heart of a major market can outweight direct cost advantages of locations away from the major centres. The benefits of low production costs do not look very attractive if firms find that they get no warning of an impending decline in the market or of the emergence of damaging competition. Markets are dynamic and constantly changing and firms need to be aware of what is going on all the time.

However, given the possibilities of modern communications and the technology of information transfer, this does not mean that all the activities of the firm need to be at the heart of the market. Indeed it is not necessary for all the activities of a firm to be in one location anywhere. It is now possible for the various functions of the firm to be located in the areas which, **to the function**, offer the greatest total advantage. For example, most of the people with most influence on policy formation and for marketing may need to be at the heart of the major market area – often, in the UK, this still means central London. Manufacturing, however, may be more efficiently located in, say, the Midlands or outside the UK, while office administration may be carried out better in, say, East Anglia. These are just hypothetical illustrations of a tendency which appears to be emerging. Large commercial services, for example, are moving their routine administrative operations away from the high cost city centre areas but keeping small offices in those areas so that some key staff remain in constant touch with the heart of the market.

Behavioural Aspects of Locational Decision-making

So far this chapter has contained an implicit assumption that the firm seeks an optimal solution to the location problem but does so against a background of future uncertainty. In earlier chapters we have discussed the view that firms rarely seek to maximise anything but rather seek to **satisfice**, i.e. to achieve solutions to problems that are considered to be satisfactory to the main participants in the decision. One of the best developed models arising from this view is the behavioural theory of the firm as expounded by Cyert and March. This suggests that the firm does not engage in continuous search activity but only institutes search procedures when faced by a problem that poses a threat to the continued existence of the firm and which is not solved by applying its present procedures based on past experience. It then seeks the nearest **satisfactory** solution to the perceived problem.

If this model is applied to locational decision-making then the firm's current locational pattern is not kept under constant review but is accepted as given until a problem arises which cannot be solved by one of the remedies that has been successfully applied in the past. For example, suppose expanding sales make it imperative that the firm increases its production capacity, but that it is not possible to expand any of the existing production sites because, say, this is prevented by official planning restrictions. Consequently a search begins with the objective of providing the increased production capacity that the firm's expanding sales appear to require. A solution is likely, perhaps, to be sought along the lines of building new plant in an area approved by the government but which is as close as possible to one of the firm's existing plants. If cost conditions require a minimum efficient size of plant and if the amount of additional capacity is below this the firm may be forced to consider closing one or more existing plants to move to the new location. The more radical solutions will be considered only if simpler and 'closer' decisions are found to be unsatisfactory. The first satisfactory solution is adopted even if better solutions might have been discovered by a more extensive search.

Notice that as long as the firm's objectives are being achieved at a satisfactory level of attainment behavioural theory suggests that there will be no move towards changing existing procedures or patterns of behaviour. Change is brought about in response to a problem and is directed towards finding a satisfactory solution to that problem as it is perceived by the decision-makers. Applied to location policy this means that the firm will continue to operate from its present sites as long as these do not appear to pose a problem.

One of the consequences of growth by takeover, a feature of business activity for much of the period since the 1950s, is that firms acquire a pattern of production sites that they would not have planned if growth had been confined to internal sales and production expansion. A common benefit claimed by companies seeking to justify a proposed takeover is that increased size will give opportunities for rationalising activities and reducing average production costs. In practice, as was pointed out by the 1978 Green Paper on Monopolies and Mergers Policy,[1] increased concentration resulting from mergers and takeovers during the 1960s and 1970s was at firm rather than at plant level and before 1978 there had been very little change in the pattern of production as a result of merger activity. In fact there was not a great deal more change in the 1980s in response to the world depression of 1980–82 and to changed political and economic policies after 1979. This lends support to the view that radical business change results from the need to solve problems and not to any continuous search for optimum profit or minimum cost.

Business Location and the Government

This section is concerned with the situation in the United Kingdom and to the policies of UK governments but the problems and policies do have a wider application as most countries have regional economic problems of one kind or another.

[1] *A Review of Monopolies and Mergers Policy, Cmnd 7198, HMSO 1978.*

Reasons for Government Interest in Business Location

The chief reason for government interest in business location is the existence of regional inequalities in living standards and the social, and particularly the political, problems that these produce. There are many indicators of living standards but the one most commonly used, most widely understood and with probably the greatest potential for political embarrassment for the government of the day is the unemployment rate. Figure 11.2 shows some regional unemployment rates for selected years (1987, 1976 and 1967). Notice that in 1967 when unemployment was low in the more prosperous regions other regions were experiencing rates that were significantly higher and these were the ones that suffered most severely when unemployment was generally at a much higher level. In each of these years South East England had the lowest rate while, leaving aside Northern Ireland, the North of England suffered the highest or was very close to the highest. The differentials between the low and high areas narrowed a little between 1964 and 1967 but were widening again by 1987.

Regional inequality is usually a very long-term problem. The areas of the United Kingdom that were suffering the highest unemployment rates in the

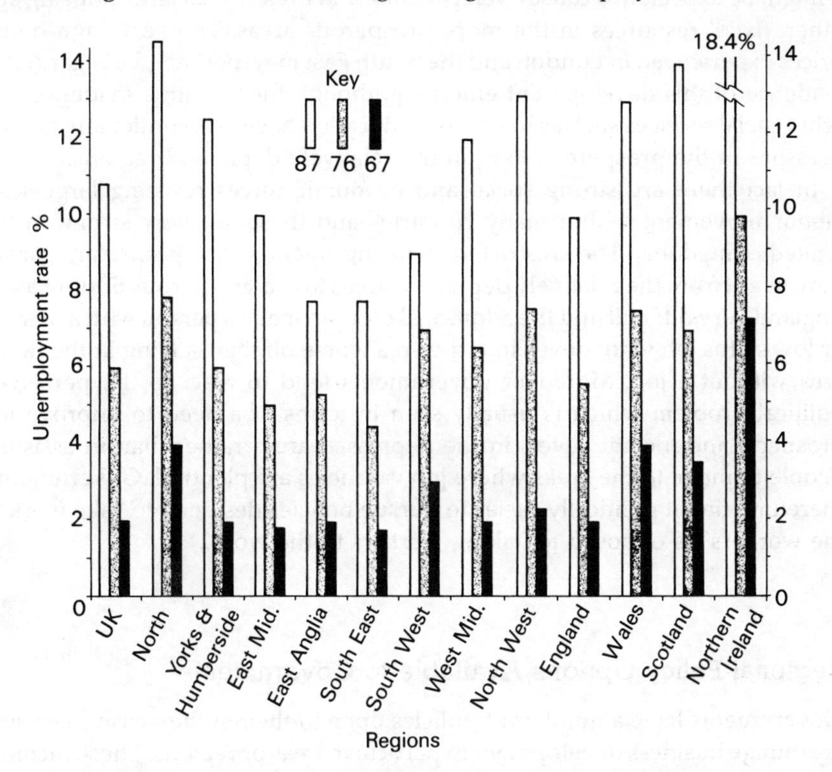

Fig. 11.2 Regional unemployment rates 1987, 1976, 1967
Note the consistency of relative levels of regional unemployment. Note, however, that the rates are not strictly comparable over these years because of changes in the way unemployment statistics are calculated.

second half of this century were very much the same areas that were identified by the Beveridge Report[1] as being the main problem areas of the 1930s.

This kind of long-term regional inequality is caused either by the absolute decline of formerly prosperous industries which had been heavily concentrated in particular regions, e.g. shipbuilding in Belfast, Clydeside and on the Tyne, and steel-making in Staffordshire and South Wales, and/or the relative decline of particular areas which appear to be unable to attract the newer economic activities with relatively high rates of economic growth. The two do tend to go together because once an area becomes associated with decline and neglect, and if it exhibits the visible signs of decaying firms, buildings and people, it tends to be shunned by those who wish to be associated with success and prosperity and by employers wishing to recruit the more enterprising and vigorous managers and skilled workers.

A regional imbalance represents an economic problem in that resources, especially unemployed labour, are being wasted. The younger and more enterprising of the people in the depressed regions are likely to move away thus depriving the area of just those people who might have helped to revive its fortunes. If this process were to continue over a long period on a large scale it might be expected to cause overcrowding and pressure on land, housing and other 'fixed' resources in the more prosperous areas. The very high house prices experienced in London and the South East may, perhaps, be regarded as evidence of this development emerging, though there is little evidence that other social services such as health and education have been under any greater pressure in the prosperous than in the relatively depressed regions.

In fact there are strong social and economic forces resisting large-scale labour movement within many countries and these are very strong in the United Kingdom. The restricted housing market, in particular, makes movement from the relatively depressed areas to the prosperous South East of England very difficult and the additional cost can make a person with a manual or low status job who moves into the area worse off than staying in the home area without a job. Moreover governments tend to react to the perceived political problem which is usually seen in terms of a need to improve job prospects and income levels in the depressed areas rather than in assisting people to move to the areas where job vacancies are plentiful. Governments, therefore, find it politically easier to pursue policies designed to 'take work to the workers' as opposed to 'taking workers to the work'.

Regional Policy Options Available to Governments

Governments have a number of policies open to them if they wish to try and encourage business development in particular areas or regions. These include: financial incentives; granting privileges; physical controls and setting an example with its own activities.

[1]Published in book form as Beveridge, *Full Employment in a Free Society*

Financial incentives

The government's aim is to reduce the cost of establishing or extending all or selected business activities in designated areas in the hope of attracting increased activity. It may channel the financial help direct to business firms or indirectly to local authorities which may then reduce certain local business costs or make available cheap resources such as land. Help targeted directly towards firms may be in the form of grants, usually for capital investment but sometimes towards the costs of employing, recruiting or training labour, or allowances that can be set against taxation, again usually made for expenditure on physical capital. In the UK considerable reliance was placed on financial incentives during the late 1960s and 1970s, but their scale has been much reduced in the 1980s although the types of economic activity qualifying for aid have been extended beyond the original emphasis on manufacturing. A significant amount of financial help for regional activity in the 1980s has come through the European Regional Fund. Although the central government in Britain has moved away from its earlier emphasis on financial assistance some local authorities have schemes for promoting local business and for stimulating new business activity. Indirect financial support, however, has been given to local authorities to assist them to make their areas more attractive and clear away the debris left by the old industrial system and generally to make their areas more attractive to modern firms and to skilled workers.

The period of active financial support for the regions in the UK was also a period when Keynesian economic policies were dominant. It was a feature of these policies at that time that great store was placed on the multiplying effect of additional, government inspired injections of expenditure. This concept was extended to include the notion of a **regional multiplier**, implying that government finance directed towards a region would also have a multiplying effect in that region. For reasons outlined later in this chapter this proved rather a false hope. A map showing the assisted areas applying in the second half of the 1980s is given in Fig. 11.3.

Privileges

The idea that firms operating in a particular area should enjoy exemptions from controls or costs that apply in other areas is not new. The most common exemption is from taxation but this, of course, would qualify as financial assistance. In the 1980s the UK government has applied the idea to the creation of **enterprise zones** where the main benefit has been intended to be release from most of the burden of planning controls combined with some relief from local taxation for a period. A further extension was made in the creation of a small number of **freeports** where firms were relieved of some import duties while goods were being processed. It has been argued that these would be much more effective if they followed the pattern of some foreign countries where freeports are also relieved of some other controls and laws, including some labour and employment protection laws but so far the UK government has not pursued this approach.

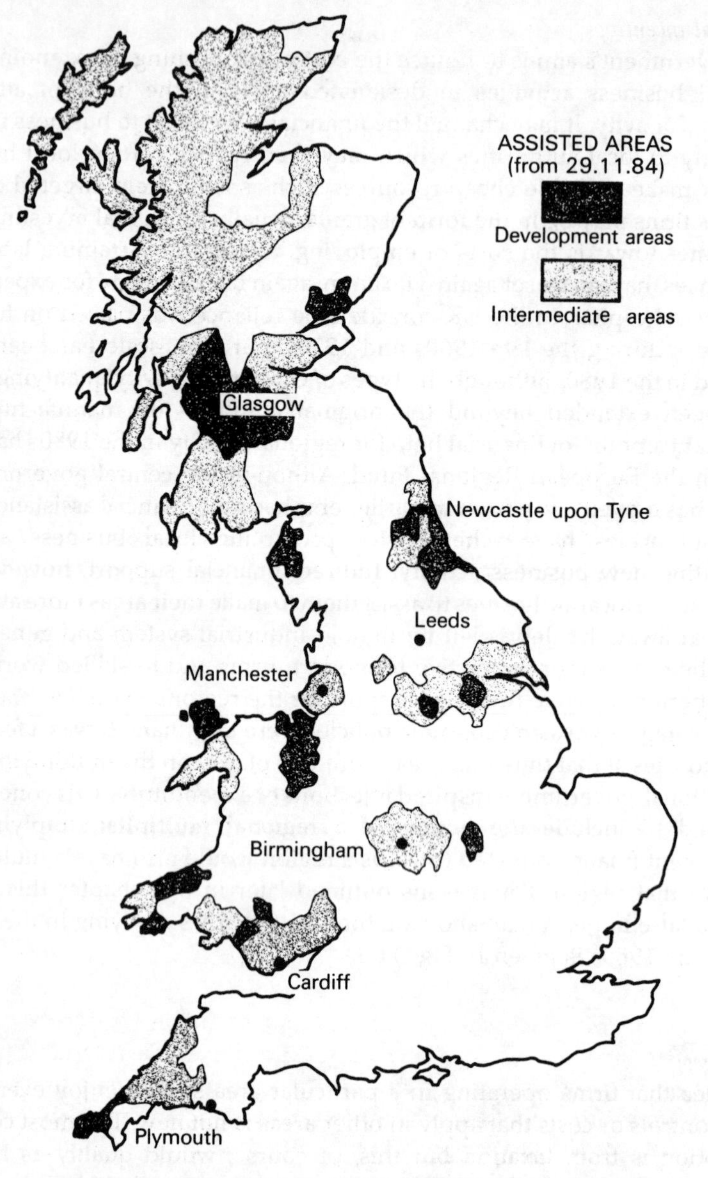

Fig. 11.3 Assisted areas in Great Britain (late 1980s)

Physical controls

A government can use its powers to attempt to coerce firms to locate in areas which they would not otherwise choose for themselves. In fact a government can only have a negative effect. It can prevent firms locating in areas of which it disapproves but it cannot force a firm to locate in a favoured area. The firm always has the option to refuse to expand or even to close down if it cannot operate in the area of its choice. International production sets further constraints to the power of government. A foreign firm considering, say, to open a factory in the United Kingdom may find itself under pressure to choose a site in an area it thinks unsuitable. Rather than submit to this pressure it may simply change its plans and build the factory in another country altogether. A UK firm may also have the option to extend its activities in other countries rather than accept direction which it dislikes.

However, physical controls were applied in the UK during the 1960s and 1970s and still persist to some extent. At one time firms had to obtain an Industrial Development Certificate (IDC) for any new building or extension to an existing building of 5000 square feet or more. IDCs were used to direct business expansion to areas that the government wished to assist. Obtaining a certificate was extremely difficult in London and the South East but very easy in the North West and North of England. These controls were gradually relaxed and were abolished altogether in the 1980s but there is still a degree of control exercised through the need to obtain local authority planning permission for all new buildings. Local authorities have to operate within guidelines established by the central government which is subject to the political pressures exercised by its supporters. Consequently the Conservative government of the 1980s resisted attempts to expand industry into the rural and semi-rural areas of the South and South East and continued to try and persuade firms to develop in the less favoured areas of high unemployment.

Setting an example

It has often been argued that governments wishing to influence business locational decisions could achieve more by setting an example of relocating more of its own operations in areas of high unemployment away from London. Recognising that this argument has some merit the UK government has done this to some extent. For example, public service pensions and motor vehicle driving licenses are administered from the North East of England and South Wales. However, exporting activities of this kind has only a limited effect while the centres where decisions are made remain in London. It can also lead to additional costs with personnel travelling frequently between regional centres and the capital for discussions, briefings and so on. An early exercise in regionalising activities resulted in a number of Royal Naval establishments moving from London to Bath and this was later found to cause a great deal of expensive travelling, problems of communications and administrative delays.

Effects of Regional Controls

Problems of Regional Policies

A fundamental assumption underlying much UK government regional location policy in the 1960s and 1970s was that growth in some prosperous regions could be diverted to the areas of relatively high unemployment to produce a more even rate of national development. It was hoped that these policies would help both to close the gaps in regional unemployment rates and to relax the inflationary pressures in the more prosperous regions. By the end of the 1970s these hopes had vanished in the midst of high and accelerating inflation and unemployment in all areas. Although it would be foolish to blame regional policies for these economic problems it is probable that they helped to aggravate rather than to check them. Moreover, a set of policies designed to smooth out growth became untenable once economic growth had ceased and moved into depression. The policies could also be criticised on a number of grounds.

1 **They favoured branch development by large firms** A high proportion of the financial assistance available for regional development was taken up by large firms which were more adept at coping with officialdom with its reliance on forms and formalities and on producing the material most likely to please civil servants. At the same time few firms moved their main activities to the assisted regions. They generally located, or relocated, subsidiary operations. If these were only just viable with government financial support they could fail to survive when the period of support was over. Large firms simply closed subsidiary operations if these did not meet profit targets and this could be more serious to the region than if they had never come in the first place.
2 **The regional multiplier rarely materialised** The belief that an injection of government financial assistance would create increased economic activity throughout the region foundered because much of the finance was, in fact, spent outside the region, often outside the country. Machines bought with investment grants or taxation allowances were frequently imported and helped to generate employment in countries outside the UK. Branch development also had a limited impact on the regions because the branches tended to buy few supplies locally. Specialised company purchasing departments made bulk purchases for the company as a whole. This applied over a very wide range of materials from paper clips to motor vehicles. At the same time the branches had to contribute profits and employee pension contributions which drew money out of the regions. Wages of workers were often the only significant benefit gained by the local area.
3 **Financial assistance reduced the cost of foreign entry** This might be considered beneficial because it brings foreign capital into the country and creates new employment opportunities. At the same time, however, the old style financial assistance available in designated regions could be claimed even if the newly arrived foreign firm proposed to set up in competition with established home industries in other regions. The financial assistance made it easier for the newcomer to compete on favourable terms. If the competition was successful the 'losing' domestic company would close, often with the loss of more jobs than had been created by the imported foreign company.
4 **Financial assistance helped to reduce jobs nationally** In some cases firms used the assistance available to establish new factories in assisted areas

using labour saving technology so that they could close down older plants. The number of jobs lost from the old factory was usually far higher than the number created in the assisted region.

5 **Too much emphasis on manufacturing** A major criticism of UK policies in the 1960s and 1970s was their emphasis on manufacturing, then believed to be the most important source of employment and the main stimulator of economic activity. This was in a period when manufacturing was becoming increasingly capital intensive so that change was leading to employment losses in manufacturing as a whole. Services were ignored for some years even though they were labour intensive and there was a general movement towards increased activity in the service industries. This bias in favour of manufacturing was dropped by the national government in the 1980s but still persisted in some local areas which were slow to appreciate the nature of the structural changes taking place in the UK economy.

6 **Assisted areas were often too wide** It was only towards the end of the 1970s that UK regional policies began to recognise that within assisted regions there could be pockets of prosperity and low unemployment while within the non-assisted, growth areas there could also be pockets of high unemployment. It is possible that the inner-city blight of cities such as London and Birmingham may have been aggravated by resistance to industrial development in these areas while new developments in the assisted regions were likely to be attracted to those localities which were already showing that they possessed attractions for business development.

7 **The creation of grey areas** If an area is granted assisted status with the intention of attracting to it business development from other areas it is probable that there will be a detrimental effect on the localities just outside the assisted region. This was recognised in the 1970s and many of these, then known as intermediate areas, were granted limited assistance. The logical result of this extension is that eventually the whole country gains the right to some kind of help and the whole problem starts again. Before this happens, of course, the escalating cost of aid forces the government to call a halt or reverse the process. In the 1970s rising unemployment brought the West Midlands to the position which would have qualified for support some years earlier but this was resisted for some time by a government worried by rising aid costs.

8 **Preservation of dying industries** Because aid was directed towards areas where industries were declining and also because of the emphasis on manufacturing much financial assistance went to firms and industries which might have been better left to face the realities of changed world markets and technology. These realities had to be faced eventually and jobs were lost in the more difficult economic climate of the 1980s instead of earlier. The belief that governments would prefer to give large amounts of regional financial aid rather than face the political problems of unemployment may well have delayed essential changes in the older manufacturing sectors.

Re-examination of the Case for Regional Assistance

In view of the formidable list of problems associated with regional help based on financial subsidy it seems legitimate to question whether or not there is a real economic case for regional aid. By the mid 1980s the UK government appeared to have reached the conclusion that the economic case was very weak but that there was a social and political case for helping those regions with the highest levels of unemployment and that this was strong enough for an economic price to be paid. The rather special circumstances of the European Regional Fund, seen as a device to reduce the net cost of the UK's membership of the European Community, also helped to keep alive the tradition of financial support for job creating developments in the areas of relative economic decline.

However, the UK government was also determined to prevent the escalation of financial support which had taken place in the 1970s and direct financial assistance was tied more closely to evidence of genuine new job creation in developments that would survive when support was removed. The problem with discretionary, selective support is that it gives considerable powers to state officials and their political masters who do not always have to justify publicly their use of these powers. The grounds on which one application for help may be refused and another accepted may seem rather obscure to outside observers. The difference may lie more in political skill and influence than on economic worth. On the other hand it is difficult to argue that regional development is best left to entirely unregulated economic markets when basic production factors such as land and labour are clearly not mobile and subject to important non-economic influences. The whole issue of regional economic development raises issues which go beyond pure economics and is always likely to produce difficult problems for national governments.

The Encouragement of Co-operation

In the light of the criticisms and re-examinations of former efforts to provide help for the regions the more recent policies of government have moved away from providing direct **financial** assistance towards using its influence to encourage greater co-operation between the agencies of government and the owners of private capital. The function of government is to stimulate activity, interest and co-operation among organisations in both the public and private sectors and to help to clear a way through the mass of bureaucratic regulations that tend to clog the normal planning processes. Private sector organisations are encouraged to find cost-effective and, in the long run, profitable ways to turn run-down or declining areas into places where economic growth can re-commence and provide new hope for increased work opportunities and rising living standards.

One example of this process has been the **Urban Programme** through which, it was hoped, local authorities responsible for inner-city areas would co-operate with commercial enterprise. Some successes have been achieved but in reality little extra funding has been put into the programme, which has largely involved redirecting existing activities and finance. There has also been disappointment with the failure of some local authorities to break free from old, long established attitudes and suspicions so that central government has experimented with attempts to work through newer organisations set up specifically to bring new ideas and methods to long standing problems.

An important move in this direction has been the creation of **Urban Development Corporations** under powers gained by the Local Government and Land Act 1980. By the end of the 1980s corporations had been set up in Merseyside, the London Docklands and the English West Midlands Black Country. They have been set up with deliberately small staffs and rely on consultants and contractors but they do have significant financial resources with which to purchase and regenerate land and improve local facilities, such as roads, to make areas capable of attracting private business. In many ways they are intended to combine the various activities referred to in earlier sections, i.e. those of providing finance, encouraging private activities and smoothing the planning process.

Considerable development has taken place in the London Docklands and few would doubt that the character of the area is changing and that it has been made capable of generating self-sustaining growth. However, the cost to the taxpayer has been considerable – in the long tradition of costly regional aid – and some observers would argue that it has contributed to inflationary pressures in the London and South Eastern region. It may even have added to these pressures over a wider area as building workers and contractors have been attracted from the South, East and Midlands.

The fundamental problem seems still unresolved. This is how to find a way of encouraging regeneration in declining areas without intensifying the inflationary pressures on wage and housing costs and skill shortages in the rest of the country, and without involving the central government (i.e. taxpayers) in massive expenditure.

Regions and Multinational Companies

The growth of multinational companies over the past thirty or more years has changed the nature of locational decision-making for these companies and this has also had considerable implications for national governments. Earlier it was pointed out that companies which could not locate in the region they desired were quite likely to decide to move to another country. They may respond in this way to any other local feature that they feel restricts their managerial freedom. For example, failure to obtain desired trade union assurances appeared to convince the Ford Motor Company that they should not locate an important new plant in the UK but build it elsewhere in Europe.

This freedom to locate in any chosen country – or at least to choose between a number of possible countries – gives considerable power to the larger multinational company which is not reliant on a particular source of raw materials but can transfer capital and highly skilled labour between countries. In a period of economic depression or of international economic competition it becomes inevitable that countries and regions within those countries compete with each other for the capital investment and job creating powers of companies from the high growth, successful economies. In many cases today this tends to mean Japan. Even politicians in the highest offices and heads of state, including members of the UK royal family, are turned into salespeople pressing for the favours of those with capital to invest and freedom to invest it in the location of their choice. There are clear dangers in this. If countries enter into this version of the 'trade war' their taxpayers will be forced into paying an increasing price for the favours of the most powerful business companies which may effectively come to dominate weaker governments and business imperialism come to replace the military empires of the past. National economic development becomes distorted to fit the needs of production and trade in the more highly developed countries.

In addition to these economic dangers there are clear social and political dangers when foreign organisations are thought to be developing too great an influence on national life and culture. Nevertheless world economic patterns and structures are constantly shifting and individual countries which try to stand aside from these changes face the prospect of declining economies and living standards – with equally dangerous social and political implications. This is a subject which you should continue to observe for yourself and to consider in the light of current trends and developments. You should, for example, be alert for any developments that appear to follow from the further freeing of trade between the members of the European Community in 1992.

Discussion Questions

1. Suggest reasons for the apparent geographical immobility of labour in the second half of the twentieth century in the UK. In what ways could the government reduce that immobility?
2. Towards the end of 1987 it was reported that the UK government was unlikely to make any further significant extensions to its early development of **enterprise zones**. Suggest reasons for the government's apparent reluctance to extend this experiment in regional aid.
3. Many of the regions of the United Kingdom which were areas of high unemployment in the 1930s were still suffering higher than average unemployment in the 1980s. Suggest reasons for this.
4. One of the criticisms of the UK government's regional policies in the 1960s and 1970s was that most of the financial assistance was taken up by large firms with very little going to small firms. Suggest reasons for this imbalance.
5. Does the growing importance of multinational enterprise make it impossible for any one country to operate a regional policy?

Suggestions for Further Reading

A number of managerial economics texts review the issue of business location and the part played by government policies in seeking to influence locational decisions. One of these is:

Reekie, W. D. and Crook, J. N., *Managerial Economics*, Philip Allan, 1982

A useful book combining modern theory and practical observation is:

Keeble, D., *Industrial Location and Planning in the United Kingdom*, Methuen, 1976

12

The State as Producer

The Need for a Public Sector

In every country in the world, whatever its politics, there are some economic and business activities that are carried out by agencies of government. These cover an enormous range of enterprises, from ambulances and banks to zoos. Indeed it is very difficult to think of an activity which at some time or other, or in some place or other, has not been carried out by government.

However, it is also true to say that there are very few activities – and this includes the police, fire brigades and armed services – which have not been provided somewhere, sometime, by private enterprise. In many parts of the world at the present time activities are being shifted from public to private enterprise in the process that has become known as **privatisation**.

In this chapter, therefore, we shall look at:

1 The rationale for public enterprise, i.e. the reasons for having activities run by government rather than by private enterprise and what is expected from this.
2 The objectives set for public enterprise.
3 The performance of public enterprise in the UK and how this matches up to the objectives it has been set.
4 Privatisation in the UK and other countries: what it actually means and what the effects have been.

Why Have Public Enterprise?

There is no simple, single reason why governments run economic activities. It is important to remember this, as we cannot assess how efficient an enterprise is unless we know what it is trying to do. To illustrate you can imagine that we are trying to decide which is more efficient, a Mini car or a Grand Prix racing car. We could not do this unless we knew whether we were to measure efficiency in terms of fuel consumption or speed.

The most important reasons for public enterprise are likely to be:

1 **Political motives** There may be a political preference for public rather than private enterprise. In some countries this might extend to most kinds

of activity, perhaps because of a particular political or economic ideology. In others it might cover just a few activities, such as defence or the provision of old age pensions, motivated by non-economic concepts such as 'equity'.

2 **Natural monopolies** It might be felt that there was no way that an industry could be organised on the lines of competition between private firms. For example, it may not make much sense to have two railway lines between the same towns. If so, the government may face a choice between leaving the railway in private hands but subject to all manner of regulations to avoid abuse of monopoly power, or to run the railways itself.

3 **Public goods arguments** Private enterprise will provide goods and services to people as long as customers not only want them but are prepared to pay for them. But there may be things which they want but are reluctant to pay for as individuals. For example, it is difficult to see why an individual should be prepared to pay for street lighting. One could simply wait for someone else to pay and then reap the benefits oneself. It is impossible to restrict the benefits of street lighting to oneself and exclude others. Everybody would end up waiting for everybody else to pay. A similar argument, for instance, could be applied to defence, policing and environmental health.

4 **Other shortcomings of markets** As we have just noted, private enterprise can only provide goods and services to people if they are prepared and **able** to pay for them. Governments may, therefore, decide to provide higher levels of unemployment insurance, health care, bus or other services than people could afford to provide for themselves. This might simply reflect a sense of social justice but it might also reflect other practical considerations. For example, if parents are poor it is difficult to see how children can make arrangements to pay for their own education even if this were likely to lead to their earning higher incomes later in life. Many governments – one of the earliest and best examples being Germany in the nineteenth century – have run public education programmes in the belief that an educated workforce will mean, in due course, a richer country.

5 **Externalities** If a commuter decides to take the train to work instead of travelling by private car, this decision will be based upon the costs and benefits to him or herself that are felt to be derived from each mode of transport. The individual can compare the cost of petrol with the rail fare, the relative speeds of each, the relative comfort of travel and so on. Paradoxically, if enough people decide to travel by train it may become more attractive for others to travel by private car. The fewer the cars on the roads, the less the congestion and the speedier the journey times.

Here we can say that a decision to travel by train has conveyed a **positive externality** to others. Their benefits have increased or their costs have been reduced. Perhaps you can think of other externalities arising out of this case. A government might wish to encourage the consumption of goods and services which give rise to positive externalities. It might also want to regulate and control the consumption of things that bring **negative**

externalities, i.e. costs imposed on other people. Examples could include traffic or factory pollution.

6 **Support for other economic policies** Governments might feel that their economic policies in respect of such matters as employment, regional development or economic growth might only be possible if the government is in a position to control, for example, the investment or production programmes of particular industries. The banking system, say, might be state controlled in order to regulate the pattern of lending. In some developing countries certain key industries such as the steel industry in Brazil, were developed in the public, state controlled, sector after they had failed as privately owned businesses.

It is worth noting that there may well be instances where activities are in the public sector for reasons which are historical and little to do with present day conditions. For example, in a number of former colonies some state enterprises are the descendents of imperial monopolies and trading organisations established in colonial days. In the UK, Rolls Royce (1971) was nationalised to prevent the financial collapse of the old privately owned company.

No list of reasons for public enterprise can be complete because there are particular circumstances surrounding individual cases in different countries. For instance, in various countries the salt, match and tobacco industries have been state controlled. Often this has been to use their profits as a source of revenue for government.

The reasons listed in this chapter are often presented as straightforward arguments in favour of the state running a particular activity. However, in view of the current interest in privatisation it is worth noting that these arguments, even if they are accepted at face value, do not make a complete case for the **public supply** and certainly not for a **monopoly** public supply of a commodity. Sometimes they can be viewed rather as a case for **public demand**. To return to the example of street lighting, we argued that, left to themselves, people were unlikely to provide this benefit through normal commercial markets. On the other hand, were the state to provide sufficient demand and the resources to pay for the service then the actual provision of the lighting could easily be provided by private contractors. This kind of thinking has led to the **privatisation** or **contracting out** of refuse collection, school meals and other services. General practitioner doctors in the UK are not employed or 'supplied' by the government although the majority provide the medical services for which the demand is mostly financed through the agency of the state.

State intervention in the supply of and demand for a commodity can thus take a number of forms. Table 12.1 sets out some of the activities in which the UK government is involved. In some cases the state is the sole or the dominant supplier. In others it supplies a product or service in competition with private suppliers, while in other cases the supply is largely in private hands. On the demand side the demand is either **collective** (determined by the

Table 12.1 Differing forms of state involvement in UK industry

Demand and supply (actual and projected in 1989)

	Demand	
Supply	*Public (collective)*	*Private*
Public monopoly or state-owned dominant supplier	Roads Education Defence Police	Railways Coal Letter post
Public in competition with private suppliers	Defence equipment Building (direct works departments)	Parcel post Shipbuilding
Private subject to regulation	General practitioner medical services	Gas Telecommunications Electricity supply Water supply and sewerage
Private	Education equipment Health service drugs	

state) or private, where the demand comes from private individuals but the government is concerned with some aspects of the market. This concern may be expressed through some form of market regulation over aspects such as prices or quality and range of services. Privatisation of some industries has sometimes been accompanied by the setting up of regulatory and supervisory bodies such as OFGAS for the gas industry and OFTEL, for telecommunications.

The Public Sector in the United Kingdom

The term **public sector** may be defined in very general terms as that part of the economy where the rights of ownership and overall control of institutions and organisations are vested in the political institutions of the state or with agencies directly responsible to these institutions. These agencies are, in turn, held to be acting on behalf of the community as a whole in accordance with authority derived from the elected representatives of the people to which they are ultimately answerable.

In the UK in 1986 the public (state controlled) sector accounted for around 30 per cent of all economic activity. Some of these activities, such as the armed forces and posts, had been state run, as either monopolies or otherwise, for very many years. Others are of much more recent origin. These include the industries nationalised by the post-war Labour government in the 1940s. It is only relatively recently, however, that there have been serious attempts to identify why particular activities are in the public rather than the private sector, and then to relate these reasons to the structure of these concerns, i.e. how they are organised and run and their declared objectives.

Note
It is only fair to point out that the way this is put rather implies that unless there is a good reason for an activity being publicly run it should be left to the private sector. This rather presupposes a particular political or economic view of the world. It is perfectly possible to make out a different, say Marxist, case that the natural place for most activities is in the public sector unless it can be demonstrated otherwise.

Structure of Public Enterprise

In the UK how public enterprise is organised tends to depend upon whether its principal objectives are commercial or non-commercial. In the Health Service, for example, the major objectives are presumably the care of the sick and the prevention of disease, rather than to sell medical services at a profit. On the other hand, the activities of the electricity industry are largely commercial, producing a product and selling it to private customers at a market price. The usual argument for state ownership in this case is that of the existence of a natural monopoly.

Where non-commercial objectives are important crucial decisions concerning the use and direction of resources are largely political in nature. Examples of such decisions would include the allocation of resources to the care of old people or to preventing an epidemic of a fatal disease (Health Service); the establishment of a national curriculum for schools (Education Service); or the replacement of a nuclear deterrent (National Defence). People expect politicians to take these decisions and to be answerable for them. These activities are, therefore, structured so that theoretically in all matters – though, in practice, in the most important matters – politicians at central or local government level are responsible for, and answerable for, the operation of the service. For example, in 1986, a number of local authorities introduced or considered the introduction of a new system of household refuse collection which involved the replacement of conventional dustbins with much larger mobile bins which householders were expected to move to the roadside for emptying. Complaints about these changes were considered by local councillors, not simply by managers of the refuse service. Contrast the position (before privatisation) over complaints about electricity supply which are the responsibility of managers of the Electricity Boards and not of the Secretary of State for Energy nor his Departmental civil servants.

It was felt that in the case of the more **commercial** activities such as electricity, the railways, coal or the previously publicly owned gas or telephone concerns, continual political supervision of, or interference in, their operations and decisions would seriously damage their ability to operate commercially and efficiently. For that reason, when nationalised, they tended to be established as **public corporations**, where government ministers appointed the chairmen and members of their Boards and exercised very general supervisory powers, but, in theory, left all operating matters and many matters of policy to the directors and managers of the corporations. The directors and managers were to be left free to operate within the broad guidelines laid down by the politicians. In many ways the position of the government could be seen as being analogous to that of the shareholders of a large public limited company. Shareholders have the right to appoint directors and to challenge policy and overall performance at the annual general meeting but they have no rights to interfere in the day-to-day management of the enterprise.

In recent years, this relationship has been underlined by the transformation of several public corporations into actual public limited companies (PLCs), although this has usually been a preamble to privatisation – the transfer of formal ownership to private shareholders. The best known examples include gas, telecommunications and British Airways. It is difficult to assess the relative effectiveness of the public corporation and the public limited company as structures for the operation of major enterprises.

Objectives of Public Enterprise

We noted earlier that you cannot assess the performance of anything, be it a light bulb, a motor car or a business, unless you know what it is trying to do. The first purpose of an objective, therefore, is to help us to assess performance. In addition, objectives serve an equally important function in business, to help people to **make decisions**. Whether or not a power station should be built, rail fares increased or a coal mine closed will depend upon what the electricity industry, railway or coal industry are trying to do and the objectives and guidelines they have been given.

You may have noticed that these examples are taken from present or former 'commercial' public enterprise. There have been a number of guidelines given to public corporations over the years. These began with the original Acts under which they were nationalised. They continued with increasing attempts to be explicit with a series of White (Government Policy Declaration) Papers.

The White Paper of 1961 focused on financial targets. That issued in 1967 detailed policies for pricing and the appraisal of capital investment, and the White Paper of 1978 switched emphasis to the financial target and a requirement that each industry should achieve a specified **real rate** of financial return on the resources invested in it. The real rate is the rate achieved after allowing for price increases caused by inflation.

Objectives for the non-commercial sector have rarely been explicit. This is not to say that tests of efficiency cannot be applied. For example, given that the objectives of the Health Service include the 'saving of lives', medical opinion may be agreed that a certain number of tests and re-tests are necessary in the diagnosis of cancer. Each successive test would tend to correct some previously false diagnosis of the presence or absence of the disease. However, one estimate of the cost of such procedures indicated that the marginal cost per life saved by having as many as six tests could be more than £30 million.

You will recall from previous chapters that, in theory, faced with a number of different ways of spending a sum of money, e.g. on resources, investments or advertising, one should distribute spending so that an equal marginal benefit is gained from each at the same marginal cost. Sometimes in commercial life it may be impractical to apply this rule but here is a case in a non-commercial activity where its application presents few difficulties. It is very unlikely that £30 million spent in other parts of the Health Service would not save more than one life!

This is the kind of logic which underlies at least some of the demands for **value for money** which are heard from those critics of the public services who are genuinely anxious to increase the efficiency with which resources are used in the public sector. Unfortunately analysis of this type is often resisted on the grounds that, 'You cannot put a value on human life', or 'No cost is too great to . . . (achieve the particular benefit such as better education, pension, motorway network, desired by the speaker)'. The result is that there is often an enormous disparity in the amounts of money spent 'for the good of the community' on different parts of the public services.

Economic and Commercial Efficiency

We have just seen a concept of efficiency which is rather different from the usual commercial criterion of **profitability**. For market-orientated concerns profitability is at least a good starting point as an objective as profits are simply the difference between revenues and costs. Success in making profits reflects efficiency both in providing customers with something they want to buy, and in keeping down costs and in avoiding waste.

There are a number of reasons why profitability, at least on its own, will not serve as an objective for state run concerns. These relate to the reasons for public enterprise outlined in the first part of this chapter.

1 Many state operations, especially the non-commercial ones such as those providing education, policing or medical care, receive very little revenue from customers paying directly for their services.
2 Even with the 'commercial' or market orientated state enterprises which actually do sell their product to customers, there are important natural monopoly and externality considerations. If enterprises such as the Post Office were fully to exercise their monopoly power there is little doubt that they could increase their profits by raising prices. However, you will recall from Chapter 10 that a major objection to the exercise of market power is that it effectively wastes resources and leads to higher profits at the expense of economic inefficiency. The diversion of commuter traffic from roads to railways is believed to give rise to valuable positive externalities in terms of savings on congestion costs, road maintenance and so on. Consequently British Rail receives a specific subsidy to enable it to run services at fares

sufficiently low to encourage commuter traffic. Here the important consideration is the saving of social cost. This does not appear in the profit calculations of British Rail.

The wider economic test of efficiency, therefore, is whether specific desired aims are being met at the lowest costs including both private and social costs.

We shall shortly turn our attention to the specific objectives and criteria that have been applied to UK nationalised industries in the light of this concept of economic efficiency. In the case of preventive health care we have already noted how the concept can be applied in the non-commercial sector, though with some problems of application. We now have to recognise that there are further problems some of which may be insuperable.

For instance, if no wide consensus exists as to the purpose of a service, economic efficiency tests have only a limited application. Is, say, the efficiency of a school to be measured in terms of the number of candidates for higher education it produces, the overall level of examination passes it achieves or the quality of 'general education for life' it provides? How does one measure 'education for life'?

Even if objectives are widely agreed success in achieving one can lead to apparent failure to achieve others. The more types of ailment that can be treated by the Health Service the more people will need treatment and the longer will be the waiting lists for treatment. If a police force puts more effort into policing 'on the beat' more crimes are likely to be reported with the result that a crime wave seems to have been started while crime detection rates (on which some police forces are judged) appear to be falling.

Planners for these activities and the politicians responsible for making decisions about the allocation of resources to them need to be aware of and to take account of these seeming paradoxes. Nevertheless there appears to be no easy way to establish objectives for many public services nor of measuring their efficiency without ambiguity.

The Objectives of Nationalised Industries

Turning to nationalised industries which in the UK broadly consist of state enterprises with a commercial orientation, we have already noted that a series of policy statements have set out criteria and objectives. The main areas covered by these policies are: prices, investment and finance.

Pricing

The 1967 White Paper put the emphasis in pricing on 'relating prices to marginal costs', a practice also known as 'marginal cost pricing'. The argument for this is that the consumer should receive a commodity as long as he is prepared to pay the extra cost that is incurred in producing and supplying it to him or her. If the cost of production and supply is greater than the price the consumer is prepared to pay then the commodity should not be supplied. The marginal cost in this analysis should strictly be the long-term marginal costs. Consumers should also contribute to the cost of the capital equipment that has to be built and maintained if the commodity is to be produced.

An example of this can be seen in comparing day-time and off-peak (Economy 7) electricity prices. During the times of heaviest electricity consumption less efficient power stations have to be brought into use so that the marginal cost of electricity rises. At off-peak times only the most efficient hydro, nuclear and low-cost conventional fuel stations need to be used so that at these times the marginal costs are reduced.

An important corollory of this rule is that there should be no **cross-subsidisation** of customers. If, for example, a single uniform tariff were charged for electricity, night-time users would be paying above marginal cost and contributing to the costs of supplying electricity to peak-time users.

Although marginal cost pricing remains the theoretical basis for nationalised industry pricing more attention in practice is given today to other objectives. Moreover, while cross-subsidisation is also officially discouraged there are clear examples where it occurs, for instance in flat-rate postal charges which do not distinguish between local and long distance letters.

Investment

Since 1967 the nationalised industries have been supposed to have adopted discounted cash flow (DCF) methods of the type outlined in Chapter 7 for the appraisal of individual projects. In addition, every nationalised industry has been supposed to have used the same test discount rate in evaluating projects. This is to avoid nonsensical misallocations of public investment of the type that would arise if, say, the Post Office were to use a test discount rate of 10 per cent and British Rail 5 per cent. A projected parcels depot might appear worthwhile at 5 per cent but not at 10 per cent. Whether or not it were built would then depend on whether it was the responsibility of the Post Office or British Rail and not whether it represented an efficient use of investment funds.

In recent years a more important criterion has been whether broad programmes of investment – not individual projects – will earn a real rate of return (RRR) on the new investment of at least 5 per cent. This is intended to reflect the typical returns on investment, after allowing for price inflation, in the private sector. In reality it is a little on the high side compared with private industry in similar activities. This suggests that projects that might have been undertaken by private enterprise may have been turned down by public enterprise. In addition the imposition of a single RRR on all nationalised industries does not distinguish between the different degrees of risk in different industries.

A further point to note is that, unlike private enterprise and state enterprises in some other countries, nationalised industries in the UK have not had a free hand in choosing investment projects in that they do not have freedom to diversify into new products. They are discouraged from doing so out of the fear of 'back door nationalisation'. For example, the National Coal Board (now British Coal) was prevented by the government from using spare computer capacity to run a travel agency. When still a public corporation, British Gas was the major innovator in developing the on-shore oil field at Wytch Farm, only to see this sold off into the private sector as an inappropriate area for its activities.

Finance

There are, in theory, three sources of finance for new projects open to nationalised industries. These are:

1 **The capital market**, particularly for finance raised in the form of long-term borrowing.
2 **The government**, either in the form of loans or equity capital on which a return may be paid if profits are made.
3 **Retained surpluses**, the excess of revenues remaining when all costs have been met.

In reality successive governments have blocked or restricted the access of nationalised industries to the capital market for a variety of reasons.

1 Nationalised industries may be at an unfair advantage compared with private borrowers. However unprofitable and inefficient a public corporation may appear, the risk of default on a loan is effectively nil as there is no instance where the government has allowed a nationalised industry to go bankrupt. Ways in which nationalised industries could raise dividend paying risk capital rather than loans with a guaranteed rate of interest were explored but abandoned in favour of privatisation.
2 Public enterprise borrowing is viewed by some economists as forming part of the Public Sector Borrowing Requirement (PSBR). According to the 'monetarist' school of economics which influenced the UK government economic policy in the early 1980s, the control and reduction of the PSBR is crucial to the control of inflation. This resulted in the subordination of public enterprise finance to this wider consideration.

Most finance, therefore, has come directly from the government although, because governments may prefer to use funds to reduce the PSBR or taxation, the public enterprises may be denied finance for wider economic policy reasons. In addition, there is an unfortunately political and popular tendency to see any money advanced to public enterprise by the state as a 'subsidy' despite the fact that private enterprises, especially those in capital intensive industries, also rely on outside finance from the capital market for about half of their financial requirements.

The emphasis in recent years, therefore, switched to self-finance through earned surpluses. The Conservative government of the early 1980s had an eventual target of complete self-financing by these industries and, before privatisation, British Gas had already achieved this target. It was able to meet all its own capital requirements and still pay a surplus to the government.

A policy of External Financing Limits (cash limits) has been developed. This indicates to each enterprise the absolute limit of funds that will be available from outside financing, whether to cover investment or any other purpose –

such as to meet the cost of a pay rise. We can see how a number of objectives may be served by this. For example, productivity gains are encouraged in so far as these reduce costs and thus increase the total of retained surpluses plus external financing available to the industry. Discipline is placed upon pay increases. Higher pay may either have to be paid for in job losses immediately or in the loss of investment programmes and thus a reduction in jobs in the long run. The limits are thus intended to reinforce the government's objectives in reducing the PSBR.

However, we can see that a cash limit system can also mean that an identical project might be undertaken by an enterprise operating inside its cash limit but rejected by another which is up against the cash limit constraint. This does not make for the best use of public funds.

The Current Framework of Objectives and Controls

These take the following forms:

1 All new programmes in nationalised industries should meet the Real Rate of Return (RRR) requirement of 5 per cent.
2 All nationalised industries are set a **financial target**: a three to five year medium-term objective, expressed in terms of an annual target rate of return on capital employed. The 1978 White Paper originally envisaged this as a criterion against which to measure performance but the financial targets as now set also reflect government determination to increase the industries' abilities to be self-financing.
3 Each industry is subject to a cash limit.

With the overriding constraints being financial targets, cash limits and the RRR requirement on new programmes, pricing policies assume a rather subordinate role. Nationalised industries have borne in mind the ideals of marginal cost pricing and the avoidance of cross-subsidies but prices have been set primarily to bring the industries within their financial targets.

Given this framework of controls, neither profits nor prices can act as adequate measures of efficiency. Additional attention has, therefore, been paid to 'non-financial targets' or 'performance indicators' introduced after the 1978 White Paper. These set targets against which performance in particular aspects of an industry's operations may be measured. Table 12.2 gives an example of these for the Electricity Council in 1985–6.

Table 12.2 Example of financial targets, cash limits and performance indicators

Financial target: 2.3% (current cost accounting) (rate achieved 2.65%)

Cash limit: net repayment £1128 million (actual repayment £467 million)

Non-financial target: Reduction in controllable costs per unit sold off: 6.1% (1983–8) (actual achievement 6.1% by 1985/6)

Source: *Electricity Council Annual Report and Accounts 1985–6*

The Efficiency of Public Enterprise

Once again, we must stress that efficiency can only be measured against stated objectives. This makes efficiency particularly difficult to measure in the non-commercial sector of public enterprise where, as previously noted, there is little consensus on unambiguous objectives. Particular activities have been the subject of efficiency reviews such as those conducted by Sir Derek Raynor in areas of the Civil Service but it is not possible to attempt generalisations of efficiency in these areas. We shall, therefore, concentrate on the commercial activities and on the nationalised industries in particular where, as we have seen, some precise criteria have been established.

Efficiency in the Nationalised Industries

It should now be clear that a simple review of profits in the nationalised industries is not sufficient to assess efficiency, although a lack of profitability might be of concern for other reasons such as the drain on resources and impact on the PSBR. More useful analysis can be obtained by looking at such measures as productivity or growth in activities where public and private enterprises are engaged in broadly similar activities. Such comparisons might be made between nationalised industries and UK based private sector firms or, where the nationalised concern is a monopoly, an overseas operation.

A number of such studies have been carried out, notably by R. Pryke, with the sort of results summarised in Table 12.3. It is worth remarking that studies covering earlier periods, including some by Pryke, suggested that, for example in the 1960s, UK nationalised industries had performed favourably in productivity terms compared with the private sector.

However, taking the results of this table at face value, what do they mean? To critics such as Pryke, they mean that public enterprise tends to be less efficient than comparable private concerns because their managers are cushioned from the realities of normal business life and the lack of a 'commercial ethic'.

On the other hand other explanations have been put forward for this apparently poor performance. These include:

Table 12.3 Examples of poor productivity in UK public enterprise

Postal services	Output per man-year: 30% higher in Holland 135% higher in the USA
Cars	BL Marina compared with Ford UK Cortina: 42% more man-hours per car to make
Coal	Output per man-year (underground workers): 45% higher in West Germany
British Rail (freight)	Train miles/man-hour: one-third of the level in France, Belgium, Holland, Sweden and Norway

Source: R. Pryke, *The Nationalised Industries: Policies and performance since 1968*, Martin Robertson, 1981.

1 It is very difficult to make valid comparisons of public enterprise performance. Comparisons with North America and Western European firms may ignore the unfortunate fact that UK industries generally have been less efficient than their American or European counterparts. Comparisons with the UK should be made with typical firms and not just with the 'high fliers' – the most successful firms in the private sector.

2 Private sector firms are free to concentrate their activities in areas where they are most productive and efficient. Airlines, for example, can concentrate on favoured routes. Public enterprise has to operate a number of services because of obligations placed on it by government. For instance, before privatisation, British Airways had social obligations to operate services to the Scottish Islands.

3 Public enterprises have often been subject to interference by government in their plans and activities. We have already seen how their financing and their investment programmes have been subordinated to wider government policies. Similarly their wage negotiations have been subject to government constraints, with possible implications for labour relations. Prices have been restrained (e.g. rail fares in the 1950s and 60s) or artificially raised (gas and electricity prices in the 1980s) to suit the policies of the government of the day. This sort of interference damages not only immediate performance but also the morale of management and workers with long-term consequences.

4 Finally, we should note that, even if we can establish that some public enterprises are indisputably inefficient, we should be careful not to jump to the conclusion that we have proved that this is **because** they are publicly owned. Inefficiency could arise for a number of reasons including:

a ownership – public rather than private;

b monopoly position in the market – no competitive pressure to keep down costs (see Chapter 10);

c control by management rather than by owners – with management possibly having objectives other than improving efficiency (see Chapter 3);

d size – organisations may simply be suffering from diseconomies of scale. This is especially likely where there is a large, labour-intensive, service element in the enterprise (e.g. gas or electrical repairs).

The last three points have nothing to do with public ownership as such.

Privatisation

Table 12.4 lists just some of the activities and enterprises which have been privatised in the UK since 1979. Privatisation has also become popular in other countries across the world. Japan has privatised its railways and telecommunications, Singapore its airlines; West Germany, Italy and Spain all have programmes for selling off subsidiaries of state holding companies. France has a Minister for Privatisation, with a programme including banks, insurance

Table 12.4 Some examples of privatisation 1979–88

Contracting out:	Civil Service cleaning; Royal Naval dockyard management; Royal Naval ship repair; local authority cleaning and refuse collection; Health Service cleaning and laundry
Sales:	British Aerospace; Cable and Wireless; Amersham International; National Freight Corporation; Britoil; International Aeradio; British Rail Hotels; Wytch Farm; Enterprise Oil; Associated British Ports; Sealink; Jaguar; British Telecom; British Gas; British Airways; Rolls Royce; British Airports Authority; British Steel
Deregulation:	Telecommunication supplies; inter-city coaches; buses

companies, industrial groups and media companies. Togo has leased its state steel firm to an American entrepreneur. Even in the Soviet Union small-scale private sector service firms are to be encouraged.

What is Privatisation?

There are at least three distinct activities which come within this general term:

1 The sale of state enterprises to the private sector.
2 The deregulation of the industry and its opening up to competition. Where a state concern previously held a monopoly, as in the supply of telecommunications equipment, parcel post or buses, private firms may be allowed to enter the market to offer an alternative source of supply.
3 The contracting out of activities to private sector firms. Examples including building work, refuse collection and warships maintenance.

It is important to note that these three activities are likely to have rather different consequences. Furthermore they can either go hand in hand or be proceeded with individually. It is possible there could be circumstances where they could conflict. For instance, it may be more difficult to find buyers for a state enterprise if, at the same time, other private firms are being encouraged to enter the market.

Why Privatise?

A number of objectives have been put forward and, again, it is possible that these could conflict. If we concentrate on privatisation in the UK we can identify certain declared objectives from official statements. These include:

> 'The desire to increase competitiveness and efficiency and the belief that the powers of the free market place can achieve this better than state control.' (H.M. Treasury)

> 'To reduce the size of the state-controlled sector of the economy (which) helps our economy work better . . . because in the state sector resources

tend to be used less efficiently . . . increase personal independence and freedom . . . have an important effect on attitudes . . . achieving value for money . . . offer a real boost to competition.' (Extracts from a speech by John Moore MP, government minister responsible for co-ordinating privatisation programmes, 18 July 1981)

These statements reveal:

1 A belief in the superiority of private enterprise and a political preference for this.
2 A desire to stimulate efficiency.
3 An aim to stimulate competition, with all that implies for efficiency, choice and so on.
4 A wish to change attitudes combined with the belief that workers with a stake, as shareholders, in their industry, may be less likely to strike.
5 The desire to provide a better service for customers.
6 The aim to obtain better value for the expenditure of taxpayers' money.

To these aims we must add:

7 The wish to free privatised firms from state interference in their pricing, investment and product policies.
8 The objective of removing finance raised by privatised firms from the Public Sector Borrowing Requirement and so remove the constraints placed on this finance by macroeconomic policies.
9 An undoubted immediate wish to raise revenue from the sale of state enterprises to the private sector.

Here you might pause for a moment and try to work out which of these objectives would most likely be best served by each of the three forms of privatisation we have identified.

The Course of Privatisation in the UK

The UK privatisation programme has been described as 'a policy in search of a rationale' (J. A. Kay and D. J. Thompson, 'Privatisation in search of a rationale', *Economic Journal*, March 1986). This may seem slightly unfair in view of all the different objectives so far identified but it is probably fair to say that the emphasis on particular objectives has changed as time has passed. Throughout the period of the Conservative government of 1979–87 there was a continuous political preference for privatisation. In that period, however, the emphasis switched from deregulation and contracting out to large 'set-piece' privatisations such as those of British Telecom, British Gas and British Airways, which have been major raisers of revenue for the government.

Success has been claimed for the policy against all the major objectives. For example:

1 Efficiency has been increased, at least to the extent that this can be measured by profits. Firms as diverse as Associated British Ports,

Amersham International, British Aerospace, Cable and Wireless, National Freight Corporation and British Telecom all report increased and, in many cases, record profits.

2 Competition and customer choice have been increased. You may now buy a telephone from a variety of suppliers, not just British Telecom.
3 Worker co-operation has been a notable feature of the success of firms such as the National Freight Corporation since privatisation.
4 Value for money has been claimed by many local authorities in contracting out services with consequent benefit for ratepayers.

In addition, several thousand million pounds each year have been raised by sales with a consequent easing of the pressure on the PSBR and assistance to the funding of tax reductions, both key elements in the economic policies of the Conservative government.

Further areas for privatisation have, therefore, been suggested. These include electricity, some elements of the rail system, British Coal, the Post Office – and even prisons, following experiments in the USA where private firms have run prisons under contract to state authorities.

The Case against Privatisation

Just as much of the support for privatisation derives from a political preference for private enterprise so much of the argument against it has its roots in a preference in the opposite direction. However, a number of non-political points have also been advanced. These basically fall into two groups: first a restatement of the arguments for public enterprise outlined earlier in this chapter, and secondly a criticism of each of the points outlined above in favour of privatisation.

We shall not repeat here all the arguments for public enterprise outlined earlier but make one further comment in respect of the **natural monopoly** argument. If an industry must be organised as a monopoly, then two alternative policies may be proposed: nationalisation or the regulation of a privately owned monopoly. The former may be preferable if it is believed that the latter will be ineffective or proof only against really serious abuses of market power or powerless to imbue the private monopoly with a sense of **social responsibility**.

Both British Gas and British Telecom were privatised as dominant firm monopolies with regulatory bodies, OFTEL and OFGAS, to oversee their operations. It is too early to make a balanced judgement of the efficiency of these bodies but already on at least two important occasions – the 1986 tariff changes and 1987 engineers' strike – OFTEL has been criticised as ineffective. Judgement on the effectiveness of these regulatory bodies must be deferred.

With regard to the second set of criticisms, the following points are among those that have been made.

1 On efficiency, as already noted, a simple increase in profits is not necessarily indicative of an increase in efficiency. For example, the quality

of the service may have deteriorated. Complaints to OFTEL appear to be running at about double the pre-privatisation level. Where productivity gains have been reported, as in the case of British Airways, the major improvements were recorded in the pre-privatisation period though the approach of privatisation may well have had a great deal to do with them.

2 On competition, the simple transfer of a public enterprise to private ownership does not affect market structure at all. For example, in the telephone and gas cases all that occurred was a shift of a dominant firm monopoly from public to private hands. Associated improvements in customer choice, such as choice of telephone equipment and business firms' ability to choose services offered by Mercury, were achieved by deregulation, which preceded privatisation and could have been carried out whether British Telecom was sold or not. The privatised firms such as British Telecom and British Airways have also developed an enthusiasm for taking over other organisations in their industrial sectors, an activity not calculated to increase the severity of competitive pressures.

   There is actually a suspicion that the sale of large state enterprises and the opening up of competition may, in practice, be conflicting aims. Senior management of these enterprises had, in the period up to 1989, always succeeded in persuading the government to sell the firms intact rather than to break them up. In the case of the gas industry this was even more remarkable in the light of an earlier Monopolies Commission report which suggested the hiving off of the gas showrooms. A policy of selling especially monopolistic firms intact rather than piecemeal may simultaneously satisfy managerial motives in respect of salaries and a cushioned market position (see Chapter 3) and government motives of raising as much money as possible from the sale. A monopoly, even if regulated, is likely to appear a more lucrative investment than a number of competing firms.

3 On worker co-operation, it is observed that the number of working days lost throughout the economy has declined (to a record low since 1967) in all sectors of the economy and not just in privatised firms. Furthermore, in 1987, British Telecom faced its worst industrial dispute for many years despite the fact that many of the participants were shareholders of the firm. In 1989 industrial disputes broke out at Jaguar, previously cited as an example of the improved industrial relations alleged to flow from privatisation.

4 On value for money in contracted out activities, critics have suggested that the cost savings achieved, even if services were maintained, arose largely through pay cuts imposed on workers who, in many instances, were already among the low paid. In economic terms there is no clear-cut welfare gain if a cost saving to one group of people is achieved only by an income reduction to another.

5 On macroeconomic considerations, there tend to be a number of sharp differences of opinion between economists. Some of the most serious points made by critics include:

   a The value of investment should be judged on its own merits and not in terms of whether it is conducted by private or public enterprise. Even if public sector investment is part of the PSBR, which is disputed, borrowing for capital purposes should be regarded as different from borrowing for current expenditure.

b Sales of public assets should be regarded as helping to fund the PSBR, not reduce it. This is not a trivial matter of bookkeeping. If your income were to lag persistently behind your expenditure you could bridge the gap by borrowing or by selling some of your assets (selling the family silver!). Neither would reduce the gap. They both simply bridge it.

c Among the reasons put forward for reducing the PSBR is that government borrowing pushes up interest rates. However, sales of public assets are likely to do exactly the same. For example, when people withdraw money from building society deposits in order to buy shares, they deprive the societies of funds and force them to raise their mortgage rates in order to make their deposit terms more competitive.

d The sale of assets has been effectively treated as a source of income by government when it really represents a capital receipt. The sale of assets cannot continue indefinitely and each sale also reduced potential future income in the form of nationalised industry trading surpluses. However, it has been pointed out that the government revenue from taxes paid by British Telecom and dividends on its 49 per cent holding of British Telecom shares in its first full year of private trading exceeded the surplus of its last full year of 100 per cent state ownership.

Conclusion

Whatever the future of privatisation in the UK, and this is likely to depend on the political future, a fresh look has had to be taken at the reasons for state involvement in industry and the form this should take where it is considered to be desirable. Nationalisation and regulation have again to be compared as practical alternatives. Where activities do remain in the public sector, increasing interest is likely to be paid to such matters as their objectives and appropriate measures of efficiency.

Where activities are concentrated in the private sector, there is likely to be increased emphasis on competition. A potential paradox which is yet to be resolved is the tension between the pressure to **deregulate**, i.e. to increase competition and give the consumer more freedom of choice and the benefit of market forces, and the pressure to **regulate** to protect the consumer from abuses of private market power.

Discussion Questions

1 Discuss the view that, while there are strong grounds for believing that the case for privatising those activities where competition exists is strong, the case is much weaker for privatising public utilities, especially those which are natural monopolies.

2 Discuss the view that while it may seem paradoxical that privatisation of public utilities such as telecommunications, water supply and electricity generation and supply actually increases state regulation, this is in the public interest because self-regulation is rarely effective.
3 Discuss the problems associated with identifying 'the public interest'. You will probably find it helpful to take a particular activity or organisation as an example.
4 How would you seek to measure the 'efficiency' of a major public utility such as a railway, telecommunications industry or water authority? Bear in mind the two meanings of efficiency defined in earlier chapters.
5 'Privatisation like nationalisation is a political rather than an economic issue.' Is this true? If it is true does this then mean that economists should not become involved in the privatisation debate?

Suggestions for Further Reading

A well known, comprehensive, but not universally accepted review of the performance of nationalised industries is contained in:

Pryke, R., *The Nationalised Industries: Policies and performance since 1969*, Martin Robertson, 1981.

The privatisation debate has generated a minor industry in academic articles on the subject. Inevitably in an issue of this nature many of these are of mostly contemporary interest and have been overtaken by subsequent events and experience but among those dealing with more durable issues are:

Brittan, S., 'The politics and economics of privatisation', *Political Quarterly* April/June 1984.
Beesley, M. and Littlechild, S., 'Privatisation: principles, problems and priorities', *Lloyds Bank Review*, July 1983.
Peacock, A., 'Privatisation in perspective', *Three Banks Review*, December 1984.
Shackleton, J., 'Privatisation, the case examined', *National Westminster Bank Review*, May 1984.

An excellent summary of the actual events of the privatisation programme is contained in *Privatisation: The Facts*, a booklet issued by Price Waterhouse. This summarises the position as it existed in July 1987.

13

The Business Firm and National Economic Policies

National Economic Policies

Policy Objectives

Most governments would probably claim that their underlying aim is to achieve the best possible conditions for their people. Many interpret this as operating a political system which they argue is in these interests. Some regard living under a particular set of religious beliefs as also achieving this same goal. Even where political, social or religious faith is the dominating force there are always implications for the operation of the economy. For example, a regime conforming to a strict Moslem code would not permit interest to be charged for the use of money. The national financial system must, therefore, be organised in a way that takes this fact into account.

However, the implications of the prevailing political or religious faith go much deeper than this. If, for example, there is a dominant belief that some suffering is inevitable, even desirable, in this life in order to achieve a more perfect existence in the next, then economic goals are likely to have a low priority and will be abandoned if they clash with the requirements of faith. This, in turn, is likely to appear irrational to those who regard the prime duty of a government as that of raising the material living standards of people in this world. It may be extremely difficult for governments at either end of these materialistic and religious extremes to communicate with each other. It is perhaps paradoxical that the nation which is usually seen as typifying the materialist extreme (the USA) actually owes its origins to religious sects which put the need to conform to their own extreme beliefs above all materialistic considerations to the extent of abandoning their own countries to face the very great hazards of pioneering an unknown land.

Whatever their political and religious differences most governments of the industrial market economies of the type described in this book give economic success a very high priority either as an end in itself or as a means to achieving political power and influence in the world. Their economic objectives, therefore, will be framed according to their view of what constitutes economic success. Here again different governments are likely to have different views. Most would agree on the elements that make up success but many would disagree on priorities. If we delay consideration of priorities we can list the various economic elements that would form part of most governments' set of objectives. These would be as follows.

The achievement of economic growth
We can define economic growth as the ability of a community to increase the total production of goods and services from the resources at its disposal. It may be objected that this ignores the quality of goods and services and there is some truth in this. However, if we can assume that increased quality is likely to increase value then an increase in total product does imply a growth in both volume and quality. At the same time many services and goods that most would consider to raise the quality of life, e.g. increased security from crime and improved health services, are likely to be recorded as increases in total production. A further objection might be made that we do not allow for the using up of valuable and irreplaceable natural resources such as oil and coal. These only appear in the national product of producing nations when they have been removed from the earth. We do not record the fall in the value of natural reserves represented by this removal. Again we have to admit that this is a substantial criticism while acknowledging that a growing number of economists and governments appear to be recognising this problem.

Maintaining full employment
By this is meant that all those people who wish to work in 'gainful employment', i.e. to gain an income, should be able to find work which, as far as possible, is appropriate to their skills and abilities provided these are relevant to the social and technological structure of the community. No person, however skilled, can expect to continue to be employed in that skill if it no longer serves any useful purpose in the community. Coal-miners in the early 1980s were understandably aggrieved at the decline of employment opportunities in coal mining. Whatever the merits of the rapid reorganisation of mining at that time no government could accept that there could never be any fall in the numbers of miners employed any more than there could be a guarantee of full employment for the charcoal burners displaced by coal and the disappearance of woodlands in an earlier age. Nevertheless unemployed people represent a waste of a scarce and potentially valuable economic resources and the community is poorer without their contribution. It is also a very great social and psychological problem in a society where the position of the individual rests so heavily on occupational status and income. All governments, therefore, seek to keep unemployment as low as possible subject to any constraints imposed by the pursuit of other economic policies.

Avoiding inflation
When the money value of goods and services deteriorates significantly and rapidly there is a loss of confidence in the financial and economic system leading eventually to a reduction in the level of economic activity and an inability to achieve economic growth and maintain full employment. Inflation, the constant erosion of the money value of goods and services, has been a

problem in almost all countries in the world for most of the second half of the twentieth century and in some countries for rather longer.

It has been argued that inflation is a problem peculiar to capitalist economic systems and that it did not exist in fully socialist economies. During the 1980s, however, it became clear that these economies were suffering from very severe problems of repressed inflation and concealed unemployment and that attempts to come to terms with these were imposing immense strains on their political and economic structures. Most modern governments would accept a need to control inflation but some might regard it as a lesser evil than some of the other economic problems which they face.

Trends in unemployment and inflation in the UK between 1984/5 and 1988/9 are shown in Fig. 13.1.

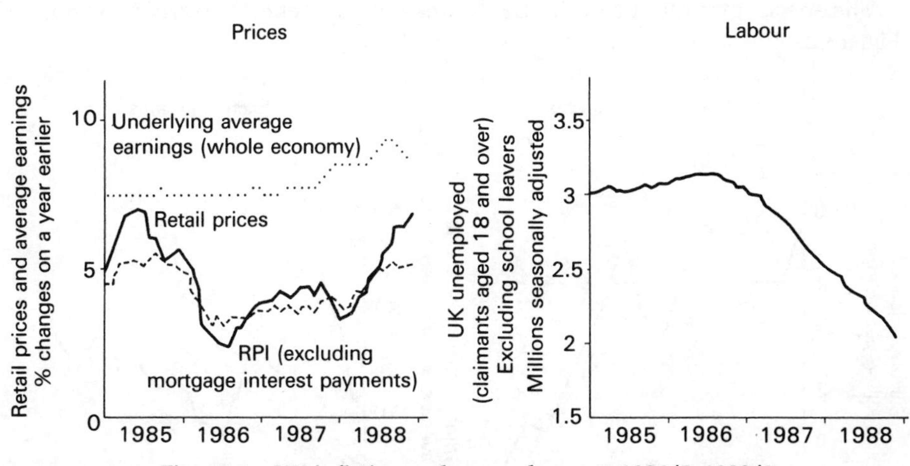

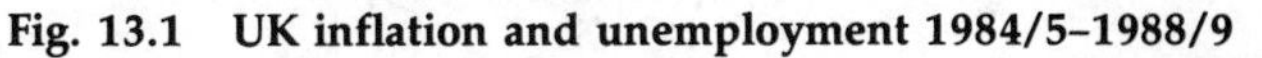
Fig. 13.1 UK inflation and unemployment 1984/5–1988/9

Notice how prices rise as unemployment falls. Source: *Economic Progress Report* (Treasury, February 1989).

Avoiding persistent balance of payments deficits

It is the **current** balance of payments that is usually of most concern to governments. A country's current balance of payments refers to the relationship between the total payments made for goods and services bought from foreign countries during the year and the total payments received from home produced goods and services sold to other countries. If payments for foreign produced goods and services are consistently greater than those received from the sale of home production then there will be a drain on the nation's financial reserves and/or an increase in borrowing from other countries to make good the difference. The final result of failing to correct a persistent balance of payments deficit is not bankruptcy in the sense that an individual becomes insolvent if living expenses constantly exceed income and exhaust past savings.

A nation's financial collapse is more complex but nonetheless devastating for its community. It is the currency that initially collapses. As the volume of money needed to pay for imported goods and services is constantly larger than that earned from exports the national currency falls in its value as a means of exchange with other national currencies. People in other countries do not wish to possess a currency whose value in exchange for 'real' goods and services is falling. This reduces its value further. Foreign exporters insist on payment in more acceptable currencies or charge very high prices to compensate for the great risk of loss. Those who have lent the country money in the past will be pressing for repayment. Pressures on the government are likely to rise until it accepts the need to reduce imports and to cut back on much of its own spending in an effort to bring about a more equal flow of imports and exports. The community then suffers from the fall in employment and living standards that arise within a country when its level of economic activity falls and it is forced to import fewer goods and export more.

The spectacular plunge in the UK balance of payments is clearly shown in Fig. 13.2.

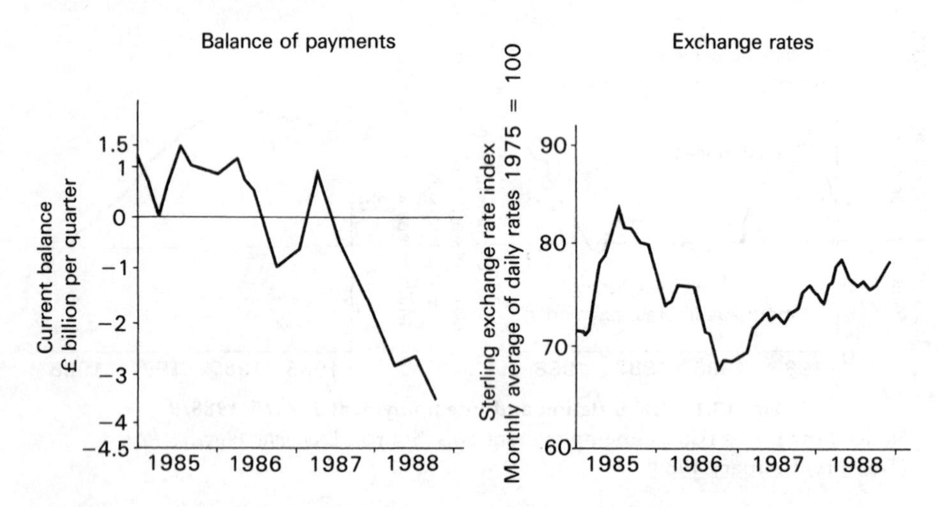

Fig. 13.2 The UK current balance of payments and sterling exchange rate 1984/5–1988/9
How long will it take for the fall in payments balance to drag down the exchange rate? Source: *Economic Progress Report* (Treasury, February 1989).

Avoiding large differences in regional living standards

In purely economic terms regional differences in people's incomes fulfil a purpose in neutralising differences in locational advantages. If it were possible to have perfect economic markets generally employers would be indifferent as to which region they chose for their business locations because differences in factor costs (land rents, workers' wages and costs of capital) would balance natural differences in locational advantages. Consequently, efforts to reduce regional inequalities in wage rates can have the effect of making the less favoured regions even less attractive to business managers, may make it difficult to reduce relatively high unemployment rates in these areas and may force more of the mobile workers to leave the area in search of opportunities elsewhere. Because these are likely to be the people with above average ability and initiative their loss further impoverishes the area and further discourages the entry of new business enterprise.

The reasons why governments seek to achieve a greater measure of equality in both income and employment throughout the regions are social and political rather than economic. Indeed there is likely to be an economic price to be paid for success in achieving this objective. It is recognised that there are strong social reasons why too many people should not be forced to leave an area too quickly and areas which are depressed in relation to others tend to breed hostility to the established political system, to the main opposition groups as well as to the government. It was the rise of the 'celtic' political parties (the Welsh and Scottish nationalists and the Liberals in South West England) in the early 1960s which persuaded the governments of that time that substantial help needed to be given to the regions in their search for new business activity. The Labour party, with its strongholds in the older manufacturing and relatively depressed regions, has tended to be more vigorous in the pursuit of regional policies than the Conservatives with their support based mainly in the more prosperous areas of England. The actual instruments of regional policy and some of its consequences were examined in Chapter 11.

Economic Policy Instruments

There is little dispute concerning the weapons available in the government's economic armoury but much controversy concerning their relative usefulness and effects. The weapons actually chosen by government depend on whichever model it assumes provides the most accurate explanation of the behaviour of the economy and the priorities it sets for the various objectives that we have outlined. The two most influential groups of economic models likely to influence the governments of modern industrial, market economies are the Keynesian and the monetarist (or more accurately the neo-classical) models.

Keynesian models

At the heart of the Keynesian economic analysis – developed from the work of Lord Keynes in the 1920s and 1930s – are the following assumptions:

1 National economic aggregates behave in predictable ways so that **macroeconomic** analysis is possible even when detailed knowledge of the behaviour of the individual units that make up the aggregate is not available.
2 Aggregate supply will respond to shifts in aggregate demand as long as there are unused resources available to enter or leave the market in accordance with suppliers' judgements concerning the relative profitability of the different options that can be chosen.

3 The most important influence on aggregate demand is the income level which the majority of people have to accept.
4 There can be long-term imbalances between the levels of economic demand and supply which will not correct themselves without the intervention of some outside force.
5 The government has the power to manipulate demand in order to bring about equilibrium between aggregate demand and supply. This is often referred to as **demand management**.

Keynesian models thus ascribe considerable powers to government to influence the economy through demand management policies. In the exercise of these powers it is assumed that the most important objective is to avoid large-scale unemployment and the personal suffering and social and political conflict that this was likely to bring. Keynes, it must be remembered, was writing and teaching (at Cambridge) against the background of the General Strike of 1926, the Great Depression of 1932 and succeeding years, and the rise of Hitler and Mussolini in Germany and Italy.

Neo-classical models

These are adaptations and modifications of classical economic models in the tradition of Adam Smith and the exponents of free, unregulated economic markets. The modern apostle of this school of economic thought is Professor Milton Friedman of the USA. The label **monetarist** is also often loosely applied to these models. This reflects their insistence on 'sound' monetary policies and preference for balanced budgets but can be misleading in that relatively few neo-classical economists would accept the extreme monetarist position that governments can and should exercise strict control over money supply and that failure to do so will lead to predictable and precisely measurable economic consequences.

Neo-classical economic models tend to contain the following features:

1 The belief that competitive, unregulated markets provide the most efficient means of providing the community with the goods and services it requires.
2 The belief that government controls, subsidies and other forms of intervention distort markets, make them less efficient and lead to lower living standards for the community. Extreme supporters of unfettered economic markets see no purpose in consumer protection regulations and argue that competitive forces are the best guarantees that producers will provide high standards of quality and service. Producers failing to meet community expectations will go out of business. The more common case for some consumer protection measures was outlined in Chapter 10.
3 A requirement for confidence in money and the stability of the financial system to ensure that markets operate smoothly. Free-market economists see governments as the main agents for monetary instability because of their chronic tendency to overspend revenues leading to borrowing and the creation of additional money. These economists believe that governments should set an example of prudent spending within their revenues,

i.e. keeping to balanced budgets, and should use their authority and control over central banking to ensure that money creation is kept within the limits of production increases. Strict monetarists consider that there is an inevitable and precise effect on average price levels of an increase in money supply above the increase in total production and, therefore, stress the importance of controlling the money supply.

4 A strong distrust of high levels of taxation which is also thought to distort the economic system and to discourage production. Consequently the combination of the desire to keep government spending within the limits of government revenues, which come chiefly from taxes, and the belief that the burden of taxation should be reduced leads to continual efforts to reduce public sector spending in order to reduce taxation. It also leads to a desire to reduce the extent of the public sector by transferring as many public sector activities as possible to the private sector where taxation would not be involved. This, of course, is the essence of the wish to privatise as many of the former nationalised industries as possible. This is one aspect of what has become known as **supply side economics**. In contrast to Keynesianism which puts the emphasis on the level of aggregate demand in the economy, supply side economists stress such factors as the competitiveness of markets, efficiency of firms and incentives for entrepreneurial managers and workers.

Because of their distrust of the effects of government intervention the neo-classical economists believe that the interventionist policies of a long period of Keynesian attempts to manage the economy have been largely responsible for economic weakness, loss of trade in world markets and constant price inflation. Neo-classical economic policies thus tend to be the reverse of those adopted by Keynesians. However, as a return to classical economic ideas has not been entirely successful in curing the weaknesses associated with Keynesian attempts at economic management more recently there has been an effort to reconcile these conflicting models. The results are often a little speculative and sometimes very complex, and as they do not yet have a major impact on the choice and use of economic policy instruments we do not propose to examine them at this stage.

The main policy instruments

Keynesians have sought to manage aggregate demand to keep it in balance with aggregate supply (production). If foreign trade is ignored, or assumed to be in balance (total value of imports = total value of exports), then aggregate demand is made up of consumer expenditure, business investment (on buildings, equipment, etc.) and government expenditure. It follows that demand management, if it is to be achieved, must be sought by influencing these elements in aggregate demand through:

1 **Manipulating government expenditure** This should be increased if aggregate supply (production) is greater than aggregate demand, i.e. if there appears to be a **demand deficiency**, and reduced if aggregate demand is greater than aggregate supply, i.e. if there appears to be **excess demand**. An imbalance associated with demand deficiency is also known as a **deflationary gap**. Levels of government expenditure are, thus, freed from restriction by current levels of taxation revenues. An unbalanced budget with a significant gap between current expenditure and current revenue is a normal part of Keynesian economic policy.

2 **Manipulating taxation for purposes of economic management beyond any simple need to finance government spending** Taxation is thus used to change economic forces and the level of the economy. This is a long way from the aim of the neo-classical economists who wish to keep taxes neutral in their effects. Government spending and taxation, which do not have to be in balance, appear to be used together to influence total demand through what are known as **fiscal policies** directed through the government's own revenue and expenditure **budgets**. Taxation may also be used to influence levels of business investment which is thought to affect both the level of aggregate demand and also aggregate supply – demand, because it is an element in the total of desired expenditure; supply, because an increase in the amount of machinery and equipment employed by business organisations increases their capacity to produce goods and services.

   In the main, however, taxation can be used to influence the level of consumer incomes that are available for spending or influencing the amount of goods and services that can be bought for any given level of spending. Direct taxes, such as income tax, corporation tax levied on company profits and national insurance contributions (which are increasingly regarded as a form of direct taxation), have a direct effect on personal or corporate (company) incomes. Expenditure taxes such as value added tax affect the volume of real goods and services that can be bought from incomes. An increase in tax is usually considered to reduce expenditure demand but this is only true if the government refrains from itself spending that tax or uses it to finance public sector activities that would otherwise have to be financed from borrowing. If the government uses the tax revenue to increase the level of its own spending then there is no change in total, aggregate demand, merely a transfer of spending power from the private business and/or personal sectors of the economy to the public sector.

   Trends in the distribution of UK taxation 1973–87 are shown in Fig. 13.3.

While not denying the general tendencies for government spending and taxation to act in the ways just outlined, neo-classical economists point to dangers in their use as instruments to manage the economy. In the first place they suggest that modern national production systems do not respond to changes in demand as readily as has been believed by the Keynesians. The structure of supply is believed to be subject to additional influences which may produce results rather different from those predicted by supporters of demand management policies. If national, domestic supply cannot or does not react to meet an increase in demand then demand will be met by increased imports and

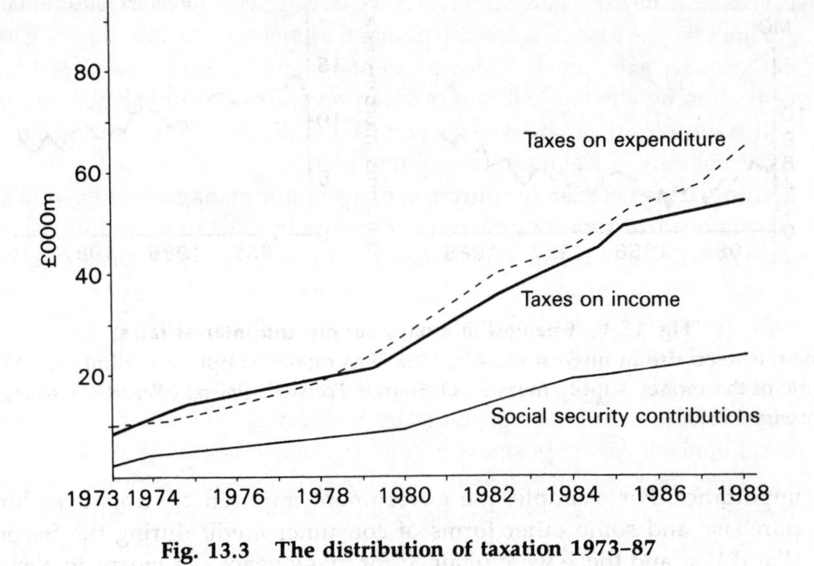

Fig. 13.3 The distribution of taxation 1973–87

there will be a balance of payments problem. There is also likely to be a general increase in the level of prices, i.e. price inflation. For these reasons the neo-classical economists are unwilling to use fiscal measures as methods of manipulating the demand side of the economy.

3 **Monetary measures** are the methods preferred by neo-classical economists to control consumer demand when this is believed to be sufficiently in excess of supply to cause inflation and/or balance of payments imbalances. Monetary measures are of various kinds. A government can seek to reduce the quantity of money in the banking system available for lending by forcing a withdrawal of deposits from the commercial banks and transferring them to the central bank within the public sector and so removing them from circulation. They can do this in ways which are explained in almost all introductory textbooks of macroeconomics. Alternatively they may push up the price of money – and hence the cost of borrowing – by forcing the banking system to raise interest rates.

   Modern classical and all but extreme monetarists recognise the very great practical difficulties in seeking to impose domestic lending controls on a modern, highly sophisticated and international banking system. They, therefore, appear to believe that the only effective monetary control under contemporary conditions is that of the **interest rate**. An example of the use of this control occurred in the winter of 1988/89 in the UK when a succession of record balance of payments deficits and the return of rising inflation rates were met by government pressure to force up interest rates. This is shown in Fig. 13.4.

4 A government can use its power to create laws to impose **physical controls** over those features of the economy which are believed to have special

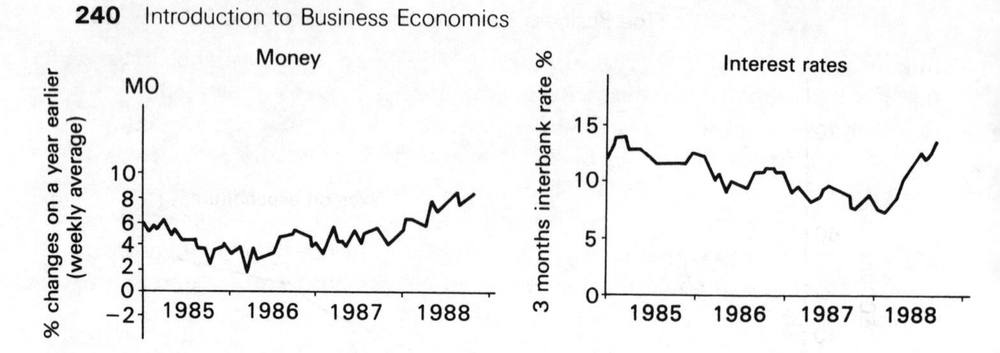

Fig. 13.4 Changes in money supply and interest rates
Note the steep rise in interest rates in 1988/9 as money supply was climbing. (M0 is one of the money supply measures.) Source: *Economic Progress Report* (Treasury, February 1989).

importance. For example, the government imposed controls over hire-purchase and some other forms of consumer credit during the Second World War and these were retained for many years as a means to control consumer spending. Better known, perhaps, were the attempts of the government between 1966 and 1979 to control prices and incomes through a number of legislative measures and agencies such as the National Board for Prices and Incomes. A reluctance to use such controls to distort or replace market forces together with a belief that they do not have the desired effects has led the government, since 1979, to abandon them. Keynesian economists have been more willing than neo-classical to contemplate direct economic controls.

Government Policies and Business Organisations

Direct Consequences of Policies

Both Keynesian and neo-classical economists and governments under their influence operate on the assumption that their policies will influence aggregate demand and or supply. Since demand conditions must influence business production decisions – after all firms only produce those goods and services which they believe they can sell – and since aggregate supply is the sum of production by individual firms, it follows that government policies designed to achieve economic objectives must have a direct impact on most individual business organisations. The impact of using each of the policy instruments can be examined without much difficulty.

Government spending
A major part of the activity determined by the public sector is, in fact, carried out by private sector organisations. A decision to build a road or a major rail

link provides work for large numbers of business organisations. Even a nationalised industry purchases most of its equipment and supplies from firms in the private sector. Any decision to expand or reduce public sector spending must have a major impact on business production in the affected sectors. It must also be remembered that government spending does not only have a once-and-for-all effect. If a motorway is built in one year it has to be maintained and kept in repair in subsequent years. Consequently a decision to increase or reduce government spending has implications for both current and future expenditure.

Taxation

This affects business firms in many ways. A change in personal taxes, whether direct on income or indirect on expenditure, changes both the aggregate level and the pattern of consumer demand. Some goods and services are more responsive to price changes (brought about by expenditure taxes) and spendable income changes (resulting from changes in income tax and national insurance contributions) than others. If, for example, the price of petrol rises following a tax increase, people may not be able to reduce significantly their purchases of petrol – they still have to go to work, go to the shops, etc. – but the extra cost of petrol will reduce the amount of income available for other forms of expenditure and consumers may make cuts in spending which have no apparent relationship with the cost of running a car. When tax changes affect either the level or the pattern of demand there will have to be a shift in the level and pattern of production. Firms can only afford to produce the goods and services they know they can sell. In some cases the pressure on prices and profits may become so great that total production is much reduced and shops find that they can only obtain replacements with goods imported from other countries.

A change in business taxes affects the amount of surplus revenue that firms have available for distribution to shareholders and for reinvestment in the enterprise. Both are likely to fall or rise less steeply than they would otherwise have done. If dividend incomes fall so do the capital values of share portfolios and shareholders – and pension funds are less well off. This will have an effect on future pensions and, therefore, on an increasingly important sector of consumer demand. There is some evidence in the USA that share values do have an effect on consumer buying but as individual share ownership is much less widespread in the UK this trend is likely to be very slight at the present time. Any reduction in company profit retentions, however, will have a more immediate impact on business investment and, consequently, on total business production. This arises partly because firms have less money to spend but also because the amount they can safely borrow depends partly on the value of their existing ordinary shares as most companies seek to keep a balance between the value of their equity (ordinary shares) and their total borrowing. Furthermore the willingness of finance markets to make capital available to business depends on the profitability of past investments. If the suppliers of capital are not satisfied with the returns on past investment they are less willing to make available new supplies of finance. They are likely to require higher rates of interest on money lent to business or expectations of higher profit returns on purchases of new shares. Altogether, therefore, an increase in corporation tax can be expected to reduce business investment, raise the cost of investment and lead to a slowing down in the rate at which total production can increase. It is also likely to make domestic industry less competitive in relation to foreign firms. We would expect a reduction in corporation tax to have the opposite effect and the events of the 1980s in the UK do suggest that this may well be the case.

Monetary measures

These are designed to influence consumer demand and are thus to some extent an alternative to fiscal measures, including the use of taxation. However, attempts to impose limits on credit creation in the UK in the 1960s and 1970s were found to distort the financial system rather than to check the total growth in the effective money supply. Business firms, aided by banks whose profits largely depend on lending, found ways to gain credit in forms that evaded the credit control measures. Multinational firms raised finance overseas and avoided repatriating profits earned overseas in order to keep them out of the controlled system. The main effects of credit controls, therefore, were to make raising finance more complex and expensive and to penalise small firms and new, innovative firms which did not enjoy the kind of financial advice and sources available to the large, established organisations.

Since the early 1980s monetary control in the UK has been almost wholly exercised through changes in interest rates engineered by the government, operating through the Bank of England. High interest rates are intended to reduce consumer demand by making personal credit more expensive. The government has also suggested that more expensive credit should make it more difficult for firms to find the finance to pay wage increases. However, there seems to be little evidence of this. What is more certain is that raising the cost of capital will reduce the volume and shorten the life of investment projects as explained in Chapter 7. There is a danger, therefore, that an interest rate rise intended to reduce excess aggregate demand to check price and wage inflation will also reduce total production so that when demand rises again it will suck in imports before the production system can increase its capacity. This is very much the same criticism that has been made against attempts to reduce excess demand by Keynesian style fiscal policies and is clearly a problem associated with any attempt at demand manipulation.

Physical controls

Physical controls tend to bring severe distortions to the markets where they apply. **Price controls** applied during a period of price inflation have to provide a mechanism for limited price rises. However, all bureaucratic procedures have to operate according to some kind of rule to avoid autocratic decisions and to provide guidelines for administrators. Business managers, especially the managers of the larger companies, soon learn what these rules are and they quickly devise methods to manipulate them to their own advantage. Anyone with experience of wartime rationing knows that this happens. A system which, say, provides that a firm cannot apply for a price increase for a particular product more often than once every six months rapidly becomes one in which most firms automatically apply for a price increase every six months and they become adept at presenting reasons which overworked civil servants find difficult to refute. Instead of studying market conditions and the wishes of consumers firms spend their best energies in studying government procedures and ways to manipulate them.

Wages are the price of labour so that **wage controls** distort supply and demand conditions in labour markets. In practice wage controls tend to reflect the view that they should allow larger pay rises to the low paid to avoid social injustice. Where trade union co-operation is sought it is usually necessary to buy the support of the large unions by favouring their members. It is in the nature of economic life that the largest unions will tend to represent the lower paid and those with relatively low levels of skill. Consequently during periods of pay controls the pay differential between the highly skilled and managerial groups and those with few skills tends to shrink. Many workers do not find it worthwhile to acquire the higher levels of skill or to assume higher levels of managerial responsibility. Business organisations find that they have a surplus of the low skilled workers and an increasingly severe shortage of the more highly skilled. This shortage can prevent a successful firm from expanding or can make it less competitive in world markets. In attempts to overcome the problem employers sometimes conspire with trade unions and even with civil servants to find legal ways of evading controls that prevent them from paying higher wages to groups of workers in short supply.

There is also a growth of **payments in kind**, allowing employees to have company cars or other benefits which have greater utility for workers than highly taxed wages. The United Kingdom is reputed to have a higher proportion of company cars used by individual workers than any other industrial country. This is the result of a long period of relatively high personal taxation, low wage differentials and pay controls. Although these distortions to the operation of the UK labour market had largely ceased to apply by the late 1980s long established attitudes and customs take time to change.

Any form of physical control which seeks to influence managers' decisions and to change their behaviour is likely to be met by attempts to manipulate the control so that managerial objectives can be achieved in spite of or even with the help of controls. Managerial efforts are diverted from the study of markets and consumers to the study of the political processes and ways of influencing political decisions. This increases business costs and turns business firms into political institutions. Economic resources are diverted from the production of goods and services wanted by consumers to the manipulation of the political machine. In extreme cases a separate 'black' or underground economic system grows up to satisfy consumer wants to the personal profit of the underground entrepreneurs. This has become evident from increased awareness of developments in the economy of the Soviet Union.

Business Firms and Rational Expectations

Modern attempts to explain the deficiencies in government attempts to manage the economy, especially economic management as developed by Keynesian macroeconomic analysis, have led to the concept of **rational expectations** as one possible explanation why government policies have not produced the results that had been predicted.

The basic assumption of the rational expectations approach is that people are rational. They do not waste or ignore information and they try to behave in the most efficient and economical way open to them in the pursuit of their own objectives.

It is also recognised that constant adjustment to changing conditions and the search for the fullest and most accurate information are costly and impractical. People make agreements in the light of the information they have and feel justified in obtaining. Because this information is unlikely to be perfect they will make mistakes but will learn from these mistakes and adjust their behaviour accordingly.

It is not difficult to apply this reasoning to behaviour in the labour market, especially where this is channelled through negotiations between large employers or groups of employers and trade unions representing organised labour. Both employers and unions will negotiate in the light of their information about present and future conditions in the labour market and current and anticipated policies of the government. Agreements will be concluded with the aim of achieving the objectives of both parties and these will be achieved if their predictions turn out to be correct. It has been argued that if labour market anticipations, including those concerning future government policies, are realised there is unlikely to be any change in real prices, output and unemployment. Only if there are unexpected shifts in demand and government actions will these change; otherwise changes will be to monetary prices and wages. Not all employers and unions will be equally well informed and skilled in their predictions so that there will be errors in particular cases but these will learn from experience.

This, of course, leads to the apparent paradox that the more consistent a government is in its policies the less successful it will be in influencing the real outcome of business activities. Only an unanticipated shift in policy by a government is likely to lead to achievement of the objectives of that policy if these include an attempt to influence the real economic variables of output and employment. Although rational expectations theory was developed to explain the breakdown of Keynesian demand management policies it is clearly equally valid in relation to monetarist attempts to influence business decisions through monetary instruments, including interest rates. We might suspect that similar reservations apply to the so-called supply side policies of the 1980s in which personal and corporation tax reductions were expected to increase the pursuit of income and profit with a consequent increase in total business production. It is not clear that this policy has been entirely successful. It is equally possible that business owners had certain net profit objectives which tax reductions had made possible at a lower level of production. Whatever their public political statements practical trade union negotiators are chiefly concerned with the real disposable incomes and job security of their actual members and are not prepared to put these at risk by pushing for business expansion in an uncertain environment.

A modern government is clearly in a difficult position. After a prolonged period of attempted economic management and against a background of public expectation that it can influence real levels of prices and employment even a decision to reduce the level of government intervention and attempt to restore competitive markets involves policies that appear interventionist. These policies are also likely to be resisted by business organisations which had become familiar with previous policies and which had developed strategies to manipulate them to their own advantage. By the late 1980s, in spite of its declared aims of reducing the size and influence of the public sector, the UK government had been obliged to resort to demand management policies using monetary rather than fiscal instruments.

Business Organisations and the European Community

Entry to the European Community has meant that UK business organisations have had to add European Community directives and policies to national laws and policies to the environmental constraints within which they have been obliged to operate. Strictly, of course, Community policies do not affect UK business activities within the UK until a Commission directive is translated by Parliament into a UK statute. Nevertheless because many firms operate in other member countries and because most directives do make the transition to UK statute law firms have to be aware of policy trends and of the political framework within which they develop.

The Community affects business activities at two broad levels. There is a large number of detailed regulations affecting day-to-day production and trade, and there are broader issues of competition which affect matters of business strategy.

Detailed Community Regulations

These concern the relationships between business firms and consumers and between employers and employees, and to some extent between business activities and the community as a whole.

Business and consumers

Most regulations of this type concern matters relating to product descriptions, to weights and measures, product labelling and informing consumers about the nature of the goods they are purchasing. In principle most people would agree that a general community body of law relating to consumer protection is a desirable concept. This might be expected to give all consumers in all member countries equal rights and protection and make all producers subject to the same body of regulations so that competition would be seen to be fair.

In practice this ideal is far from actual achievement. The effectiveness of consumer law, like any other area of legislation depends as much, if not more, on the way it is enforced as in the wording of the law. Patterns of enforcement vary enormously from country to country. In addition there is a very long tradition of the use of 'consumer safety' provisions as methods of securing hidden or indirect protection of domestic producers from foreign competition. All member countries, including the historic trade rivals, West Germany, France and the UK, are guilty of these measures. Long-standing habits are not changed easily, and on these issues national governments are subject to the united political pressures of firms, organised labour and regional political forces.

Employers and employees

The general trends of Community labour policies are towards the equal treatment of men and women employees and towards employment protection for workers. The political motivation underlying these trends is clearly social. Although national governments are expected to have considerable responsibility for the economic health of their countries, Community government in so far as it exists does not – so far – appear to have attached to it any measure of responsibility for the economic health of the whole group of member countries. It responds to the political pressures of influential interest groups with little apparent awareness of an overall community group interest.

The cause of equal pay and conditions for female workers has benefitted from appeals to Community law and UK labour law has had to be amended to take into account wider interpretations of what is meant in practice by the requirement that there should be 'equal pay for equal work'. Women have also won the right to avoid compulsory retirement at a lower age than that applying to men in the same organisation. On the other hand there has been no similar pressure to oblige the UK government to pay state pensions to men and women at the same age – the one major area in which women workers enjoy superior conditions.

The area of employment protection law and trade union rights is an interesting one given that most of the UK government's employment legislation of the 1980s runs counter to Community policy. This is likely to cause some friction given the proposals for trade harmonisation in 1992. It should also be recognised that the effects of 'social' labour legislation are different in different countries. It has much less practical effect in countries with a high proportion of small family owned and controlled business units than in the UK with its preponderance of large public companies. This difference is unlikely to have been overlooked by Community politicians many of whom are highly skilled in the manipulation of Community regulations to favour their own national interests.

However, as part of the process of the creation of the single market in 1992 there is likely to be increased pressure for harmonisation of employment law. Advocates of this point to the danger of what is termed 'social dumping' – firms concentrating activities in countries where workers enjoy relatively few rights.

In this context, social or legal systems affording few rights are seen as a form of unfair competition similar to the provision of subsidies or other financial incentives.

Business activity and the Community

In this connection the term 'business activity' is used in its widest sense and can be extended to include such issues as expenditure taxes and environmental issues. Tax harmonisation appears to be a logical aim in the pursuit of an ideal common market area in which all producers can compete on equal terms. However, it overlooks the different ways in which taxes are collected and tax laws enforced. It is much easier to evade taxes in some countries than in others and expenditure taxes cannot be considered in isolation from the general tax environment including personal and social security taxes or near tax 'contributions'. The harmonisation of one kind of tax only could increase rather than reduce market distortions and differences.

There is also a danger that fashionable environmental issues can be treated very selectively. The concern of Community politicians with conditions in the UK water industry has come as something of a surprise to many people in the UK who have had experience of the water, plumbing and lavatorial arrangements within the countries of some of the most vocal of these politicians. Similar reservations may be held concerning Community concern over bathing beaches!

The European Community and Competition

Community policies on Competition and restrictions on trade competition are stated in Articles 85 and 86 of the Treaty of Rome. The Commission has established its right to investigate major mergers which threaten competition in areas of the Community and to challenge these. The Commission also has the power to investigate abuses of monopoly power. Nevertheless it is proving difficult to establish any clear pattern of case law to indicate precisely what kinds and levels of market power should be discouraged and the suspicion remains that much depends on whether individual countries or firms with political influence feel threatened by foreign competition. If they do then efforts are likely to be made to invoke the Treaty of Rome. If not then mergers and business practices remain undisturbed. It is also possible that the Commission may prove to be more ready to challenge entry to markets by US or Japanese producers than to prevent the build up of mainly European business groups. Nor has the European Commission shown a great deal of enthusiasm for opening up the restricted markets of the professions or for encouraging more competitive markets in services such as insurance, house purchase and retail banking. Political enthusiasm for competition both internationally and nationally often appears to be rather selective and sensitive to established political pressure groups.

The ideal of a truly European competitive common economic market area with a high degree of harmonisation of social and economic policies is attractive from many points of view, particularly in a world where trade is increasingly likely to be influenced by superstates such as the USA, USSR and China. Nevertheless the practical difficulties of harmonisation among countries of different economic and social traditions should not be taken lightly, nor should the tendencies of individual states to use Community institutions for nationalistic ends.

Discussion Questions

1. Although the majority of business firms support the Conservative Party it is often said that many business managers find life more comfortable and profitable under a Labour government provided that this is subject to the influence of Keynesian economic policies. How would you explain this attitude?
2. 'Governments cannot pursue all their objectives at the same time but their attempts to do so do a great deal of damage to the business environment within which firms have to operate.' How far is this statement justified?
3. 'Most business firms can cope with the problems created by inflation. What they find much more difficult to handle are the policies employed by governments to deal with inflation.' Explain and discuss this view.
4. Are multinational companies immune from national government economic policies?
5. Discuss the view that business managers have more to fear from government attempts to solve economic problems than they do from the problem themselves.

Suggestions for Further Reading

Most modern, general textbooks on economics will contain an explanation of the Keynesian and monetarist models of the economy and explain their differing implications for policies towards inflation and unemployment. In addition you should be alert for discussions and reviews in the financial press and business sections of the serious daily and Sunday newspapers. You should also analyse the speeches on economic issues made by leading government and opposition politicians and work out for yourself whether they are making assumptions based on Keynesian or neo-classical economics.

14 Business and the Changing World

Sources of Change

Among the key areas of change which firms have to cope with are those in products, markets, technology and production methods, the business environment and the structure of firms. Many of these are closely interrelated. For example, new technology has given rise to new products. Very often these might be products such as calculators, for which an international market exists. Firms that may previously have found themselves operating in a stable, perhaps even 'cosy' business environment might then find themselves challenged by competition from imported goods. One way a firm might respond to this might be to adapt its structure to enable it to become more responsive to competition.

Here we have traced just one line of causation but we shall show how the dynamics of change may have its source in any one of the areas we have identified. This is illustrated in Fig. 14.1.

Product Changes

New technology may clearly give rise to new products, but it is not necessarily the only source and indeed the pressure may be the other way about. For example, much of the impetus to the development of microelectronics came

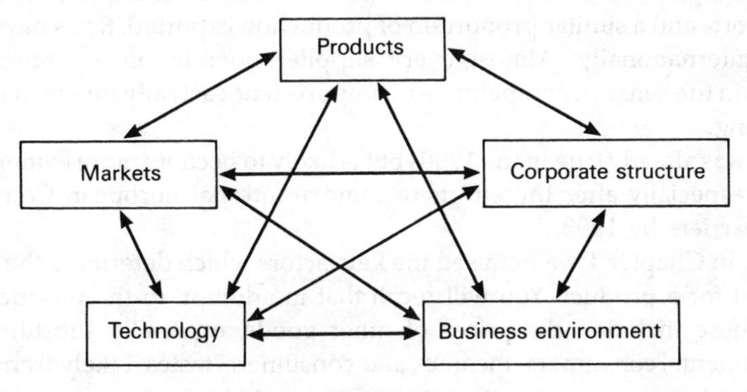

Fig. 14.1
Change in any one factor may spark off changes in the others.

from the US space programme, and many other high technology developments have their roots in the drive to produce more advanced military hardware. War-time pressures are often a powerful spur to new developments which need not always contain very advanced technology. Radar and the cathode ray tube are products which originated in war. New products are also developed in response to market changes.

For example, the nature of world tourism has changed under the pressure of rising incomes. Tourist travel is a particularly income-elastic product, that is its demand tends to increase more than proportionally as incomes increase. With a higher volume of tourism there has been more traffic to conventional holiday centres and increasingly exotic and far-flung destinations have been developed.

This has also had an effect on other industries. For example, the pattern of world air transport and types of aircraft have adapted to the tourist trade. A significant and successful insight by some commercial aircraft manufacturers in the 1960s was that larger rather than faster aircraft were required. Consequently, in the 1970s, commerce prospered with the **jumbo-jet** while governments spent huge sums of their taxpayers' money on the supersonic **Concorde** with its commercially inadequate payload.

Another set of services that tends to increase in importance as incomes rise are financial services such as banking, insurance and investment management. Here the development of larger domestic markets, a world financial market and computer-based technology forced changes in the structure of financial service firms. These were epitomised by the **Big Bang** that transformed the City of London in 1987.

Market Changes

In the previous section we remarked how the financial services industry had reacted to changes both in the UK domestic and international markets. In the UK, in particular, where nearly 30 per cent of all consumption is provided by imports and a similar proportion of production exported, firms have had to think internationally. Almost every supplier operates in an international market in the sense of competing with imports if not actually involved in direct exporting.

This was already true in the 1980s but is likely to become more evident in the 1990s, especially after the efforts to remove internal European Community trade barriers by 1993.

Early in Chapter 1 we itemised the key factors which determine the level of demand for a product. You will recall that in addition to the product's own price these included the prices of other goods, especially substitutes and complements, consumers' incomes and consumers' tastes. Likely trends in all these must be the focus of attempts by firms in their efforts to forecast market movements and estimate future levels of demand.

Technology and Production Methods

New technology gives rise not just to new products but also to new production methods. In the past there has been a tendency for new production methods to revolve around the exploitation of economies of scale and thus encourage a drive towards bigger business organisational structures. In recent years some key developments in technology have worked in the opposite direction. This has been most marked in the area of microelectronics. As noted in Chapter 4, applications of microtechnology have been a major factor in encouraging an increase in the number of small firms, not just in fairly obvious areas such as the writing of computer software but also in less predictable activities such as printing. Numerous very small desk-top publishing firms have appeared throughout the country. Many are able to offer printing facilities that previously would have required large firms with very substantial capital support and numerous highly skilled people.

The Business Environment

Market changes are clearly a major factor in the business environment. Others include:

1 The structure of the industry within which the firm operates. By this we mean such things as the number and size distribution of firms and thus, by extension, whether the market is becoming more oligopolistic or more competitive.
2 The structure of markets within which the firm acquires inputs such as raw materials and components and whether these are likely to become more or less freely available in the future and what their price trends are likely to be. The structure of the labour market from which the firm recruits most of its labour is another important matter. In the late 1980s, for example, certain key trends were becoming apparent in labour markets. Among these were shortages in many areas of skilled workers, an increasing reliance on female and part-time labour and a fall in the number of new entrants from full-time education.
3 Government policy, as shown in the previous chapter, influences important matters such as interest rates, exchange rates, employment legislation, financial and other help for the regions and some rules governing business conduct in such areas as restraints on competition and mergers.

The Structure of Firms

A feature of recent decades has been the way many firms have experimented with the manner in which they actually organise their processes. Fifty years ago, for example, management texts and handbooks would proffer advice on the 'one best way' to run firms. Even if they differed on the nature of that 'one best way', most clearly had a concept of the structure of the typical firm which was basically similar – a hierarchically organised pyramid, with individuals and departments within the organisation responsible for areas of functional specialisation. They would be sales, production, purchasing specialists and so on.

Management and organisational specialists today may disagree about much but they are fairly unanimous that there is no such thing as an 'ideal' organisational form. Instead, a variety of types of structure are thought to be suited to different situations. If anything, the traditional hierarchy seems best suited only to mass-production in stable markets and, as we have seen, this is an area of declining relative importance. It is a structure that seems rather rigid and ill-equipped to deal with change and a number of other structures can now be observed. One of these is the multi-division firm where the organisation is subdivided into semi-autonomous units, each responsible, for example, for a particular product or geographical area.

Other types of organisation may be described as 'organic' in contrast to the machine-like 'mechanistic' system of the traditional hierarchy.[1] In organic systems the role of individuals is much less clearly defined. Traditional authoritarian structures are largely replaced by the maximum of advice and information. Expertise may reside anywhere inside the organisation in contrast to the traditional view that wisdom flows only from the top. Communication within the organisation may be lateral, across the firm as well as up and down vertical hierarchical lines. It is argued that the newer types of organic structures are better able to cope with change.

Many other structures and devices have been introduced, all of which seem to work under certain circumstances but fail to live up to expectations in others. They include matrix structures as described in Chapter 2. These depend on project teams formed out of functionally organised departments for the duration of a particular job. Other structures include group based systems in which a hierarchy of individuals is replaced by a network of interlocking cells of workers of various types, and quality circle systems in which groups of workers are encouraged to take greater responsibility for their own work and to make suggestions for change.

Coping with Change

In the previous section we have identified just some of the most important sources of change facing firms. The question that arises is: 'How to cope with this change?'

It is facile, however, but none the less true to remark that a changing environment is a fact of business life. If there were not change, running a business would be just a matter of administering time-worn and tested policies, rather than a real job of management which has been described as the art of 'taking decisions under conditions of uncertainty'. Change is a major

[1] These terms were popularised by Tom Burns.

cause of this uncertainty. Businesses have always had to cope with change. Nevertheless it is also true that businesses are also one of the main agencies through which changes take place. After all, the basic activity of **all** firms, taking resources and transforming them into something else, is an activity which, by its nature, causes change.

A firm's response, therefore, to a changing environment must be twofold:

1 to anticipate and respond to change;
2 to investigate change and itself attempt to influence the future.

Forecasting and Planning

These two activities, both of which deal with the future of the firm and its environment, are sometimes, wrongly, regarded as synonymous. Forecasting is an activity carried out, consciously or unconsciously, by every firm. Even an unthinking assumption that tomorrow will be the same as today is a forecast of no change. We have looked at some forecasting techniques earlier in the book, attempts to forecast demand, for example. Forecasting, however, is only part of the planning process. Planning is less concerned with forecasts of what is likely to happen in the future than with what a firm should do **now** in order to be better placed to cope with the future.

This is especially so because forecasting is known to be fraught with potential errors. It is probably not too strong to say that if a forecast can be made with great certainty it is probably fairly uninteresting and offers little potential for striking business innovation, whereas the more speculative and, possibly, potentially erroneous the forecast, the more interesting it becomes and the more likely to suggest a process of strategic business change.

Regression Analysis and Forecasting

In Chapter 5 we looked at the application of some fairly simple statistical techniques to the forecasting of demand. One of these was the application of the **least squares** regression technique. This method can be used to make much more complex forecasts, producing predictions based upon a number of variables rather than just one, and predictions for many things other than just demand. Such **econometric** processes involve a number of steps.

1 Formulating a **model** based upon economic theories to predict, in qualitative terms, how one economic variable may affect another.
2 Identifying cross-linkages in the system. For example, higher incomes may stimulate higher demand, which, in turn, is likely to feed back into higher incomes. This is likely to result in the variables to be forecast being represented by a system of simultaneous equations, all requiring solution.
3 The modelled system of equations is then tested against existing data – normally past time series for the explanatory variables in the system. It is then hoped to identify the **quantitative** links between the variables. With

these it becomes possible to make forecasts, for example that an *x* per cent increase in incomes will result in a *y* per cent increase in the demand for a particular product.

4 The modelled system, and the relationships identified, are subjected to a number of statistical tests, designed to show:
   a whether there are significant flaws in the model suggesting, perhaps, that some significant variables have been omitted from the system;
   b whether the relationships estimated have any real significance. It is possible, for example, to draw a line of best fit through **any** scatter of data on a graph, whether the estimated relationship between individual variables has any real meaning. In addition it can be estimated what proportion of the total observed variation in the model is really likely to have been 'explained' by the relationships modelled and how much remains unexplained.

Problems of Econometric Models

Econometric methods are widely used and their value should not be decried but even enthusiastic users of these methods will admit that they do have limitations. Apart from technical problems associated with statistical methods and economic theory there are problems such as the reliability of the data that has been used as a foundation for the calculations. This is particularly true of aggregate data and if it is unreliable then any predictions flowing from it must be highly suspect.

Other relevant problems include the following.

1 There can be a potential conflict between the way econometric models are constructed in an effort to explain and predict relationships and the type of analysis business planners may wish to undertake in order to improve their understanding of the environment in which they operate. For example, in econometric investigations the number of explanatory variables is normally reduced to the minimum possible. It may seem a good idea to include every imaginable variable but the result would simply be to make the results statistically meaningless. In contrast the business analyst may want to scrutinise every possible factor in a market because even a trivial point may sometimes be significant. Simply to estimate likely trends in the consumption of low alchol beer a very basic econometric model using the variables incomes, price and the prices of other competing beverages would probably be sufficient. However, to understand and attempt to influence the nature of the market for the product, the analyst would probably want to consider a wider range of variables, including changing patterns of social and leisure behaviour and so on.
2 Some of the most important changes that the firm might want to examine, such as technology or the introduction and diffusion of new products, may be less suitable for handling by this kind of technique. Forecast trends tend to be of smooth, linear change. Although some success has been achieved

in attempting to model product and technology changes in linear models they tend to arrive in more irregular and non-linear patterns.

3 An econometric forecast, by its nature as a prediction of the most likely event, gives an extrapolation of existing trends. But the forecast should be taken to mean that a range of possible outcomes could occur so that what is forecast is only a kind of 'midpoint'. Figure 14.2, for example, shows a forecast of possible future sales. At time *t*, existing trends have been estimated and then extrapolated into the future as forecast F_O. In reality, however, this forecast represents only the most likely of a range of possible future values, the highest and lowest of which are represented by the broken lines F_U and F_L. What the business manager really wants to know is whether it is possible for the firm to encourage F_U and avoid F_L and, if it is, how might it be possible to plan **now** to exploit the possibilities of achieving the higher trend.

4 Some of the most intriguing relationships can be modelled but not estimated or predicted in a quantitative sense. It may be possible to analyse and make some fairly confident statements about the ways in which some variables are linked but not to have the data necessary to apply meaningful econometric analysis. However, it might still be feasible to make fairly confident **qualitative** predictions, i.e. that this or that is likely to happen, without being able to put figures into the predictions. For example, the sterling exchange rate is subject to such a variety of forces, including market forces arising from the balance of payments, government policy and the 'sentiment' of financial markets, that it becomes extremely difficult to give a realistic econometric forecast for its future value, though macroeconomists may build models to attempt to do this. However, in the

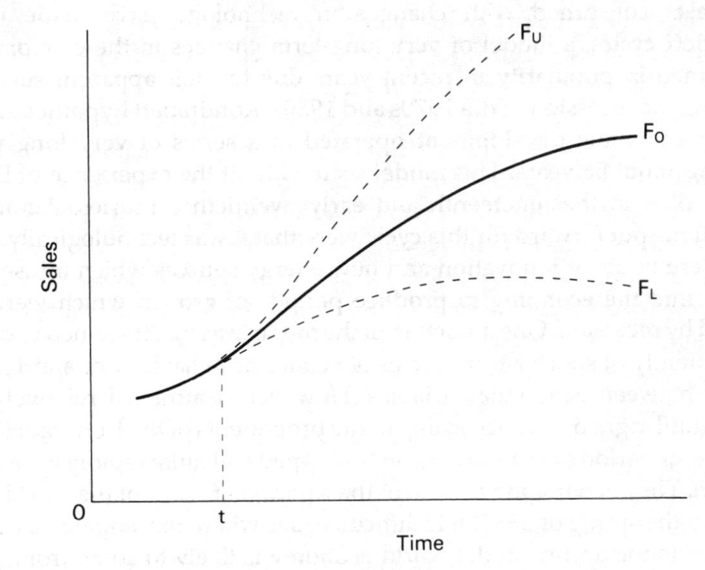

Fig. 14.2
The forecast F_0 may represent a mid point between F_U and F_L.

spring of 1989, with the UK running a balance of payments deficit of unprecedented proportions, it was reasonable to predict that, in the medium term, the exchange rate would fall during much of the rest of that year and remain lower for a further year or so. (You will be able to judge for yourself if this forecast proves to be correct!) Firms engaged in foreign trade or in competition with imports would, therefore, be able to build this forecast into their models for the early 1990s.

5 As noted earlier, the business firm is concerned with instigating as well as reacting to change. When using forecasts derived from econometric multiple regression techniques or other sources, there is a danger of confusing a **forecast** of what the future **might** be if existing trends continue, with a **plan** of what the firm wishes it to be and is prepared to act to encourage.

Other Forecasting Techniques

Multiple regression analysis may be augmented or even replaced by a number of other techniques. For example, some insights into the changing structure of markets and the business environment may be obtained from the use of **input–output** analysis, a technique pioneered by Wassily Leontieff. The heart of this technique is a matrix showing how the output of each industry feeds into the production activities of other industries. It is a technique which can handle, and indeed requires, vast amounts of data, but an input–output matrix for the economy can reveal valuable information. It can show how changes in one sector can ripple through others and it can alert business decision-makers to significant changes likely to affect their own industries.

Forecasts concerned with changes in technology have made use of **Kondratieff cycles**, a model of very long-term changes in the economy that have gained in popularity in recent years due to their apparent success in predicting the recession of the 1970s and 1980s. Kondratieff hypothesised that capitalist economic development operated in a series of very long waves, averaging about 56 years. This model seemed to fit the experience of Europe and the USA in the nineteenth and early twentieth centuries. Among the explanations put forward for this cycle were that it was technologically based. There were bouts of innovation and new energy sources which infused new strength into the economy to produce periods of growth which were then followed by recession. One attraction of the model was that it seemed to operate independently of shorter-term cycles of economic behaviour or shorter-term linkages between economic variables. However, it attracted relatively little interest until, right on cue according to the proponents of the Kondratieff view, the post-war period of economic growth stopped and quite rapidly gave way to recession. The encouraging feature of the Kondratieff view of the world is that even if (in the spring of 1989) it is difficult to see where the 'engine' of the next major economic upturn in the world economy is likely to come from, it **will** appear in the next few years. It might also be relevant to remember that during the very depth of the 'Great Depression' of the early 1930s there was one industry expanding – the motor vehicle industry – and it was the motor vehicle that was to prove one of the most powerful instruments of economic and social change and development in the following forty or so years.

Quantitative analysis of whatever type may also be augmented by various non-quantitative techniques designed to tap the knowledge of experts in various fields as to likely trends and changes. Probably most famous, or notorious, among such efforts are those of 'futurologists', but less spectacular though quite productive attempts can be organised within firms. One possibility is to ask various managers and experts to produce 'scenarios' of the firm's possible position in say, ten or fifteen years' time and then circulate these among the contributors to stimulate further discussion and insight into the strengths and weaknesses of the firm's current position.

Planning

It is worth repeating that the point of planning is not simply to forecast the future and then respond to it. Nor it is to attempt to draw a 'super blueprint' for every action that the firm is to take in the future. Just as forecasts are prone to error so it is with plans.

Some of the leading proponents of planning as an activity from Stafford Beer, the systems expert, to Dwight Eisenhower, the American war-time supreme commander and later President who, as a general, was famous for his attention to planning, have explained that plans are of limited value as they will almost certainly fail to work out exactly. Nevertheless they emphasise the value of planning **as a process**.

To explain this more fully we can refer to the discussion of investment in Chapter 7. We suggested that any business decision consists of certain stages:

1. Recognition and identification of the nature of a problem.
2. Formulation of courses of action.
3. Evaluation of courses of action.
4. Choice between optional courses of action.

Most systems of **corporate planning** reflect this model. Against a clearly defined **corporate objective(s)** are compared various forecasts of the future. The forecasts are made on the assumption that there is no marked change from the present pattern of corporate strategy. Differences that these reveal between the objective and the forecast define areas for attention. A **range of optional strategies** is then developed. These are evaluated and choices made so that a coherent plan of action can be drawn up. The **planning process** does not stop there. Once the plan is **implemented** the outcome is carefully **monitored** and compared with the corporate objective. As divergencies appear – and they inevitably will – **the entire process is repeated**.

Planning, therefore, is not seen as a once-and-for-all activity but as a continual process in which plans represent only a temporary situation report. Among the virtues claimed for this process are:

1 It forces firms to think clearly about their objectives and, in the course of forecasting, to attempt a better understanding of the nature of the environment in which they operate.
2 It establishes a continual and creative process within which there is conducted a search for improved and useful business strategies.
3 Properly conducted the planning process can act as a focus for the whole of the firm's activities and help to motivate the activities of all within the organisation.

Corporate planners are often at pains to stress that there is more to planning than a collection of forecasting and quantitative decision-making techniques and that it is particularly important that elements crucial to the well-being of the organisation, but less amenable to quantitative analysis, are considered in the process.

One such area that is often stressed is the organisation structure. Given the uncertainty with which the future abounds it is argued that organisations should plan to meet this uncertainty with a structure having maximum flexibility and adaptability. The firm may not know what changes are likely to happen but puts itself in readiness for change when it comes.

This point has been emphasised even by those who are disillusioned with corporate planning and whose disappointment often arises from the misapplication of the planning process and from attempts to draw up over-precise and detailed blueprints. For example, it has been noted that Japanese companies have very often built up resources beyond the level required for their immediate activities, while, at the same time, exercising only general guidance from senior corporate management. In contrast, many US firms have practised strict corporate control, coupled with efforts at 'streamlining' to cut out 'unnecessary' and 'wasteful' hoarding of resources. The latter approach, it is argued, is appropriate where the environment is either unchanging or where changes come in predictable and discrete steps. Where change is continuous and gradual, the Japanese model is more flexible and appropriate.

Product and Market Research

In Chapter 5 we examined some techniques that could be employed in the process of market research. These were mostly techniques of gathering and interpreting information. Market research is an important element in the marketing mix as explained in that chapter. You should recall that marketing is not simply a question of finding a way of selling a given product. The product is **itself** one of the elements of the marketing mix. The results of market research must feed back into the product planning process just as the firm will adjust the focus of its market research to reflect the fact that it is developing new products and wishes to assess the market for them.

Suppose a firm is aware that a particular product is not selling very well in the market. Market research, it is hoped, will reveal information about

consumer attitudes towards the product that may help to explain this poor performance. If negative attitudes are identified then, put at its starkest, there are two possibilities:

1 The negative attitudes are **incorrect**. Consumers are attributing to the product characteristics which it does not have. For example, it may be perceived as being of low quality, or be overpriced, or unfashionable, or injurious to health, or some other negative attribute. If, following an **honest** appraisal of the product's characteristics, it is decided that these perceptions are incorrect then there is a role for marketing strategy to change these perceptions.

   Such an appraisal can be undertaken, for example, through **double blind tests**. A proprietary food can be tested with consumer panels under conditions where neither the panel nor tester knows which brand is being sampled. This removes the possibility of bias. If the reaction to the product is more positive than that revealed when the brand name is known it would seem that the brand name is itself responsible for the negative attitude.

   It is the experience of the marketing profession that it is circumstances where the product is 'right' but attitudes are 'incorrect' that offer the greatest possibilities of achieving successful results through marketing methods such as advertising and branding. Results are likely to be much less successful and much more fleeting under the reverse circumstances.
2 The negative attitudes are **correct**. The product really does fail to meet the requirements and expectations of consumers. When this is the case, the more appropriate strategy is to bring forward a product which meets more effectively the needs of consumers.

Of course, to develop new products and to launch them successfully on to the commercial market is not a straightforward process. We speak of **research and development** in recognition of the fact that the process involves not just producing new ideas, but also bringing these ideas forward to a point where they are transformed into commercially viable projects.

There are a number of ways in which this process can be analysed. For example, research and development (R&D) can be classified as **basic research** – research for its own sake; **applied research** – that geared towards specific commercial ends; and **development** – turning new knowledge into new products and processes. The third of these typically accounts for much greater expenditure than the first two combined and basic research itself accounts for far less than applied.

The economist F. M. Scherer has suggested that it is useful to view the process of R&D as consisting of a number of elements:

1 **Inventions** In which a new idea is conceptualised and then worked out in basic detail.
2 **Development** In which the basic idea is then tested, adapted and prepared for commercial exploitation.

3 **Entrepreneurship** The process involved in deciding to proceed with a particular idea, organising and arranging finance for it.
4 **Investment** Actually backing it with funds.

The value of such an analysis is that it highlights the importance of each of these stages and the fact that they need not be undertaken by the same person or group of people or even by the same organisation. It deserves emphasising and repeating that the invention stage, though typically the most glamorous, usually places far lower demands on resources than the other stages of R&D, and a firm engaged in R&D must be prepared for this. This explains why many inventions have their origins in smaller firms but are only brought to commercial fruition by larger ones after they have either bought up the idea or entered into a partnership arrangement.

In this discussion we have not distinguished between innovations relating to **product** and those relating to **process**, i.e. improved ways of doing the same thing. In practice, they are often identical. For example, the word processor represents a process innovation for office work but a product innovation for the business machinery industry. This has an interesting implication for corporate strategy. A firm may research a process innovation in order to improve its efficiency and improve sales of its product by reducing its price. But if such an innovation is developed, it is at least worth considering whether the firm should diversify by starting to market the innovation itself, either to other producers of the same product or in other markets and industries if it has a wider application. Scherer describes the example of Xerox, which began with the efforts of a lawyer to increase efficiency in copying legal documents, efforts which led to the development of the photocopier with its far wider applications.

The work of research and development has often been regarded as a particularly high-risk commercial activity which has led some observers to argue that it is only larger or even quasi-monopolistic firms with plenty of resources and comparatively safe market positions which can afford to undertake it. Academic investigation, however, tends to indicate that the returns from R&D are by no means as uncertain as this; that the technical and commercial success rates from R&D bear comparison with those from other types of investment.

To understand this, we need to refer again to Scherer's analysis. We are **not** saying that money thrown at R&D will bring predictable results. The key to understanding the reality of R&D lies in seeing that only a tiny fraction of total R&D resources are applied to the invention phase. This is where the greatest uncertainty is concentrated. Would-be inventors can spend a lifetime of effort without producing a single worthwhile idea. Basic research, whether in academic or commercial establishments, is noted (or notorious) for its capacity to throw up ideas and results with applications, where they exist, far removed from the original problems being investigated. Hence the familiar academic complaints when it is suggested that research funds should be concentrated on areas where there are known practical applications. The academic response is often to point out that no one knows what the results of research are likely to be.

But, after the modestly resourced invention phase, the crucial **business** activity of **entrepreneurship** is needed to assess the practicality of the new idea and its potential technical and commercial prospects. This helps to explain the high success rate for R&D. It is not a blind activity but one that involves the application of market and investment appraisal and other techniques at an early stage to check the viability of projects before major resource commitments are undertaken.

This is not to minimise the importance of the invention phase, or the creativity that must go into it. Many firms have implemented procedures to try to stimulate and channel creativity. These include sponsorship of academic research, running 'brainstorming' sessions among their staff and making use of the opportunities now afforded by the **science parks** attached to some universities. Although we began the discussion by suggesting that much innovation comes from an attempt to improve the product in response to market research we must recognise that, with many new products, the process is reversed. The invention of the product **precedes** the investigation of the market. This, after all, is how many smaller firms came into being. A single individual was convinced that he or she had a product that would appeal to a worthwhile market and then struggled, not always unsuccessfully, to find that market.

In larger firms a similar process of production-led innovations may also occur. It is not always the case that an invention is a response to an identified market problem. Sometimes the product may be the result of a piece of basic scientific research, sometimes it may be a by-product of something else. In these cases there is an entrepreneurial problem to be solved along the lines of: 'Here we have a product; what is it and will anybody buy it?' The oft quoted classic case of this is Teflon non-stick material, developed originally in the US space programme. A product which, once invented, took longer to find widespread commercial applications (eventually in transmission systems) was the super-bouncy rubber for which, for many years, the only use seemed to be in small balls for children's playthings.

Sometimes the origin of products may be even more bizarre. One way of encouraging creativity is **morphological analysis** which involves analysing a product into its basic constituents, altering one or more of these, and then examining what results. A recent (alleged) result of this process came about from a consideration of what one had if a tape recorder was produced which would not record but would only play back. The resulting, very successful commercial answer can now be seen attached to the belts and ears of students, commuters, joggers . . .

The past two centuries have seen an explosion in human aspirations. To reach for the moon and, indeed, the stars, now seems more natural and inevitable than to believe that the great mass of people should be doomed to plod along the paths trod by generations of their ancestors. If these aspirations are to be met and if the lot of the majority of the world's population is to be improved, industry and commerce must continue to innovate, continue to find new ways to use resources and to find new resources to meet demands. It must do this in ways that do not destroy the world on which we all depend. Change and development are now an inevitable part of modern life. The certainty that tomorrow will be different from today is, perhaps, the only certain element in the modern business environment. This is the challenge that every business manager must face but it is a challenge that offers many worthwhile rewards to those who meet it successfully.

Discussion Questions

Instead of posing questions of the type that have appeared in most previous chapters we suggest that you examine the processes of change taking place in your own work and/or study environment. What developments of modern technology are likely to alter the structure of your own industry and the activities in which it is involved? What, for example, may be the implications of modern communication technology on the structure of education? We have an Open University and an Open College. Will there be Open Schools? What is the future for small and large business organisations – or is the future likely to be one of greater co-operation between both small and large organisations within 'loose federations' which seek to take advantage of economies of scale while avoiding the diseconomies? How will changes affect you and how can you prepare to meet their challenge?

Suggestions for Further Reading

For an interesting discussion of many aspects of change as it affects business organisations – and the people in them – see:

Handy, C., *The Age of Unreason*, Hutchinson, 1989

Most of the leading management texts consider the topics introduced in this chapter. One such text, with extensive sections on corporate planning, is:

Stoner, J. A. F. and Freeman, R. E., *Management*, Prentice Hall, 1989

For stimulating material read:

Ackoff, R., *A Concept of Corporate Planning*, Wiley International, 1969
Ackoff, R., *The Art of Problem Solving*, Wiley International, 1978

Index